In the Company of Radical Women Writers

In the Company of Radical Women Writers

Rosemary Hennessy

University of Minnesota Press
Minneapolis
London

The University of Minnesota Press gratefully acknowledges the generous assistance provided for the publication of this book by the Margaret S. Harding Memorial Endowment, honoring the first director of the University of Minnesota Press.

Every effort was made to obtain permission to reproduce material in this book. If any proper acknowledgment has not been included here, we encourage copyright holders to notify the publisher.

Poetry by Claudia Jones reproduced from *Claudia Jones: Beyond Containment*, ed. Carole Boyce Davies, with permission from Ayebia Clarke Publishing Limited, Banbury, Oxfordshire, UK; copyright Ayebia www.ayebia.co.uk. Meridel Le Sueur, excerpt from "The Origins of Corn," from *Ripening: Selected Work*, 2nd ed.; copyright 1975 by Meridel Le Sueur; reprinted with the permission of the Permissions Company, LLC, on behalf of the Feminist Press at the City University of New York, www.feministpress.org; all rights reserved. Excerpts from "Gyroscope," "The Lynchings of Jesus," "The Book of the Dead," "To Be a Jew," and "An Unborn Poet" in *The Collected Poems of Muriel Rukeyser*, copyright 2005 by Muriel Rukeyser; reprinted by permission of ICM Partners. Excerpts from "Under Forty" (1990), *Willard Gibbs* (1942), "Women of Scottsboro" (n.d.), and correspondence and diary entries from Muriel Rukeyser Papers (1933 and 1975) and any other published or unpublished prose copyright Muriel Rukeyser, reprinted by permission of the Estate of Muriel Rukeyser. Excerpts from letters from Nancy Naumburg to Muriel Rukeyser (1932, 1933, 1934) courtesy of the Berg Collection of English and American Literature, New York Public Library, Astor, Lenox and Tilden Foundations, New York. Excerpts from Muriel Rukeyser, *The Life of Poetry*, copyright 1996 by William L. Rukeyser; published by Paris Press / Wesleyan University Press, Middletown, Connecticut.

Portions of chapter 5 were previously published in "Toward an Ecology of Life-Making: The Re-membering of Meridel Le Sueur," in "The Politics of Social Reproduction," ed. Cinzia Arruzza and Kelly Gawel, special issue of *CLCWeb: Comparative Literature and Culture* 22, no. 2 (June 2020).

Published by the University of Minnesota Press
111 Third Avenue South, Suite 290
Minneapolis, MN 55401-2520
http://www.upress.umn.edu

ISBN 978-1-5179-1489-9 (hc)
ISBN 978-1-5179-1490-5 (pb)

A Cataloging-in-Publication record for this book is available from the Library of Congress.

Printed in the United States of America on acid-free paper

The University of Minnesota is an equal-opportunity educator and employer.

32 31 30 29 28 27 26 25 24 23   10 9 8 7 6 5 4 3 2 1

To Mary-Jane Carson Hennessy
(1924–2019)

Contents

Preface

During the great Covid-19 pandemic, when people were in lock-down and lonely, I found myself in the company of radical women. I was on a long leave from my regular work, often away from family and friends. With life as we had known it falling apart, so much was at stake. Living through the Great Depression, these women knew about surviving in a time of crisis. They had something to say, and I had time to listen. Their writing reached out to readers hungry for stories of courage and struggle against greedy power brokers. They took chances in that writing and in their lives. As fierce women can, they dared me to pursue a new path. Returning to literature after a long journey with feminist theory, I discerned in their writing an expansive critical knowledge and a timely invitation to pursue the unimaginable.

Learning about the risks they took as women, artists, thinkers, and lovers and about their turn to life writing, I became absorbed in their stories as well as their work. Sometimes I found myself reading between the lines, following clues or probing the strategies of concealment and desire that punctuate their prose and poetry. Their attention to history led me to discern its imprint in images, metaphors, and syntactic choices: the telling features of form. I found myself reflecting on the meanings of that history in my own life as well.

"And so we marched," Louise Thompson announces in the title of her article on the massive gathering of women she led to Washington, D.C., in 1935. They came to protest state-sanctioned violence against nine Black teenagers. That history of public dissent lives on. Almost a century later, women and those who love women still take to the streets to claim control over our bodies, our children's lives, and the future of the planet. In one another's company even in the darkest times, we generate the energy to make and remake life.

Introduction
Life-Making Essentials, Life-Writing Inventions

> We see, in this moment of the world, the lives of many people
> brought to a time of stress. The streams are challenged, all the
> meanings are now in question. It is at this moment that we turn.
> —Muriel Rukeyser, *Willard Gibbs*

This is a book born from a world in crisis. When capitalism faltered under Covid-19, the labor of life making collapsed into the
home, and the exhausting burden was shouldered by women. As
the numbers of dead Black and brown bodies mounted, the pandemic offered yet more evidence that Jim Crow in the United
States is alive and well. While these national and global emer-
gencies unfolded, drought, wildfires, and floods devastated communities across the United States, Europe, India, and China—
more proof that the planet is ailing, its illness perhaps terminal.
The alarms are loud and clear: we must reclaim the means of our
reproduction—our homes, the land we live on, the energies supporting our mutual dependency, and the capacity to decide the
kinds of human beings we want to be.

In another time of global crisis, the Great Depression, thousands were also unemployed and evicted. Then, too, middle-class
people found themselves in food pantries for the first time. It is fair
to say that the Depression of the 1930s was one of the greatest pe-
riods of crisis that Americans had ever faced. Women shouldered

the work of holding families together then as well, their efforts often invisible. The murder of Black men at the hands of the state then, too, ignited a mass movement that spilled into the streets and kindled a social awakening. Violent and bloody strikes rolled across the country as workers joined the unemployed crying out against capitalist inequality.[1] During 1934 in San Francisco, Toledo, and Minneapolis, striking dockworkers, autoworkers, and truckers closed down their cities, almost simultaneously. Midwestern farmers blocked delivery of their products and demanded fairer pricing. By 1934, millions of acres of cultivated land had become useless because farming on the Great Plains had destroyed the prairie and large areas of grassland had been laid waste by overgrazing. With the onset of the drought, the land began to blow away, and the American heartland became a vast dustbowl. It was clear to most observers that something had gone very wrong with the economy and with American society. A reexamination of the values that had plunged the nation into unprecedented material catastrophe and its citizens into despair was inevitable.[2]

The seven women writers gathered here launched their political lives during the Great Depression. Four of them—Marvel Cooke, Louise Thompson Patterson, Claudia Jones, and Alice Childress—lived those years in Harlem. Josephine Herbst and Meridel Le Sueur both came from the Midwest and wrote about the Depression years there. Muriel Rukeyser grew up on New York City's Upper West Side and participated in national campaigns that took her to the South. They all knew something about a world in crisis. To keep company with them is to be reminded of persistent forces: the labor that takes place at home, the violence of white supremacy, an essential relationship to the land, and the energies of interdependence that maintain the web of life. Their bold voices and audacious lives are eye-opening and thought-provoking, as are their efforts to expand what the radical Left stood for.[3] To linger with them is to learn from their aspirations and efforts, even when they failed. You could say their lives and writing are a primer for our time.

As crises often do, the losses and upheavals of the Great Depression enabled these women to recognize that life is sustained across a web of dependencies that humans have a responsibility to maintain. In simple terms, this is what life making means.[4]

The making and remaking of life is the baseline of survival. If life forms—both human and nonhuman—do not reproduce and are not nurtured, they become extinct. Not only do they need to replicate, they also need the means to do so. These means entail resources *Resources* as well as relations that provide nourishment, shelter, and care. If *Relat'ns* we understand that, we can see that capitalism as a way of life has succeeded only at a fatal cost because it promotes relations that violently deregulate life. The drive to accumulate capital began on a world scale in the sixteenth and seventeenth centuries when the first Western explorers opened the New World to Europe for plunder and extraction. Plunder and extraction remain integral to capitalist development. It takes place in the privatization of communal assets like bodies, air, land, and water. Many thinkers call these assets "commons." As capitalism's drive for profits increasingly converts life forms into market relations, it continually extends the frontiers of accumulation. In the twentieth century, the bioeconomy became a new frontier, expanding resource extraction to biomass in addition to fossils. Plant life and genetic modification, for example, became profitable resources for pharmaceutical firms and agribusiness, but often with no regard for relations not compatible with the capitalist organization of work.[5] The global economy's late twentieth-century restructuring continued this concerted attack on our most basic centers of reproduction—the home, the land, and the body. In each case, the pattern of continual accumulation has deepened the destruction of our common wealth.[6] Lands able to maintain life are increasingly turned into private property, and more people are being displaced from their homes and jobs. The labor of care is being more and more commodified and devalued, as are women's bodies. As capital enclosure progressively penetrates the biosphere and modifies cells and neurons, lands, and bodies, these new enclosures, like the older ones, consolidate control over natural resources into the hands of a small group. The new enclosures shrink living space and time and disrupt the reproductive rhythms of all life forms and of the earth itself, making holes in the ozone, polluting the air, seas, and beaches.[7] As the planet warms, it is becoming clear that capital is no longer able to provide even the minimal conditions for reproducing life.

Across history, both individuals and groups have resisted this erosion of life, alerting people to injustice and ruin even when they were hidden in plain sight, broadcasting the truth for those who had no voice and whose deprivation was enriching a few. These messengers made clear the positive value of life making and broadened understanding of it as a human survival endeavor. Even as capital imposed constraints, organized resistance efforts were inventing alternatives. Young women on the left during the Great Depression delivered that message. They knew that capitalism had seriously failed to support the reproduction of life. The crisis made dramatically evident life's fragility. Like the more recent economic depression of 2008–9, that crisis threatened to tumble the entire system. As crisis often does, however, it also created openings for widespread discussion of the damage, for dissent, and for consideration of alternative ways the remaking of life might be organized.[8]

The political climate of the Left in the 1930s offered opportunities to comprehend the harm to the dependent relations of life making, a process capitalism had been propelling for centuries. The disruption of the metabolic relation of social and biological life was on full display during the Depression, when the wealthiest were cushioned while those whose labor built their empires were standing in breadlines and in "slave markets," their factory jobs gone, their fields of wheat and corn depleted. American Communism in the 1930s explained the fault lines underlying the catastrophe; it also enabled people to work together toward solutions and alternatives.

As the country sank deeper into the Depression, organizing efforts in northern cities moved beyond factories and union halls as people assembled local organizations to address their survival needs. Before New Deal relief came from the federal government, communities were forming unemployed councils. In New York City, Harlem was the epicenter of these efforts. Women came together to boycott butchers who increased the price of food. Flying squads intervened in evictions, moving furniture that landlords had dumped on the curb back into homes. Professionals put their skills to use, too. The journalist Marvel Cooke was one of them. Reporting on the "slave markets" where Black women gathered on the street corners of the Bronx waiting to be hired for a day or more of domestic work inspired her to join their unionizing efforts. She was one of a handful of women who brought their protests over work conditions into the national spotlight.

By the middle of that decade, the case of the Scottsboro Boys summoned widespread attention to what many called a legal lynching. These nine Black teenagers, accused of raping two white women in Alabama, had been swiftly sentenced to death by an all-white jury. Support for their case sparked a national response and propelled an unprecedented period of antiracism. All these events required organization and planning. At their forefront was the Communist Party in the United States. Perhaps like me, you may be surprised to learn that the party was unparalleled in fighting racism, both in its own ranks and in society, and that it promoted attention to what was then called "white chauvinism."[9] These antichauvinism campaigns personalized race politics for many white Communists and led the party to develop a more complex explanation of racial oppression than a strictly class-based analysis afforded.[10]

Much of the party's antichauvinist history is vibrantly evident in the writings of these seven women, who were young adults on the left in the 1930s. The Communist Party's attention to racial oppression left its imprint on each of them, shaping in different ways the political commitments they pursued as Black, Jewish, or white, as immigrant or settler. Their writing often advanced the party's stance on race even if at times they also succumbed to the powerful pull of race ideology. Marvel Cooke and Ella Baker's bold attention to the neglected problems of Black domestics in 1935 prefigured a feminist approach to class, race, and gender that would not be fully recognized for decades. At times, however, their groundbreaking investigation reiterated anti-Semitic tropes. If that fact indicates the fraught relationships between Blacks and Jews, it also points to the powerful impact of race as an imaginary and material force even for the Left. Although American Communism prioritized the struggle against racism, it could not obliterate racism's deeply rooted history and influence.

As a hierarchical cultural system, race was born in the late eighteenth century. Think of it as a technology or cultural instrument invented to protect the accumulation of wealth in an emerging democracy. At the same time the American Revolution was declaring a government by and for the people, the most profitable commodity in the colonial economy was slaves. As a system of difference tied to biology, race justified that contradiction. The violence it wrought seeped into the colonial world and became a powerful rationalization of slavery as an institution that provided cheap labor. It also served as a wedge to keep working people from recognizing their common lot and claiming their collective power.

I only gradually saw race as a through line in what I was learning from the women who kept company with me. To different degrees, each confronted the corrosive impact of race and racism. At times, their writing reiterates racial and ethnic stereotypes that undercut their radical interventions. Rather than dismissing or ignoring these stereotypes, I realized that these fissures in their awareness present opportunities to learn about the psychic and social potency of race. At a time when the violent maintenance of white supremacy is once more openly championed and reinstituted in the United States, reckoning with the wide reach of that potency is instructive, even imperative.

The opening and closing chapters of what follows are in this respect bookends. In each, the instability and material force of racial categories come into view. Both are especially evident in the case of Jews, and I pause here to say a bit more about the place of Jews in American culture and on the left. The racialization of Jews in the United States shaped their history, and that history is particularly significant for what it reveals about whiteness as a tentative and fraught identity. From the late nineteenth century until after World War II, and still today, Jews have an uncertain relationship to whiteness.[11] As the historian Eric Goldstein puts it, "Jews were a racial conundrum."[12] Native-born whites had a difficult time seeing them as part of a unified, homogeneous white population, and whiteness sat uneasily with many central aspects of Jewish identity (Goldstein, 1). Their unstable relationship to whiteness makes clear that the racial history of the United States cannot be reduced to a Black-versus-white dichotomy, even as that dichotomy has been marshaled at crucial points to control a much more complex social landscape (33). That European immigrants to the United States did not automatically become white has been well documented. Research has demonstrated that whiteness, like other racial categories, is neither biological nor monolithic but cultural and constantly reshaped (4). The deep history of anti-Semitism in the West implanted anti-Semitic stereotypes into modern culture. Like other groups, some Jewish immigrants to the United States asserted the white–Black color line in an effort to distinguish themselves from the nation's most oppressed group (3). From a Black perspective, Jews appeared to be relatively successful outsiders with access to influence and assimilation that African Americans did not have. These resentments were real, and yet the two groups also accepted a degree of mutual identification.[13]

During the 1920s, the Ku Klux Klan expanded operations in the North and the South and targeted Blacks, Jews, and Catholics. By 1933, the rising tide of anti-Semitism inspired by events in Nazi Germany compounded persistent discrimination against Jews in the United States. Universities limited enrollments or enforced quotas, neighborhoods excluded Jews, and professional fields barred them from employment or promotion. The contradictory pulls of exclusion and assimilation permeated the Jewish experience, as did their differing histories as migrants. In contrast to migrants from urban western Europe, eastern European and Russian Jews, who suffered violent segregation, had a sharpened commitment to social justice. In the early decades of the twentieth century, Jews from both groups were assigned to the not fully white side of the racial spectrum.[14] Across an array of U.S. organizations, from the liberal National Association for the Advancement of Colored People (NAACP) and Urban League to the Communist Party, Jews organized for the defense of Blacks because they recognized in them an even more oppressed group and identified with Blacks' exclusion from a mainstream America whose racism was directed at Jews as well. Many Jews gravitated to unions, to socialism, and, by the 1930s, to the Communist Party's antiracism campaign. Jewish socialism was hegemonic in New York City's immigrant Jewish communities, and all wings of the radical movement across the United States experienced a considerable influx of Jews during that decade, when they gravitated to Communist Party leadership positions.[15] The case of the Scottsboro Boys drew support from Jews across the political spectrum.

• The uncertain relationship Jews had to whiteness played out in their experience on the radical Left. For some it meant separating from a Jewish community bound by religion and tradition. As Irene Paull put it: during her years in the party, she provisionally vacated her Jewishness, a stance others adopted as "non-Jewish Jews."[16] We can hear it in the opening line of Vivian Gornick's memoir _The Romance of American Communism,_ when she declares, "Before I knew that I was Jewish or a girl, I knew that I was a member of the working class." For second-generation American Jews involved in American Communism in the 1930s, the movement's aspirations toward a sweeping internationalism opposed to assimilation held out the dream of overcoming Jewish parochialism and Gentile anti-Semitism even as they negotiated the persistent tensions promoted by the ideology of race and its systemic structures.

These seven writers documented divisions and blurred lines on the left that continue to resonate in the present. Their efforts to address them, even when imperfect, drew me in and buoyed me up in a time that felt hopeless. Like a smitten lover, or at times a sleuth, I tracked the enthralling details of each life, intrigued by these women's overlapping paths and inspired by the power of their writing. I became attached to them as individuals, and I began to see how much they each contributed to the common commitments they fought for. Their insights about the activities of life making were daring, innovative, and provocative. They took risks and broke from convention, at times from family expectations and respectable norms, at other times from the terms of the radical Left they joined. They put available forms of writing to new uses, reshaping them to tell stories that expanded the political scope of the party that inspired them. The life adjustments they made during the 1940s and 1950s left an equally compelling record as, bolstered by their political education from the 1930s, they navigated the state's brutal Cold War arresting power. Several of them aged fiercely into the closing decades of the twentieth century, relentlessly confronting the crises of those times and exercising their talents for organizing, public speaking, and writing.[17]

They might have been astonished to be called public intellectuals, but that is what they were. Their writings were pointed contributions to public discourse, at times pitched to a mainstream audience, on other occasions directed to the Left, often in the form of a call for sustained attention to women's labor and experience. All were innovators who enlarged the critical perspective they gained from their association with American Communism. Five of them were Communist Party members, and all were involved in

Communist-supported organizations. It is fair to say that all these women were radical left feminists, although none of them identified with that label or with the feminism of their time.

In the 1930s, the U.S. feminist movement focused on appeals for rights directed to the state. From the 1920s until the early 1960s, "feminism" was the domain of the National Women's Party (NWP), whose members and supporters campaigned for the Equal Rights Amendment. The NWP claimed the term "feminism." Consequently, Communists wanted nothing to do with it because they saw "feminism" as representing white middle-class women's interests, some of which were racist and anti-Semitic.[18] In varied ways, however, all these writers challenged the patriarchal expectations of women that undergirded their lives, and they summoned the Left to confront them.

In the 1930s, Communism was a vibrant political force that put forward a broad vision of social possibility that filled the air of the Left. You learned about it through party newspapers, chief among them the *Daily Worker,* but also from scores of magazines and periodicals—the *New Masses, Partisan Review,* the *Nation,* the *Anvil, Freedom,* and *American Mercury,* to name a few. Distilled through social networks and countless organizations, Communism became what Josephine Herbst once described as a political sensibility defined by what you read, who you talked to, the "we" you invoked. One objective of this book is to shine a light on that history. The American culture scholar Alan Wald puts it succinctly: Communism touched the lives of millions as the largest and most coherent expression of twentieth-century rebellion by workers, women, people of color, and committed intellectuals prior to the 1960s.[19]

How did Communism gain such support in the 1930s? The answer is fleshed out by the life stories and writings of these women who recognized the disparity between the promise of democracy and the inequalities people lived under in the United States. Communists offered an explanation and proposed that life could be different. These writers amplified the scope of that explanation. They confronted a Left dominated by men, and they foregrounded women's lives in their writing, raising issues that American Communism had marginalized. They made visible the fact that Black women's domestic labor was worth less because it was women's

work and racialized. They exposed the persistence of racial violence, confronted the social advantage offered by settler heritage
and whiteness, and probed the structures of U.S. imperialism and
colonial conquest.

In the 1930s, the political climate of the Left, salted by American Communism, disclosed the distortions and fragmented relations that capitalism had been promoting for centuries. It spoke to
peoples' unmet needs and helped them come together to address
those needs. It gave these writers a map for reading their country
and the world as well as a vision of possibility that each of them expanded in her work. More than anything, it is this fact that made
them captivating figures for me.

It can be hard to comprehend or even to imagine the widespread support among ordinary working people that Communism
had in the 1930s. Until Bernie Sanders's presidential campaigns in
2016 and 2020 put democratic socialism back into the U.S. political vocabulary, "socialism," no less "Communism," had been unspeakable, implanted in the national psyche during the Cold War
as demonic threats. In the 1930s, Communism spoke to the disparity between the promise of the American dream and the desperation most people were suddenly living, and it asked why. Why
is our life organized as it is? When so many are poor or work all
their lives for so little, why are a few so wealthy? Communists examined capitalism as an essentially unequal market economy fed
by the accumulation of human and natural resources over hundreds of years of colonial conquest, and it suggested there might
be an alternative.

That alternative emerged from nineteenth-century uprisings
against the capitalist way of life when working people began to
propose systems of governing that would control the accumulation of wealth.[20] Across Europe, reform movements struck com-
promises with ruling groups. In Russia, revolution aimed for more
transformative change. The enactment of those changes shaped
American political struggles in the early decades of the twentieth century. The history of the various forms of American Communism was complicated and tumultuous, beginning in 1919 when
U.S. Communists severed ties with the more moderate Socialist
Party.[21] By the 1930s, as historian Bryan Palmer aptly puts it,
American Communism's uniqueness was the effect of many forces.

Among them were generations of American radicalism, immigrant Marxism, the example of the Russian Revolution, and the material and programmatic aid and advice of the Communist Party's international organization, known as the Communist International or Comintern.[22] The shifting policies of the Comintern were shaped by developments in revolutionary Russia, a bureaucracy in Moscow, the Communist Party's transnational reach, and eventually the rise of fascism in Europe. Some of the women of the radical Left were drawn to American Communism's broad understanding of social justice. They called for an even more capacious analysis of capitalism, one that took into account women's devalued domestic labor and its relation to racial oppression. A handful summoned Communism to address the depletion of the land as a common resource, and an even rarer few believed the dependent relations of life making entailed energy transfers across human and nonhuman life forms.

One of the salient features of the women writers I bring together here is their attention to these issues, which were marginal in left politics. Their interest in addressing them was not to call for state reforms or for expanded rights but, rather, to call for a more expansive and less fragmented organization of the relations that the reproduction of life requires. Under capitalism, these relations had been shaped into divisions between owners and workers, public and private arenas of market and home, white and Black people, human and natural worlds. Inciting a perspective that thinks against the grain of the divisions that capitalism's class relations thrive upon, these writers summoned a way of seeing beyond the commonsensical.

During and after World War II, a systematic campaign of state violence and widespread propaganda effectively repressed their efforts. Members of the U.S. Congress, the Department of Justice, the Federal Bureau of Investigation, the American Legion, and a network of citizen informants led that campaign. It employed state power to imprison, blacklist, intimidate, and silence anyone connected to the Communist Party or the organizations it supported. In 1956, the FBI launched a counterintelligence program that aimed to obliterate American Communism through infiltration and division. Informants joined organizations in order to disrupt activities and inflame divisions, among them Black–Jewish tensions.[23]

The result was that in generations to come, "Communism," the name of a set of principles for how American social life might be organized, was distorted into a vilified code word for something evil. Eventually many people knew little or nothing about its underlying political philosophy that people can make a way of life that provides what everyone needs, about its history as a leader in antiracist struggles, or about its endorsement of the democratic dream of equality for all. Because the possibility of realizing that dream was a threat to the wealthy who control the levers of power, Communism was distorted beyond recognition in public memory and in the history books. The repression was systematic and continues to this day. However, it did not entirely succeed.

The aspiration underlying American Communism, as formulated in the philosophy of historical materialism and reshaped in decades of collective action, remains alive. It continues to propel movements calling for human needs to be met more equitably; for unbridled greed to be contained; for a democratic form of government to be instituted, more just and not run by corporate interests; for people of color and women to be valued. Organizers and writers emerging from street corners and fields, kitchens and classrooms, continue to expand its scope. They are evidence that even against powerful forces that try to contain them, people rise up to address such common needs as better working conditions, housing, education, health care, childcare, and eldercare.

Many of these unmet needs pertain to the broad range of activities that fall under the umbrella term "social reproduction." At its most basic, social reproduction entails the acquisition and distribution of the means of subsistence (food, shelter, clothing, health care) as well as the reproduction of the workforce at a certain level of differentiation and expertise.[24] These are activities essential to reproducing social life, yet they are historically unpaid or underpaid. All kinds of labor fit into this category—food preparation, cleaning, laundry, shopping—but so do education and activities that constitute care. Increasingly, this work is commercialized and done by low-wage workers, most of them women of color. A considerable number of these activities are done for free, again most often by women. Women bear the burden of reproducing life as domestic laborers, and their reproductive bodies have been a battleground from the earliest phase of capitalist development. That struggle continues today as control over women's bodies is increasingly returned to the state and as lucrative industries appropriate women's knowledge and self-determination.

In the midst of crisis, people experience the contradictions and disparities in their lives more sharply. They awake to the need for a more sustainable and equitable way of life. When this awakening occurred in the 1930s, American Communism was already several decades old, and modern revolutions were a lived experience for many immigrants. The Russian Revolution followed a century after revolutions in France and the United States that had replaced life-making systems controlled by an aristocracy with democratic forms of government. In principle, the Communism of the Russian Revolution aspired to supersede those democratic experiments. It had become all too clear throughout the Industrial Revolution of the nineteenth century that an economy based on wealth accumulated by a few through the sweated labor of many could never be a true democracy. So long as people were enslaved or worked to death for a pittance in order to produce the wealth that a small group owned and controlled, equality for all was a myth. The state could proclaim that myth, but the people knew that its laws protected and benefited the wealthy.

The alternative inspired by the Russian Revolution spurred new social experiments across the Americas. In the United States, the ideals of socialism and Communism called for government that would rein in or eliminate capital greed. They built upon a long history of resistance manifest in slave rebellions and abolition movements, Native uprisings, and labor strikes. Communism and socialism found support especially among an unskilled immigrant workforce fleeing persecution in Europe. Immigrants to the United States played a major role in shaping the many factions and sectors of American Communism. The influence of the eastern European Jews in the garment industry, the Italian women in the needle trades, the Irish in the mines, the Finns in consumer cooperatives, and many others brought a mix of labor militancy, highly politicized ethnic cultures, gendered social relations, and fierce battles over Communist versus social democratic sensibilities.[25] Meanwhile, in the newly formed Soviet Union, the revolutionary new government was splintering. Leon Trotsky and his allies who supported the Bolshevik revolutionary leadership and policies were marginalized as Joseph Stalin rose to power and eventually executed or exiled them.

People Erst

What I refer to as "American Communism" in fact spanned a spectrum of political positions on the left, from actual members of the Communist Party USA (CPUSA) to those who allied with a Communist and socialist opposition. Differences turned on many questions, including whether revolution could take place effectively if it was confined to the Soviet Union or whether it had to be an international undertaking because capitalism as a colonial venture had a global reach. In the 1920s, a ruling bureaucracy was solidifying a governing power bloc in the newly formed Soviet Union. Led by Stalin, that bloc would rule by terror, exiling and executing dissenters and undermining the revolution's ideal of a workers' state and the potential to build international social transformation.[26]

Pressure to conform to direction from Moscow divided the American Left. By the mid-1930s, Trotsky had broken from the Communist International. Followers of his International Left Opposition in the United States condemned Stalin's direction and rigidly absolute sectarianism as the antithesis of revolutionary principles that aimed to unite the masses. There is ample evidence that the Communist Party USA held dogmatically to pronouncements from Moscow, but this is not to say that American Communism was monolithic or ineffective.[27] The reality of the Communist Party's positive impact on the Left and beyond cannot be ignored, and many who aligned with the party did not do so dogmatically; in fact, quite a few, like these writers, actually developed and augmented its ideals.

These seven women were part of the party's effort after 1935 to pursue a coalition of alliances that would bring together a diverse range of left-leaning organizations in order to fight the rise of fascism in Europe. Even as this "popular front" consolidated a political coalition, its success was also a cautionary tale. By ushering in a new phase of cooperation with the federal government, it failed to reckon with the state's role as handmaiden of the wealthy few.[28] The shifting geopolitics after World War II became a justification for state repression of revolutionary leftists and further undermined American Communism as a political discourse that called capitalism into question.[29]

As this brief history shows, the period between the two world wars was an extraordinary time not only because of the devastation of the Depression but also because American Communism flourished then as a political discourse and practical response to the crisis in capitalism. Many of those who worked with Communist-supported organizations did not engage in heated debates between factions, but they did begin to understand the underlying relations of capitalism and its ties to the state as well as the commonsense ideas that furthered corporate interests by obscuring them. Moreover, when people were traumatized by the economic crash and thrown out of their jobs, homes, and farms, they found help from the Communists. College students across the country, some, like Muriel Rukeyser, forced to leave school, joined party-supported relief efforts. African Americans came to trust the organizing offered by the party's white supporters because they saw their efforts to combat poverty and racism.[30] By the 1930s, Black steelworkers and farmers across the U.S. Black Belt were organizing, many supported by the party's ability to mobilize. Others joined because organizers in their neighborhoods, many of whom were white, supported Black people's needs. Trust was reinforced when the party adopted a policy of fighting what today might be called white privilege.

One of my aims is to highlight that history and women's place in it. In the early 1930s, the Communist Party encouraged women's efforts to form women's councils and neighborhood committees. Women became "the foot soldiers of the Great Depression," although their experience was not readily noted as such by historians of the decade. More than two million women, including heads of households, faced homelessness and joblessness and gathered in unemployment offices. They slept in vacant lots, on subways, and in boxcars.[31] Some led milk, meat, and bread boycotts. They made clear that all the resources provided by homelife were tied to production in the wage economy. Housewives' militant actions politicized the family, making its social roots public and renarrating the meanings of housewife and mother. Women's neighborhood actions redefined the boundaries of working-class struggle. Not until the mid-1930s did the party fully realize the significance of this organizing through neighborhood councils.[32] It then developed campaigns for lower rents and prices and equal access for African

Americans to relief programs and public housing. By mid-decade, women's membership increased somewhat in local and national party leadership. As they wrote for party publications, women pushed for access to free and legal birth control and abortion and challenged men's domination in the workplace.[33]

Women received an education from joining Marxist study groups, labor colleges, John Reed Clubs, union meetings, and other Communist-supported organizations. They learned the reasons for forms of consciousness that promoted property ownership, the autonomous (white and male) individual, and the notion that reason is the center of knowledge, a notion that severed humans from the web of life. Encountering in the radical Left an alternative understanding of life making, they noted the party's partial accounts. They brought into focus women's domestic work as valuable labor integral to the wage economy. Their attention to the land dispelled the mythic conception of nature as separate from human life. Some attended to sexuality as a political discourse and explored ways of knowing attuned to a life-giving energy that spans human and nonhuman bodies and relations. In tandem with their documentation of privation, their narratives enacted a layered remembering that illuminated the life-sustaining value of dependent relations across the so-called social and natural life worlds. Indeed, they disclosed that the division between social and natural life was itself one of capitalism's creations.

I was not the first to be inspired to find the women writers of the Left in the missing years between the waves of twentieth-century feminism. Feminist scholars, the Feminist Press, and the West End Press initiated recovery of their work in the 1970s. By the 1980s and early 1990s, a flowering of marxist feminist literary scholarship on the period was probing the history and groundbreaking contributions of women writers between the wars.[34] Among those scholars are Constance Coiner, Elaine Hedges, Linda Ray Pratt, Paula Rabinowitz, and Alan Wald. My own research stands on their shoulders and is deeply indebted to their dedication to making visible the Marxist and feminist legacy of the radical writers of the 1930s. That this legacy continues to resonate in the twenty-first century is evidenced by the republication of Charlotte Nekola and Paula Rabinowitz's anthology *Writing Red*, the reissue of Vivian Gornick's memoir *The Romance of American*

Communism, and the re-release of Tess Slesinger's 1935 novel *Time: The Present.*

It took a long time for me to find these writers from the 1930s. Like others who came to feminism through higher education in the turbulent late 1960s, I navigated a fractured political landscape. In college, I fought hard for my emerging feminist commitments in debates with antiwar Marxist friends. It was only in graduate school, in the wake of my growing existential desperation with post-structuralism, that I encountered marxist feminism. Here was a way of making sense of the world that attended to survival, that opened a coherent path through feminism, history, and my own lived reality as a woman, a young scholar, and by then a mother. The work of Margaret Benston, Michele Barrett, Hazel Carby, Angela Davis, the Combahee River Collective, Christine Delphy, Gayle Rubin, Lise Vogel, and others addressed the material realities of women's lives and labor. They offered an analysis that explained *why* women are oppressed and the relation of gender and race to capitalism.

In tracking down the women writers of the radical 1930s, I only gradually realized that I was looking not only for a lost generation in the history of feminism but also for an absence in my own family. When he was eighteen months old, my father's mother left him with her parents and ran away. Born in the first decade of the twentieth century, as were most of the writers gathered here, Grace Mildred Godfrey was pregnant and only seventeen when she married my grandfather, Peter Hennessy, also a teenager in 1923. The story goes that after they married they lived with his parents. Neighbors whispered about the violence they overheard. One of them later told my mother that Mildred had wanted a job; perhaps it seemed a way for her to escape an insufferable situation. On New Year's Eve, 1926, she packed her mother-in-law's suitcase, took the Sunday school cash, and left. The only evidence of her life after that is a letter she sent from Chicago the following September. She wrote that she had traveled across the north and west and had paid dearly for leaving her baby. She begged Pete to take her back. He never answered the letter.

I have spun many tales of what Mildred did in those eight months and after. How could a teenage girl in 1926 with little money get all the way to Chicago from the working-class life she lived in a mill-town neighborhood in Philadelphia? Where was she by the time the dark days of the Great Depression descended on the country? I see her in the anonymous protagonist of Meridel Le Sueur's novel *The Girl,* unskilled and a dreamer new to the big city. Drawn to a ne'er-do-well man, she eventually found herself living on the streets and pregnant. I see my grandmother among the forgotten women in the breadlines of the 1930s, those who sold their bodies to survive, rode the rails, and held the picket lines. Perhaps like these seven writers, she found her people among others who refused their assigned positions, maybe even turned to American Communism and wrote under an assumed name.

Women's control over their own sexuality and reproductive bodies features in the lives of all the women I assemble here. Le Sueur's mother was an ardent champion of women's reproductive rights on the lecture circuit, where she taught birth-control methods and was arrested for doing so. Several of these writers, perhaps like my grandmother, dealt with the trauma of unexpected pregnancy and faced family rejection for taking their reproductive options into their own hands. Several of them had abortions; Josephine Herbst's sister died tragically from a botched one. Muriel Rukeyser intentionally set out to have a child as a single mother and was disinherited by her family for doing so. Meridel Le Sueur wrote from her experience living in a Minneapolis community of women squatting in an abandoned warehouse. In her fictionalized account, they deliver a baby in the midst of the city's general strike of 1934 while strategizing how to put women's needs and desires into political language.

Mothers appear often in the writings of the women of the 1930s, and those works prompted me to consider what may seem obvious: mothers have a fundamental bearing on life making, even when mothering is refused or when its commonsense meaning is reconceived. "Mother" is a social position that situates "woman" at the threshold of life, a linchpin between culture and nature. To be "woman" is to be in some sense always understood in relation to "mother," regardless of one's refusal to bear children or one's experience of childbirth or parenting. Every woman, even those who are unable or choose not to be a mother, navigates the capitalist assignment of women to the persistent patriarchal gender structure that expects motherhood of all women, idealizes mother and nature, and at the same time devalues mothering along with all feminized and gender-nonconforming bodies, subjects, and activities. Thus, like it or not, all women are aligned one way or another with mothers as agents of procreation and care, signature figures of life making.

"Mother," however, like "woman," is a historical term, which is *tell that* to say that its meaning is neither natural nor fixed. Not all who *the Gop* mother give birth to children, and few women with children do that labor exclusively or without conflict. Similarly, "nature" is historical. It is not an external and eternal realm that humans manipulate and to which human meanings are attached. The web of life crosses nature and human life, each shaped by and shaping the other over the course of social and natural history. Idealized meanings of mother, nature, and woman are entangled with each other and often stripped of their history. The history of mothers, like the history of nature and woman, is conditioned by centuries of capitalism as a way of life, which is to say, it is class specific and racialized. The social position of mother was denied enslaved women when their children were taken away or procreation was forced upon them. For disproportionate numbers of Black women, maternity is still a deadly risk. Coercion is interlaced in the class history of motherhood, making clear that "choice" can be an option for women only when the material conditions of all women's lives are altered. Women have had motherhood stolen from them against their will. Meridel Le Sueur wrote about working-class *Eugenics* white women who were sterilized during the Depression if they were considered "feebleminded" or promiscuous.[35] Those sterilized through government-sponsored eugenics plans were mostly women of color.[36] "Woman," like "mother," defines a particular place in the capitalist division of labor, but that is not the end of the story. That assigned place is also a standpoint for redefining what "woman" means, and you do not need to have a uterus to do that.

As I lingered in the company of these seven women, I began to see that women's historical assignment to domestic labor resonates throughout all their work when the essential labor of care comes into view.[37] I address it most fully in my section "Labor," but in fact, it is a thread running through the whole of their lives and work. At times, domestic labor is a source of income; at other times, it appears as unpaid work, as an intimate complement to the reproduction of life in the natural world, or as an obligation to be refused or contested. Its spaces—the home and the female body—crop up as recurring arenas of life making.

I began researching the radical women writers of the 1930s with an interest in this labor of social reproduction. The concept of social reproduction was developed by marxist feminists in an effort to explain the material contribution of women's domestic labor to capital accumulation, a reality that was being addressed neither by liberal feminism's campaigns for rights nor by Marxists.[38] Initially, feminists used the concept of social reproduction to refer to women's unpaid labor outside the wage economy. It entails bearing children but also doing a host of other life-supporting activities for a household. Much of this labor reproduces the human capacity of wage earners to sell their labor power in exchange for money to buy consumable goods. Domestic labor converts the goods purchased with wages into meals, clothes, and a clean house; it educates and cares for the well-being of future wageworkers as well as of those unable to work, the sick, and the elderly. It ensures a ready labor force through care that extends for years before and after employment, yet the capitalist resists paying for that insurance. Invisible and unpaid and in that sense devalued as work, this labor is nonetheless extremely valuable to capital. Without the procreation and caretaking that occur in the home, there would be no able wageworkers. Despite adjustments to the patriarchal gender hierarchy, by and large this labor is still women's, an assignment many even now still understand as a natural inclination.

Social reproduction also takes place outside the home in schools, churches, and community centers where people learn how to comport themselves and how to make proper sense of their world. It has a special relation to home, however, because of the extensive and necessary labor that takes place there. No matter the claims that machines are replacing people; capitalism cannot do without workers, and home is the place where they are mainly reproduced. The crisis of the 2020 pandemic dramatically unveiled the fragile relationship between capitalism's wage economy and the home, and it revealed the intense and essential labor of maintaining life that takes place there. When capitalism faltered under

Covid, much of the labor of life making normally handled by consumer services, including schools, day-care centers, and eldercare facilities, was off-loaded onto the home. Home-based domestic labor exponentially increased, and the women redirected there to do it shouldered the burden, with children on their laps and laptops on their desks.

Even as the domestic arena harbors women's exploited labor, it is also a place where women plot rebellions. Feminists enacted this rebellion when they called for wages for housework in the 1960s, a strategic demand aimed at making visible domestic labor *as* labor. Trudier Harris remarks that the kitchen has long been a gathering place for women to voice their resistance by telling their stories while shelling peas for dinner. The women who named the first press run autonomously by women-of-color "Kitchen Table Press" knew this well. The kitchen table is where generations of women have come to resistance by sharing their yearnings with one another. It is still where they question and teach, and often do so through storytelling. Seeds sown at the kitchen table can take decades to flourish. It was certainly such a learning place in my growing-up house. My mother and grandmother presided in the kitchen, and the table was the place where food was served and homework was done, where visitors sat down with their stories and jokes. Young ones learned there how to listen, and eventually it was there that they spoke their rebellion. When my mother had her sixth baby (there were eventually seven of us), money from my grandmother's pay in the mill went to hire a woman to help. Then for a few months, every two weeks Sarah Johnson came to clean. Later, when another baby arrived and Sarah had gone, Mrs. Dougherty arrived to iron. They each brought to the lunch table stories of their families. Sarah and her husband, Clarence, were raising twin girls in North Philadelphia; Mrs. Dougherty was an elderly widow who lived in the neighborhood.

For domestics, an employer's home can be an uncomfortable space, situated as it is both inside and outside the wage economy, the family, and the homemaker's domain. Norms that apply in the formal workplace are less certain here. The absence of regulations (mandating minimum wages, overtime pay, safety standards, provisions for Social Security and unemployment benefits) can open the door to abuse. Even when the pay is fair enough and the job short-lived, as it was for Sarah, employer and employee often navigate their different relationships to domestic spaces awkwardly. I am sure my mother felt that strain and tempered it with conversation. I remember feeling it sitting across from Sarah at that kitchen table. Watching my mother open the fridge, set out plates, and pour my milk while Sarah carefully unwrapped her tuna sandwich, my mother insisting she could make Sarah a sandwich next time, I sensed in Sarah's reserve and that sandwich a well of history. I think now this was my first lesson in whiteness as a spatial relation suffused with energies I still struggle to name.

The writing of the seven women I gather here often reaches out to the reader, provoking a heightened awareness of one's place in history. The lives they wrote about had that effect on me. Life writing was also for all these women a literal undertaking and, as such, part of their political work. Three of them wrote memoirs: Meridel Le Sueur published one about her parents. Louise Thompson left one unfinished, as did Josephine Herbst, who also wrote a fictional trilogy based on her family history and a biography of the botanist John Bartram. Muriel Rukeyser published three biographies: on the founder of physical chemistry, Willard Gibbs; on the naturalist and astronomer Thomas Hariot; and on the politician Wendell Wilkie. Alice Childress's newspaper columns and her novel featuring a Black domestic's account of her working day are surely forms of life writing, as was Marvel Cooke's series on domestics and sex workers. Each reinvented conventional narrative forms for representing a singular life. Their innovations underscore that *life writing* is a crucial feature of the cultural production of *life making*.

The lives they render are captivating precisely because they defy the commonsense division between theory and story, public and private. In them, concepts come to life in naked and bold arguments, at times dressed in empirical fact or outright advocacy, at other times cloaked in detailed plots or shrouded in metaphor, the language of dreams. They open windows onto the Communism that propelled them as writers during this extraordinary decade and illuminate its stamp on American history. It is precisely because of this interest in life writing as a political aesthetic that I pay considerable attention to their own biographies. Although some scholars and members of a certain generation of the Left are familiar with several of the writers, many readers have never heard of most of them. The forthcoming republication of Nekola and Rabinowitz's collection *Writing Red* should help make more of their writings known. The biographical details in the following chapters also bring these women to life as complex persons whose lives informed the "feminism" and Communism they advanced. Embedded in their life stories are also interconnections among them, another salient feature of the history here.

In their lives, these writers either turned away from conventional expectations of women or navigated them strategically, sometimes painfully, in order to make time for research, fieldwork, community organizing, family care, friendship, and love. They knit these activities into their writing, including when the cost of the effort meant a life's unraveling. For some, these commitments implied constantly seeking a way to make a living from writing. A few lived on earnings from their publications; others found support from a patron or life partner, from paid work with party-supported organizations, as a journalist, teacher, waitress, or domestic. Most struggled financially at various points. Woven into all their writing lives were the intimacies they sought, fostered, and lost. These relationships complemented and sometimes complicated their political commitments, entered their work, inflected their political vision, and broadened their conception of life making.

Because these women's lives were entwined in the politics that inspired their writing, the biographical details I offer in each chapter are an important part of the story that each tells. The more I learned about these writers, the more convinced I became that the history they pass on is incomprehensible without some reckoning with this biographical material. It is entangled in their relationships to American Communism and to the labor, land, and love they navigated. Its truth, of course, I could not document in any absolute way, and I did not aim to do that. Indeed, they taught me that this truth only can be captured through what Muriel Rukeyser called "presumption." Presumption, as she puts it, is an imaginative process, propelled by "a passion to know people and the web in which they, suffering, find themselves." It leads one "to look for the sources of energy, sources that will enable us to find the strength for the leaps that must be made."[39] As I kept company with these writers, passionate to know them more, I began to presume and wonder. What common energies inspired them? When did their inventive paths cross? What shaped their desires, deceptions, and betrayals? Because each does life writing that brings neglected subjects into focus, my attention to them set out to do the same. As I trace absences and contradictions, fractured temporalities and parallel lives in their work, I aim to let presumption's audacity enable buried relations to emerge. "For there are meanings here," as Rukeyser wrote in her introduction to the biography of Gibbs, entitled "On Presumption":

> [They] blaze up for our moment, meanings of struggle and wish and loneliness, meanings of war, and structure and democracy that tie in with what we shall be doing tomorrow, meanings that must be reached.[40]

Much of the political work of the life writing gathered here lies in the use of story and poetry, and I occasionally pause over them to note a text's formal characteristics and to consider the relations of language where many of the encrypted processes of life making await. In chapters 1 and 2, they summon attention to masks and discretion, to the discourses of spectacle and performance, fact and dissemblance. They appear in the form of allegory (chapter 4), parallel syntax (chapter 5), and analogy (chapters 6 and 7). At times, I reveal the impact of these effects on my own life in the making, prompting me to consider relations I had not paid attention to and to take up the task of remembering. In chapter 3, for example, I confront my own background as it chimes with Josephine Herbst's and Meridel Le Sueur's efforts to recognize the parameters of whiteness, something they wrestled with both obliquely and head on. My story speaks to the challenges and failures of that effort as someone who grew up treading the very ground in Pennsylvania that Herbst and Bartram did. As you keep company with me, perhaps you will be drawn in as I was by these extraordinary women and by the gifts they offer from a long-past decade for the life making of today and tomorrow.

What follows is organized into three parts: "Labor," "Land," and "Love." Each part focuses on one or several writers as their life and work illuminates what life making entails. In each part, race, gender, and sexuality appear as vectors of capital accumulation lived in the flesh. I introduce each part with an initial shorter chapter that explains beyond this general Introduction the significance of each key term. These initial chapters highlight concepts that underlie the ensuing narrative. In this sense, they offer vestibules of historical context and thought for each new section. Chapter 1 introduces the section "Labor" and sets the stage for the gathering of writers from the Black feminist Left in chapter 2. That they are a gathering is part of the point. Marvel Cooke, Louise Thompson Patterson, Claudia Jones, and Alice Childress knew about each other; some were friends. They lived in the same vibrant neighborhood of Harlem off and on over many years, a proximity that makes their attention to Black women's domestic labor a striking statement about Harlem's radical history and an extraordinary intervention into American Communism. Being in the company of these writers who shared a common concern reinforced for me a sense of the collective community of ideas and action that characterized the Communism they embraced.

In the next section, chapter 3 introduces land as a source of life making as represented in the lives and writings of Josephine Herbst (chapter 4) and Meridel Le Sueur (chapter 5). Their attention to the land amplifies American Communism's East Coast focus as they draw out capital's imposition of a property relation on the land, on women's bodies, and on sentient experience. I am especially interested in the imprint of the 1930s on their writing in the 1950s, when they turned Cold War repression into an opportunity to reflect on American history. Each confronted then the settler's relation to the dispossession of Indigenous peoples, a history entwined in her own family legacy. The perspectives on that history that each developed unsettled common conceptions of property and rights and disclosed the relation of "whiteness" to the land. In so doing, they inserted a critical wedge into a persistent national story.

The topic of the final section, "Love," is Eros, an ample term that refers to the energy of many relations. That energy might be characterized as living attention, curiosity, desire, or imagination. Muriel Rukeyser invites twenty-first-century readers to grasp that erotic essence and its reach, to politicize the connections it enables and those it interrupts. She maps some of those connections in her exploration of the erotics of race work. In chapter 6,

I introduce Rukeyser by way of her extraordinary 1939 biography of Willard Gibbs, the founder of physical chemistry. It is, surprisingly, a powerful formulation of Eros, the energetic infrastructure of what she later designates "ecology—the study of the interrelations of living things and their environment" where "particles of intense life" circulate across multiple intimate environments.[41] In putting forward Eros as essential energy, Rukeyser enacts a critical turn at a time when the Communist Party had suppressed Alexandra Kollontai's attention to the erotic and its international political strategy was coalescing around the so-called Negro question and support for the Scottsboro Boys. Rukeyser was involved in the Scottsboro campaign, and she wrote about it in terms that expanded Kollontai's suppressed legacy. The final chapter, chapter 7, teases out the erotics of race work that Rukeyser conducted from the 1930s in the company of her friend Nancy Naumburg, the photographer, who shadows her writing on the Scottsboro case and appears in her magisterial poem "The Book of the Dead."

Like Rukeyser, Naumburg was allied with Communist film and photography organizations, and she traveled with her to West Virginia to report on a mining disaster there. One of the questions I raise is how to read her presence in Rukeyser's poetic documentation of race. By way of an answer, I read a section of Rukeyser's "Book of the Dead" in conjunction with one of Naumburg's three surviving photographs from the trip. Each calls upon the reader/viewer to apprehend investments in distinctions that some might call "race" even as they blur into something else. The process touches other unspeakable relations that condition the incomplete project of photographer and poet, and I turn to that unprocessed material in the chapter's final section. Here Nancy's shadow clings to erotic traces in Rukeyser's relationship to her student, Alice Walker, and conditions her rendering of race in her last published poem.

Although each section has its particular focus on labor, land, or love, these topics are never discrete. They all appear in the relations that preoccupied these writers: the laboring bodies in fields, on street corners, in kitchens, and in mines they witnessed; the eroded lands and slow violence of surveillance, silicosis, or amnesia they reported. Eros as life-giving energy also circulates throughout. It punctuates the intimate distances of a racialized

colonial history and is embedded in the dependencies of survival
and revolt. As such, it is a force to reckon with in any effort to work
a collective way out of crisis toward an interdependent responsibility to the future of life on planet Earth. Lingering in the company of these seven women writers brings home the radical potential of that energy.

Certainly these women taught me how to read at a point in my
life as an English teacher and scholar when I thought I knew all
there was to know about that. I learned anew to decipher history's
vestiges in a text's loose threads, to decode the strategic use of
story and spectacle, and to ponder the power of performance and
silence. As I allowed myself to follow the loose threads of a tale or
a life and to speculate on where they led, I found in life writing
from the past seeds for the present. Keeping company with these
extraordinary writers brought to life for me in absorbing, salient,
and luminous detail a history I had never known much about. This
is a book about the past, then, but it is a past they taught me to
know as restless, one that never stays put in the long ago but in-
serts itself into the here and now and perhaps into somewhere else
tomorrow.

As I learned more about these women's lives and writing, I soon
realized that the past did not stay put for them. Their alliances
with a changing American Communism as young women during
the decade of the 1930s followed them into unexpected places in
the decades that followed. Across this arc, their work is prescient
and timely. As Natasha Trethewey remarks of Rukeyser's "Book
of the Dead," "she could have been writing about the Tuskegee
experiment, lead in the water supply in Flint, Michigan, or the
impact, across the U.S., of the COVID-19 pandemic."[42] The same
might be said of all these writers. They each offer

> roads to take when you think of your country
> and interested bring down the maps again.[43]

These roads conduct us to street corners where women still wait
for work and to farmlands where agribusiness continues to poison
the land. They connect the American heartland to the cane fields
of Cuba, the back roads of Alabama to Harlem, and migrants in
Greyhounds to a restive past.

What can we learn from these writers today when these roads

remain much the same and we, too, are tied to their meanings? Each of them reminds her readers that crisis reveals what is essential. Almost one hundred years later, the pandemic clarified the meaning of essentials when the normal operations of capitalism teetered on collapse. It put reproductive labor in the national spotlight when feeding, teaching, and providing for children, the sick, and the elderly suddenly were all happening at home. These writers who came into their own as young women in the 1930s lived in similar times of crisis when capitalism was no longer able to provide the wages for consumer goods to keep bodies alive. They offer maps for reading crisis and for understanding the labor, land, and love that capitalism as a way of life is eroding to the breaking point. They also document the ways, in a crisis, women summon the collective strength to fight for essentials and alternatives. What they wrote from the 1930s and beyond spills into our present with messages that incite us to confront the contradictions of a way of life we still inhabit. At this time in national and world history, when the lives of so many are stressed to exhaustion and the earth itself is sounding alarms, they remind us that it is at this moment that we turn. We get to work with the people.

Labor

One
Black and Red

In the early dawn light of a chilly November in 1935, two women trudged toward the corner of 167th and Jerome Avenue in the New York City borough of the Bronx. They had made the trip again today from Harlem, and although not admitting it, each was nervous about the project they had taken on. Neither had ever done this before. Up ahead several women were already visible. This corner was one of the more popular ones where women gathered hoping to be hired for day labor as domestics. As they approached, the two could already see why it was one of the better spots. Here there were benches. At Simpson Avenue, the street across town where they had gone the day before, women had to scrounge around for a box to sit on or lean against a lamppost or storefront while waiting for a potential employer to drive up in her car.

Nearing the group, they breathed a sigh of relief. Unlike at the Simpson Avenue corner, where the stench was overwhelming, here they could draw a breath of fresh air. The women at the corner were a mixed group—some neatly dressed with trim hats and gloves, others in jackets too light for the season. Each clutched a paper bag bundle concealing her uniform, and each waited expectantly for a Bronx housewife to buy her energy for an hour, two hours, or even for a day at the measly rate of fifteen, twenty, twenty-five, or, if she was lucky, thirty cents an hour.[1] The two newcomers were not for sale, however. They were there to investigate, to write up what they saw, and to find out who these women were. What brought them to the corners? Why did they keep returning? The answers would become a story published later that month in the *Crisis* under the title of the local name for the corners: "The Bronx Slave Market."[2]

We might well ask these questions of the reporters: Who are they? What brings them to these street corners? In the next three decades, each would become a key figure in the Black Left. The taller of the two was Marvel Cooke, a journalist on the staff of the Black-owned and operated *New York Amsterdam News.* The other was Ella Baker. The two had met when Cooke was working for the *Crisis* when W. E. B. Du Bois was editor. In her work for the Young Negroes' Cooperative League, Baker was already developing a reputation as a clever strategist. She would become the most influential woman in the civil rights movement, a mentor to many leaders and best remembered as the founder of the Southern Christian Leadership Council and convener of the conference that would lead to the creation of the Student Nonviolent Coordinating Committee. Unfortunately, Cooke would be less well known. She was a canny investigator who used journalism as a medium for changing the way people see their world.

Her experience that day in the Bronx captured Marvel's attention and would not let go. She recalled later that she became fascinated by the slave market. "As a matter of fact," she recounted in an interview, "I've threatened several times recently to go up there and see if it's still going on."[3] The story she and Baker wrote captivated readers, too. The *Amsterdam News* republished it in 1937, and it may well have inspired the series on the slave markets written for the Federal Writers' Project in 1938 by the mysterious Vivian Morris.[4] Cooke wrote about the corners again fifteen years later, and in the intervening years, she wrote about women's labor across a range of occupations. Her stories expanded the common understanding of what domestic labor entails, and in amplifying readers' conceptions of Black women's labor, she made visible the broad scope and significance of their essential contributions to life making.

In her attention to domestic labor, Cooke laid the groundwork for some of the most significant contributions to feminist thought. Louise Thompson Patterson, Claudia Jones, and Alice Childress would carry forward that task and inaugurate what Mary Helen Washington would later call "Black left feminism."[5] Like Cooke, all these women writers from the 1930s were Communist Party members. All in different ways were also public intellectuals, theorists, and warriors. They turned to the party for the principles it forwarded and for the support for Black people it enacted during the decades when they were the ones most affected by the Great Depression and its aftermath.

Only a year before the stock market crash of 1929, at the 1928 Sixth World Congress of the Communist International, the Communist Party adopted a position that called for multiracial workers' solidarity and self-determination for the so-called Black Belt (the area of the southern United States in which over 50 percent of the population was Black). The American party's endorsement of the position provided the impetus for unprecedented levels of antiracist activity in the United States throughout the next decade. This commitment encouraged some Black women to suspend their suspicions of this mostly white organization. As the country sank into the Depression, in northern cities like Chicago, Philadelphia, Newark, and New York, Black women sought assistance from Communist-supported organizations that addressed their survival needs. When faced with unemployment and housing evictions, it was not unusual for a Black mother to shout to the children, "Run quick and find the Reds."[6] The Black women who joined the party in northern cities tended to be members of the working class, professionals, or members of nationalist groups like the African Blood Brotherhood and the Universal Negro Improvement Association. Those in the South were mostly working class and poor. Although Black women who committed to the party were a minority and were often dismissed, they endorsed structural change for relieving the suffering that people experienced during the Depression, and their strategies differed from women's more typical reform efforts.[7] As LaShawn Harris's research highlights, those women who allied with the party challenged the middle-class norms associated with Black women's clubs and church groups, and they offered alternative images of Black women's political agency.[8] In their varied alliances with the party and in their writing, Cooke, Thompson, Jones, and Childress all challenged respectability. In that regard, each in her own way was what Saidiya Hartman calls a "wayward" woman.[9]

In chapter 2, I consider selected works by these four Black

left feminists that are focused on domestic labor. Each writer makes visible Black women's domestic labor as a form of social reproduction—that is to say, as labor needed for survival or the remaking of life. Each also addresses the life-arresting investments of the capitalist state as it controlled the devaluation of that labor through legislation, policing, imprisonment, and even death. In doing so, they confront the fragmenting impact of capitalism. This fragmenting takes form in ways of thinking that separate and divide—Negro from woman, domestic from state, private from public; the list goes on. As Erik McDuffie points out, these writers also challenge the fragmented assumptions of the Communist Party's approach to the so-called Negro question while taking seriously and elaborating, as few had done, the Marxist-Leninist approach to the woman question. Thus, they forced consideration of an alternative that made visible Black women's triple oppression as Negro, woman, and worker.[10] In their writing, each discloses the conditions of the Black domestic whose undercompensated labor benefits white families (and *their* employers) while depriving her of time to care for herself and her family.[11] By centering Black women domestics in their writing, each allows us to see that the essential service of a domestic's labor is devalued and underpaid when it is racialized and feminized as a Black woman's work. To say, as they all do in other words, that a Black woman's domestic labor is exploited is to claim that her labor creates value for capital precisely because it is cheap. I want to pause to explain the significance of that claim.

Exploitation refers to a social relation in which the material benefit of some is made possible *through* the material losses of others. The domestic labor of cleaning, laundering, cooking, and caring is essential because it enables those in the wage workforce to return to work each day fed, clean, and cared for, ready to exchange their labor for a set time. In many cases, both historically and still, this labor is unpaid, considered the natural duty of enslaved women or of mothers, wives, and daughters. That notion keeps the wages for paid domestic labor low. When the cost of domestic labor is off-loaded to families, along with many of the other costs of social reproduction (think of health care, day care, or eldercare costs), we might consider that labor exploited because the capitalist benefits. Struggles over wages often address the unmet needs of social reproduction, and the state is a major actor in meeting or not meeting those needs. The state sets the minimum wage for the services and consumables that enable workers to return to work. It sets the allotments for those unable to work and for the social security of the elderly and the disabled, and it provides many of the other requirements of social reproduction unaddressed or only minimally met by the wage economy. In one of their most radical contributions, these writers make visible the state's role in managing capital's appropriation of the labor of social reproduction. So long as the state does not establish minimum wages or require overtime pay for domestic workers, it enables individual household employers to pay the lowest possible wage. Although some domestic workers are employed by families who actually control big capital, most work for middle-class households; they are in this sense caught in their class struggle. Moreover, and importantly, as these writers disclose, ideologies of race and gender legitimize ways of seeing that cheapen not only the intrinsic value of domestic work but also the women who do it.

Embedded in these narratives on domestic labor is astute analysis of what Karen Fields and Barbara Fields call "racecraft." "Racecraft" refers to ideas about race that circulate as social facts through the fabric of our lives. It governs rituals of deference and kinship, codes for common notions regarding what goes with what and with whom, and how people see each other. It sets routines and rules of evidence, belonging, sight, and value.[12] Such a crafting of consciousness under capitalism construes "Black" and "female" as worth less. To call racecraft "ideology" is to go one more step because the concept of ideology invites us to ask *why* and *to what end* these differences, rules, and practices take hold.

Marxists answer that ideas lived as social facts help reproduce relations of labor and ownership. Historically, racecraft legitimizes the devaluation of some workers' labor as "unskilled" or "low wage." It narrows the scope of who they can be while helping guarantee access to property, wealth, and opportunity for those regarded as naturally respectable, reliable, capable, and good. The state's apparatus—stretching from the family to school, church, media, and law—helps guarantee that this value system is reproduced, and if need be coercively enforced, through the ideology of racecraft and the arresting power of the criminal justice system.

Both race ideology and the repressive power of the state continually managed the dehumanization of Black people under slavery and the criminalizing of freed Black people in the wide net cast by Jim Crow, in the 1930s and still. Black women's collective resistance, especially in the form of cross-race organized alliances, posed a powerful threat to this arrangement, and the arresting power of the state was poised to prevent that.

The institution of slavery enacted the most extreme collaboration between life-arresting state power and capital accumulation from Black women's domestic labor. A more surprising historic example is the probation system. From early in the twentieth century, probation was directly tied to Black women's domestic labor. Women arrested for any number of petty crimes—vagrancy or prostitution, for example—would serve time and be put on probation for their wayward acts.[13] Probation meant being sent into white homes as domestics. In this respect, the state colluded in a system of involuntary servitude for Black women that resembled the convict-leasing system or indentured bondage.

All these writers were directly involved in domestic service and were touched by the state's arresting force. Childress worked as a maid, and Cooke, Thompson, and Jones had family members who worked as domestics. The FBI surveilled and kept files on all of them. Several of them were denied passports, and all at some point in their lives were arrested. The state's surveillance and harassment added a new twist to the meaning of domestic violence, as it surely disrupted family life and the ability to hold a job.

Nowhere were the relations entangling the arresting state in the domestic arena more in the national spotlight than in the case of the Scottsboro Boys. Exploding on the national stage in 1931, it became a lightning rod for the Left. The case provided the catalyst the Communist Party was seeking to address the "Negro question" and to realize the priority the Comintern gave to "Negro self-determination," especially in the Black Belt.[14] The Communist Party's legal wing, the International Labor Defense (ILD), defended the nine young men who were accused of raping two white women and sentenced to death. All the writers I consider in chapter 2 worked in some capacity to support their case. Thompson, a leading figure in the national organizing effort, wrote about the case, as did Jones, Herbst, and Rukeyser. Their writings draw out the relation of race, gender, and sexuality to property and to domestic labor. They highlight the use of racialized sexuality and white womanhood as pretexts for the state's power to arrest Black life, disrupt Black families, and criminalize Black men through the police, the courts, and state-sanctioned vigilantes.

In their attention to domestic workers, each of these writers expands the party's—and the Left's—theoretical and political scope by renarrating the commonsense understanding of "domestic." They counter the notion of home as a private arena of social life and reveal the state's policing power over it. Through the figure of the domestic worker, they center Black women politically and thus radically recast them as the vanguard agent of change. As Jones forcefully asserts, when Black women, the most devalued of actors, organize against exploitation, domination, and state repression, they become a militant force. That force is especially threatening when it defies race as an instrument of control and crosses race's imaginary yet violent lines of difference to forge collective alliances. In making this point, these writers put forward a radical left feminism that would not be recognized as such for decades.

The iconic actors in this broad conception of domestic violence are mothers and prostitutes. Mothers figure both in the lives of the Scottsboro Boys and in the party's handling of their case. They also appear as prominent figures in the lives of these writers and across their writings. The presence of mothers in their work is invariably strategic, challenging conventional abstractions and idealizations of motherhood by politicizing the meaning of "mother" from a radical Black left feminist perspective. In their representations, Black mothers become critical figures, situated at the threshold between private and public life. That they appear adjacent to prostitutes is purposeful. Their alignment discloses the fact that both are workers—indeed, domestic workers—whose labor goes unacknowledged. Moreover, as these writers suggest, both are intimately familiar with the state's arresting force, the propertied interests that force serves, and the manipulative language of morality that mystifies their labor and devalues their lives.

In the following chapter, I consider the historical and social forces that enabled these four writers to find their way to the American Communism of the 1930s and the impact it had on their representations of domestic labor. I discuss the various formal and rhetorical forms they employed to convey their groundbreaking arguments. Cooke's undercover investigative strategy as a journalist is one. Thompson's use of public spectacle is another. As a national organizer of a 1935 march on Washington, D.C., in support of the Scottsboro defendants and in her essay about the march, she effectively reorients a national sensation that was being played out through two spectacular icons of domestic discourse, the mother and the whore. Her essay "Toward a Brighter Dawn" uses a national stage for Black women to launch domestic workers' demands.

The Black left feminist who endured the most direct and intense state violence was also its major theorist, Claudia Jones. Her rhetorical prose strategies are neither subtle nor undercover. Growing up in the 1930s, Jones was inspired to affiliate with the Communist Party by their defense of the Scottsboro Boys. Her 1949 essay "An End to the Neglect of the Problems of the Negro Woman!" remains a far-reaching theoretical statement delivered to the Communist Party in the rhetorical mode of critique. Highlighting its inattention to Black women's problems, Jones reveals the "superexploitation" of their reproductive labor and places Black women at the vanguard of international revolution. Punished with imprisonment for her outspoken political activity and unsparing critical writing, Jones resorted to more nuanced strategies in her poems, one of which I read for its coded commentary on the entangled relationship between the arresting state and women's life-supporting domestic labor.

An apt coda to these writers is Childress's *Like One of the Family*. Originally published as a running column in the newspaper *Freedom* and then assembled into a novel, this work draws upon undercover, performative, and critical strategies. Although closely allied with American Communists and party-sponsored events, Childress never publicly acknowledged any party affiliation. Perhaps the terrorist tactics of the Red Scare prompted her to protect her professional life by keeping her Communist credentials undercover. Her novel spotlights an outspoken Black domestic worker, Mildred Johnson, whose dramatic monologue is a clever performative masquerade, at times a searing assessment of her employers and at times a song of praise to unions. In making visible the lived realities of doing housework for pay, Mildred enacts a compelling instance of progressive popular education.

Two
Centering Domestic Workers

*The Harlem-Based Politics of Marvel Cooke,
Louise Thompson Patterson, Claudia Jones,
and Alice Childress*

Soon after Marvel Cooke became a member of the Communist Party in January 1936, her mother came to visit her in New York City. She joined a gathering at Marvel's 409 Edgecombe Avenue apartment in the Sugar Hill neighborhood of Harlem where friends, mostly white and a few Black, were celebrating Marvel's membership in the party.[1] One of them went up to Cooke's mother, Amy Brown Jackson, and asked what she thought of her daughter joining the party. Unsurprised by the question, her mother retorted that Marvel had been brought up on Marx and Lenin.[2]

If not an entirely accurate representation of Marvel's upbringing, Amy Brown Jackson's spunky reply reveals her quick-witted character and hints at the left-leaning politics that infused Marvel's childhood. Born in 1903 in Mankato, Minnesota, Marvel was still an infant when the family moved to Minneapolis. Her mother, Amy Wood Brown, was the daughter of a freedman from Northumberland County in eastern Virginia. Amy's father, Charles Wood, was a miller and a preacher on Sundays. He worked on the Underground Railroad, sending enslaved people who came through Northumberland County to his brother in Cape May, New Jersey. As a young woman, Amy Brown was in service for a white family in Washington, D.C. The household summered in Great

Barrington, Massachusetts, and it was there that she met W. E. B. Du Bois. Although he was over ten years older than Amy, Du Bois took her out from time to time and they developed a close relationship. She returned to Washington eager to find work outside of service, received some training in cooking, and took a government test for a job as cook on an Indian reservation near Pierre, South Dakota.[3]

Marvel's parents were both light-skinned. She believed that her father's mother was a white woman with blue eyes and blond hair who was the daughter of the master's wife on a Virginia plantation, born when he was off to war and given to an enslaved family to raise.[4] Marvel's father, Madison Jackson, was the grandson of Henry Jackson, the brother of Andrew Jackson, president of the United States. Henry was a freedman whose family, also from Northumberland County, Virginia, was given land in Ohio along with their freedom when Henry Jackson died. Eager for an education, Madison left home to attend high school and went on to graduate from law school at Ohio State University while working to support himself as a Pullman porter. He met Amy Brown when she was on the train to Pierre. Madison Jackson was very close to his eldest daughter, Marvel, throughout her childhood. He spoke with her often about politics, especially the thinking of the socialist Eugene Debs, whom he greatly admired.[5]

When the Jacksons moved from Mankato, Minnesota, to Minneapolis, they were the first Black family to move into Prospect Park, a neighborhood near the university, where Madison built a house along the Mississippi River.[6] Growing up in an all-white neighborhood and attending all-white schools, Marvel learned early about racial discrimination. In 1909, a "race war" broke out in Prospect Park when William Simpson, a friend of Madison Jackson's, purchased a nearby lot. That October, a crowd of over a hundred people descended on the Jackson home, where Simpson was staying while overseeing the construction of his house. The Prospect Park Association decided they did not want a Black family in the community and came to deliver the message to Simpson and the Jacksons.[7] Neither family moved away, however. Years later, Marvel still remembered her mother standing her ground that day and turning the hose on the crowd.[8]

In keeping with her father's dreams, Marvel attended the Uni-

Marvel Cooke testifies before Senate Investigating Committee, September 7, 1953. Bettmann Collection, Getty Images.

versity of Minnesota, where she majored in English and was one of five African American women in her graduating class. During her college years, she met Roy Wilkins, also a student there, and they became engaged. Although Marvel eventually broke off the engagement and in 1929 married the Jamaican athlete and science teacher Cecil Cooke, she and Wilkins remained friends, and he went on to become the editor of the *Crisis* after Du Bois left. When she graduated from college, Marvel moved to Harlem, which in 1926 was still the center of a renaissance in American Black life and culture.

Soon after her arrival in New York, and at her mother's suggestion, she visited the offices of the *Crisis* to introduce herself to Du Bois, who was then editor of this widely read magazine, the flagship journal of the NAACP. When she mentioned that her mother knew him, Du Bois expressed surprised delight and said he would help her in any way he could. Soon after, he offered her a position as his assistant. Eventually she was promoted to a position on the staff of the magazine, where she wrote a column and began to learn what would become her lifelong profession as a journalist. Through friends, she met Zora Neale Hurston, Langston Hughes, and other prominent Harlem figures. Thanks to the *Crisis* and Du Bois, she was also introduced to the broad network of political figures connected to the NAACP. At Du Bois's suggestion, in 1932 she secured an apartment in the building at 409 Edgecombe Avenue where he and many other notable Harlem figures were living.[9]

Cooke's decision to join the party and to write about the slave markets was conditioned by her upbringing and relationships with some of her new friends, but it was also influenced by the swirl of events in Harlem in the mid-1930s, by then the hub of the Communist Party.[10] In 1928, the party designated Negro self-determination in the southern United States as one of its strategic international organizing targets, and Harlem became the northern center for that effort, beginning with the end of ethnic segregation in the party's local affiliates (Naison, 17–19, 34–35). In the North, the party was instructed to bring Black and white workers together for joint actions, and it "initiated a campaign of self-criticism and discussion aimed at mobilizing membership to destroy white chauvinism 'branch and root'" (46). According to Mark Naison, "Never before has a political movement, socialist or otherwise, tried to create an interracial community that extended into the personal sphere, and defined participation in this community as a political obligation" (47). After 1929, the party became the principle site for organizing in Harlem that was not centered on a club, a church, or national background. As the Depression's economic crisis intensified, the Communist Party in Harlem recognized people's immediate survival pressures and became involved in consumer needs by leading food boycotts and blocking evictions. Linking these struggles to a broader vision was a shift from the false distinction between the wage market and the home. This attention to the needs of Black women as mothers and workers was another striking contrast to the party's official stance on women and race and its ambivalence on consumer movements (87).

The historian Erik McDuffie's brilliant scholarship on Black women's organizing in Harlem during those years documents this new focus on survival issues and its appeal to Black women. Championing survival attracted public attention, drew people to the party, and gained their allegiance. As he shows, many Black women became prime movers in efforts to meet people's needs, and the party supported those campaigns. In June 1935, a "housewives' revolt" took place in Harlem when one thousand protesters, most of them Black women, pressured white grocers on 135th Street, many of them Jewish, to lower their meat prices. Bonita Williams, a charismatic working-class Communist from the Caribbean, led the protest. She headed the Harlem Action Committee against the High Cost of Living, a group affiliated with the Communist Party.[11] Marvel Cooke certainly must have been aware of this event because it took place just a few blocks from her home. During the previous summer, tenants in her Sugar Hill neighborhood protested rising rents, an event that was reported in the paper where she was working.[12]

News of other party-supported direct actions where women were key organizers certainly circulated through her social networks.[13] One of the chief housing champions was the Harlem Tenant's League (HTL). Unlike other tenant organizations, it linked poor housing to broader struggles against white supremacy, capitalism, and imperialism.[14] It became a model for the party-led unemployed councils that were the infrastructure of Communist-supported mass movements throughout the decade. In recognizing the connections among Black women's exploitation, consumption, unemployment, and racial discrimination, the HTL challenged the party's concentration on the shop floor as the key site for organizing.[15] With a membership of mostly Black women and with Black women in prominent leadership positions, the HTL politicized the prescribed roles of women and mothers. One such leader was Grace Campbell, an HTL founder and officer. Another was Audley "Queen Mother" Moore, who, like Campbell, was a Harlem working-class organizer who blocked evictions and led rent strikes. She also helped organize domestic workers. An ardent Black nationalist, she decided to join the Communist Party in the early 1930s after attending a mass demonstration in Harlem in support of the Scottsboro Boys.[16] Bonita Williams, like Moore, was a working-class woman steeped in the traditions of Harlem's southern and Caribbean Black life, and again like Moore, she spoke the political language of the streets. With their organic connections to the neighborhood, Moore and Williams operated in a different political world than did Cooke and other professionals. Their experience as women who cleaned the kitchens of white women under the constant threat of sexual assault by white men shaped their message and its medium. Several were "stepladder speakers" on neighborhood corners. Campbell went on to be the first Black woman elected to the New York State legislature, but in the 1920s she was a social worker in the criminal justice system. Her years working in the women's prison, the courts, and the probation system gave her a critical perspective on the state's punitive relationship to Black women's survival needs and the forces that led them into sex work and into the system.

I want to think that Marvel Cooke may have crossed paths with some of these women when walking back and forth to work at the Black-owned and operated *Amsterdam News,* whose offices were off 135th Street. After Roy Wilkins became editor of the *Crisis,* he frequently visited Marvel's apartment because he also lived in the Edgecombe complex. In the fall of 1935, he suggested that if she did a story on the Bronx day-laboring domestics, he would publish it in the *Crisis.* The offer of a story for the *Crisis* was especially timely for Cooke because the journalists at the *Amsterdam News* where she worked had just gone on strike. The editorial staff had joined the Newspaper Guild, the first all-Black unit to do so. From the outset, Marvel was a leader in the union organizing effort and opened her apartment to the Newspaper Guild's meetings. When the editorial staff asked the owners of the paper to recognize the union, their response was a lockout. On October 8, the picket line formed on Seventh Avenue outside the building housing the *Amsterdam News.* At that time, there was a police directive that no more than two people could be on a picket line. When a thousand people showed up, police intervened, and on October 10, Marvel Cooke was arrested.

The strike was still underway when Cooke and Ella Baker went to the corners in the Bronx. The byline for their story in the November issue of the *Crisis* mentions that Cooke and fifteen others were locked out of their jobs at the *Amsterdam News* because they sought recognition of their unit of the guild.[17] Writing the slave market story while confronting the resistance to organized labor in her own job probably helped propel Cooke to join the Communist Party. The newspaper strike also inspired her to support the domestic workers' organizing campaign. She later recalled that after the newspaper strike, she said, "I've got to work with the people," and she chose to work with the Domestic Workers Union.[18] That union began when a club of domestic workers in the Bronx decided to bring all the workers in private families into an organization for collective bargaining. They established themselves as the Domestic Workers Union of New York, which they launched publicly at a mass meeting in June 1936.[19]

Baker and Cooke's 1935 *Crisis* story makes clear what is often opaque in commonsense understandings of wage work: that working for wages entails a literal exchange of abstracted labor capacity over an amount of time in return for pay, and in that exchange, the employer will try to reduce the pay and extend the time for the work. Part of the force of Baker and Cooke's story is its disclosure of a restless history that shaped the terms of that bargain as a recent and a more distant past converge in the present.[20] We learn that the corners were in one sense a new marketplace. By 1935, the security, such as it was, that Black women once obtained in the form of long-term steady employment as domestics in the wealthy white homes of Manhattan, Long Island, or Westchester had all but disappeared. With the onset of the Depression, these employers let go their Black maids and turned to newly available white help. Black women who were once employed in industry were also now on the corners looking for day labor. By 1935, women of the predominantly middle-class Jewish population in the Bronx who could not have afforded a maid before the Depression now could boast that they had one, given the rock-bottom wages offered for day labor. Desperation drove a day laborer to accept these terms, which often approximated outright servitude. Glorying in the status of having a maid, the new breed of white employers coming to the corners chiseled down wages even after the terms were set. Some robbed their employees of the agreed-upon wages by changing their clocks. Other wage-theft tactics included charging for room and board, offering rides home that never materialized, and deducting from pay for the meager lunch they provided.[21] Some employers paid no wages at all in lieu of carfare, a uniform, and lunch for a day's work.[22]

An older past also haunted the corner market. Only a generation or two earlier actual slave markets had operated, and their
legacy lived on in northern-style practices. Veiled and explicit references to slavery in Baker and Cooke's narrative underscore that
its vestiges saturated the relations of Black domestics and their
employers. Once hired, the narrator explains, women work under
the "scrutinizing eye" of "Mrs. Simon Legree," a reference to the
infamous plantation owner of *Uncle Tom's Cabin*. The narrative
skillfully renders this insertion of slavery's legacy into a theater of
work where the embodied performance of white control and Black
subordination mingled with an ironic nod at "free" labor. "Under
a rigid watch," we are told, the maid is "permitted" to scrub floors
"on her bended knees, hang precariously from window sills cleaning window after window, or to strain and sweat over steaming
tubs of heavy blankets, spreads and furniture covers" (Baker and
Cooke, 340). The myth of the white middle-class home as a sanctuary from the toil of the marketplace is dispelled as a racialized
space comes into view where whiteness is reproduced through a
Black woman's performance of her subordinate place.

The domestic space was racialized in another respect as well.
The *Crisis* highlights in bold type that the northern borough of
New York City "was known for its heavy Jewish population," and
the story mentions that business on the corners would flourish
during the approaching Jewish holidays. Even if women in these
households were used to cleaning and cooking, hiring the casual
labor of a Black maid offered the opportunity, if only provisionally, to secure middle-class white status. The narrator introduces
the first of would-be employers as "a squatty Jewish housewife,
patently lower middle-class," and later remarks that "exploiters"
like her "are the wives and mothers of tradesmen and artisans
who militantly battle against being exploited themselves" (340).
The contradiction inadvertently discloses what the narrator does
not: the corrosive effect of race distinctions. The equation of the
"squatty Jewish housewife" with Simon Legree underscores her
oppressive treatment of her employees, but her relation as housewife to the battle against exploitation remains obscure. Describing
her as "patently lower middle-class" carries a tinge of scorn, perhaps resentment, for her access to class mobility and whiteness,
assets that Black women were barred from and that were attained

at their expense. The encounters on the corners and in the home enact the proximate competitive social positions of Jews and Blacks and the white–Black binary that structures them. The narrator concedes that the women waiting for work are "a study in contradictions" because they cling to the American dream that those who work hard will succeed. In fact, the entire scene is such a study. The pall of "whiteness" cast over the Jewish housewife excludes her from the collective organizing Cooke and Baker recognize among tradesmen and endorse among domestic workers. Her treatment of her employees is indeed oppressive, even as she is also a scapegoat. As women often do, she, too, bears the scars of a profound historical wound—an American dream forever deferred by the invention of race, a weapon that cuts differently, albeit deeply, across groups, inciting the belief that security rests on the subjection of another or by competition that obscures a common cause.

One of the most stunning features of their story is their attention to sexuality as an integral component of the exchange taking place on the corners. Just after announcing that, rain or shine, the day-laboring women wait expectantly for Bronx housewives "to buy their strength and energy for an hour, two hours, or even for a day," the narrative tucks in the added detail that human love is also a marketable commodity here. "If not the wives themselves, maybe their husbands, their sons, or their brothers, under the subterfuge of work, offer worldly-wise girls higher bids for their time" (340). The casual mention of men soliciting sex from Black women makes visible an all-too-familiar pattern from slavery here reiterated as a feature of the marketing of Black women's domestic labor. Indeed, it suggests that the very concept of "domestic labor" may be incomplete without mention of sex work. The effect is to draw back the veil over the respectable private space of the white family home to expose this other labored activity sharing a commercial marketplace with it.

Layers of undercover action proliferate when the reporters posing as domestics realize that another undercover agent, "one of New York's finest" in plain clothes, is trailing them. Suspecting the cop is trying to arrest them for soliciting, they stage a cat-and-mouse game and cleverly elude him. This encounter between undercover agents is more than a moment of ironic levity, however. It firmly situates the market for domestics and prostitutes at an ideological crossroad where sex work is not presented as an immoral sideline but is unmasked *as* work and as an all-too-intimate companion to women's devalued domestic labor. The specter of sex as a need for men and a domestic service the housewife or her proxies provide hovers in the margins.[23] Moreover, this detail in the story underscores that the arena of private life is policed. The effect is to shatter the mystique of home and sexuality as private by situating domestic labor and sex work in the crosshairs of state surveillance and control.[24]

A decade and a half later, Cooke probed the sexual dimensions of domestic labor in her five-part series on the Bronx slave markets for the *Daily Compass*. In researching for this story, she once again went undercover, this time actually hiring herself out as a maid.[25] The narrative she crafts cannily draws out the relationship between Black women's commercialized domestic labor and sex work and highlights the policing of both by a life-arresting state. In her research for this series, Cooke joined a group of women gathered in front of Woolworth's on 170th Street, between Jerome and Walton Avenues. By then this Bronx corner had its counterparts in Brighton Beach, Brownsville, and other areas of the city.[26] Reform efforts during the intervening years when Fiorello La Guardia was mayor of New York City (1934–45) brought a more benign liberal state to the corners when his administration opened the first free hiring hall on Simpson Street on May 1, 1941.[27] By 1949, however, more Black women were facing unemployment after the war and the corners were again back in business.

Eager to get away from the sensationalism of the *Amsterdam News,* Cook had accepted a position as assistant managing editor at the Harlem-based *People's Voice,* where she essentially ran the paper.[28] After several years, she joined the newly founded mainstream *Daily Compass,* where she was able to pursue her investigative reporting on the "slave markets." In this version of the story, she reports in stirring detail the scandalous conditions that Black domestic laborers were still forced to endure, embellished by her own eyewitness experience and undercover strategy. She traces the fluctuating existence of the corners and the wage rates for domestic labor following the Depression and highlights the sobering fact that in the intervening years not much had changed. Her account goes on to draw out the lived experience of day labor, beginning with the humiliating impact of seeking work on the corners.

She begins with the viewpoint of the arriving employer, who sees "the drooping shoulders" of the waiting women, "the worn hands," and "the look of bitter resentment on their faces" as they quietly gather, "leaning on store fronts or lamp posts, waiting for anything—or nothing at all" ("I Was Part," 1). Slavery's imprint on this market and the bodies assembling there comes into view as the auction block is summoned and a relationship of humiliating domination is sexualized in the employer's gaze. The housewife who arrives at the corner where the women gather, "almost undresses them with her eyes as she measures their strength" (1). By her third day on the corners undercover, Cooke reports, "hundreds of years of history weighed upon me. I was the slave traded for two truck horses on a Memphis street corner in 1849. I was the slave trading my brawn for a pittance on a Bronx street corner in 1949. As I stood there waiting to be bought, I lived through a century of indignity" (4). History saturates the racecrafting of Black women's commercialized labor in the public marketplace. Once she enters an employer's home, Cooke renders the employer's gaze as an instrument of sexualized control as the employer "watches" Marvel change into her work clothes. When one employer insists she scrub the floors on her knees, she refuses and rebukes the woman with the charge that "this method of scrubbing went out with the Civil War" (7). These details in the story mark a bold shift. Here sex is a relation of power exercised by white women and integral to the domestic workplace. Cooke captures its deployment in the white gaze and the relative body positions of the two women. Making visible this vector of power as crucial to the affirmation of whiteness is one of the narrative's most potent critical moments.

The fact that the corners are also places for another kind of sex work is also made explicit when the narrator reveals that she was approached there more than once by men soliciting sex. In this story, sex work is also policed, but new undercover state agents have replaced the plainclothes cop. Civic and social agencies now "point to this shameful act" and warn, "Slave Market areas could easily degenerate into centers of prostitution" (15). The narrative skillfully recodes this moral discourse when domestic workers report that they "are still humiliated, day after day, by men who frequent the market area and make immoral advances." While they "resent and reject" this treatment, they do not judge the prostitutes, who are just "looking for an honest day's work to keep body and soul together" (15). In April 1950, Cooke once more went undercover to do a twelve-part investigative series for the *Daily Compass* on prostitution. In a narrative that ranges from sex workers' personal lives to the workings of the vice squads, courts, and prisons, "Occupation: Streetwalker" describes every facet of these women's labor, once more addressing who they are, why they do it, and why they stay.[29]

Cooke published these stories in 1950, but like so much of the writing that I consider in this chapter, they emerged from the 1930s, inspired by her visit to the Bronx corners in 1935. The 1950 "slave market" series ends by spotlighting the Domestic Workers Union and the efforts of the women who began to organize collectively in 1937 under the leadership of Dora Jones. The New Deal essentially dealt out domestic workers, who, along with farmworkers, were not included in the Social Security Act of 1935. In 1950, a domestic worker could receive workers' compensation for injuries only if she worked for a single employer for at least forty-eight hours a week. She could receive unemployment insurance only if she was one of four or more workers employed in that home for fifteen days in the calendar year.[30] The shocking fact is that in 2022 these restrictions are still in place. In closing with the voices of the Domestic Workers Union leaders, Cooke brings domestic work into the arena of collective political struggle.

Cooke did much of her investigating undercover. Going undercover was for her more than simply performing or putting on a disguise, however. It raised the question of what is seeable as a central social problem that set the terms of her investigative practice. Sadly, this tactic also characterizes her place in history, where until recently she remained largely unrecognized in genealogies of feminist thought and in the annals of the American Left. I confess that I knew nothing about her when I began researching the history of Black women from the radical thirties. I came to recognize, however, that working "undercover" was a critical practice integral to her political work and an apt strategy for discovering the relationships she teases out in her writing. She invites readers to see Black women's domestic labor as taking place across activities in which their bodies are dominated, devalued, and worn down as someone else profits from their labor. She reveals the "domestic" as a broad workplace shaped by race, gender, and sexuality. Not least of all, she spotlights the state's power to survey, control, and arrest as a constant presence for Black women performing domestic services for money. These relations are largely invisible when commonsense distinctions invite us to consider home and work, race and labor, sexuality and the state as distinct and separate entities. Cooke's stories make Black women seeable in a new and potentially revolutionary way. In short, they are a stunning advance in feminist thought, a conceptual leap that was as significant an intervention in ways of seeing as was the invention of the electron microscope four years earlier.

A few months after publishing her first undercover story, Marvel Cooke joined the Communist Party. She later described the decision as unplanned, but any casual quality to that choice was deceptive, for she went on to embrace this commitment for the rest of her life. Her story about her party membership, however, is in keeping with her choice of a low profile, a choice that took her undercover to the corners in November 1935. Cooke says that she joined the party after being goaded by the well-known Communist lawyer Ben Davis, who used to come to strike headquarters when the *Amsterdam News* editorial staff were on lockout. When he saw her on the picket line Davis told her, "You have a much better reason to be a member of the Communist Party than I have" and asked, "Why aren't you a member?" She replied, "Because no one ever asked me."[31] By January she had joined the party. Over the next decades, she would become an effective recruiter, precisely because her preference was to do that through one-on-one relationships rather than to do high-profile party work. She did not become a leader in the party, and she never held an office in any of the organizations it supported. She did not wear her party membership on her sleeve, but neither did she deny it, even when later called upon to name names before the House Un-American Activities Committee. Her Communism was there in plain sight if one knew how to see it.

LaShawn Harris, one of the few scholars who has written on Cooke and whose outstanding recent work on the Black feminist Left has recovered her contributions, speculates that some of

Cooke's lesser-known activism may have been the effect of this discreet approach, what I am calling her "undercover" tactic. Harris characterizes it through Darlene Clark Hine's concept of a "culture of dissemblance" that some African American women cultivate as a form of protection. It creates the appearance of openness while actually shielding the truth about their inner lives from friends as well as from whites.[32] Whether for self-preservation or expedience, Cooke's "dissemblance" allowed her to filter her left convictions through both the Black and the mainstream press and to reach a broad reading audience where her ideas might be heard and make a difference.

Linking Struggles on the Popular Front

In September 1930, Charlotte Osgood Mason, a well-known wealthy patron of the arts in New York City, consulted the spirits. She was distraught and unable to recover from her break with Langston Hughes. Accompanied by her goddaughter Cornelia Chapin and Cornelia's sister Katherine, and holed up in Katherine's room on School House Lane in Quakertown, Pennsylvania, the trio asked the spirits if letting go of Langston had been the best decision. Mason had informally "adopted" Hughes (and later Zora Neale Hurston) and insisted that he call her Godmother. Long a devotee of Spiritism, Mason believed that her special sensitivity to the paranormal made her a conduit for Native Americans and the primitive peoples of Africa.[33] Delivering their guidance via automatic writing, spirits known as "the Friends" advised her not to regret her decision to cut ties with Hughes. However, they added, Louise Thompson, who worked as Mason's assistant, "is one to be wiped off the slate of Godmother's existence."[34]

Without the help of spirit guides, Louise Thompson was already making plans to leave her employment under Mason and to bid good riddance to the philanthropic world of the Harlem Renaissance. In 1929, Alain Locke had introduced her to Mason, knowing that she was in need of a job that would offer flexible hours. Her mother had been diagnosed with cancer, and the position with Mason offered Louise the possibility of working from home while caring for her mother. She was to be Mason's assistant and was to help one of Mason's latest protégés, Langston Hughes. He had just

Louise Thompson at the podium, circa 1930s. Louise Thompson Patterson papers, Stuart A. Rose Manuscript, Archives, and Rare Book Library, Emory University.

arrived in the city from Howard University and needed someone to type the revisions to his novel. In the ensuing months, as Louise typed a mountain of pages, she and Langston formed a close and lasting friendship.

In early 1930, the flamboyant and spirited Zora Neale Hurston arrived on the scene, back from two years of fieldwork and weighted down with the folklore materials she had collected. Hurston was another of Mason's "adopted" talents whose research she was funding. Assigned by Mason to help Hurston assemble her materials, Thompson typed up her notes, working long into the night in Hurston's apartment, near where Hughes was living in Westfield, New Jersey. A dispute between Hughes and Hurston over the collaborative authorship of their play *Mule Bone* soon ensued and led to a now-infamous falling-out between them, perhaps inflamed by Hurston's jealousy over Thompson's close relationship with Hughes.[35] As the dispute unfolded and Hurston left town, Thompson's work for them dried up. That fall, Mason summoned Louise to her New York apartment and formally fired her, chiding her for betrayal and for not being an "authentic" Negro.[36]

I imagine Louise leaving that meeting incensed by Mason's arrogance. She had worked in service jobs before, and she knew the submissive behavior they required. She recognized the deference Mason demanded, and she would not give it. Mason was not her patron, and she refused to call her Godmother as Hughes and Hurston did. The job for Mason had drawn her into a close-knit circle of Harlem Renaissance literati, perhaps too tightly. They were an exciting but also a cloistered set, one she navigated smoothly, but it was time to expand her life's work and find a way to address the inequities that made possible the wealth and arrogance of the world's Masons. In New York City, there were a lot of them, even when many of the mighty were falling in the wake of the crash. Working for Charlotte Osgood Mason confirmed Louise's antipathy for philanthropy, a distaste with deep roots in her own family's humiliation. She was relieved to be moving on and had a hunger to do more. Perhaps being around Hurston helped convince her to risk and dare more openly, even if her aspirations were also practical. She needed employment to support herself and her mother. The skills she brought to working for Mason—reporting on events and organizing materials as well as typing—were assets that could allow her to spread her wings. Within the next few years, she would put those assets to work in prominent national and international organizations as well as in Harlem, where she would become the most influential Black woman shaping the Communist Party's popular front in the 1930s.

At that time, caring for her mother was also a significant fact of Louise's life. She had witnessed her mother's sacrifices as a single parent working in low-paying jobs while also taking care of her daughter. A lifetime of mutual support was a mainstay for both of them. Lulu, as Louise's mother, Lula Mae Brown Toles Thompson, was known, was light enough to pass for white but she saw no reason to do so. Lulu's own mother, Emma Colwell Brown, was the daughter of a white heiress in Ohio who was given to a Black family to be raised.[37] She married a fair-skinned African American man, Moses Brown, who was Lulu's father. Lulu moved to Chicago in 1899 and a year later met and married a brown-skinned bartender; they divorced soon after Louise was born in 1901. Lulu supported herself working as a domestic and a seamstress. Her networks in the Black community introduced her to a prominent Black family in Seattle, and with an offer to live with them in hand, she and little Louise moved west. Their stay in Seattle was short-lived, however, because of Lulu's discomfort with her own meager means. They went on to Goldfield, Nevada, where Lulu married John Thompson. The trio moved often across the West, and it was in these western towns that Louise developed race consciousness when she suffered from rejection by other children. She was admitted to the University of California, Berkeley, but had to defer for a year because she fell ill with influenza during the 1918 epidemic. Lulu helped her through her studies for a degree in business administration, moving to Oakland to be near her, and later joined her when she became a teacher in the South.[38]

As a member of the faculty at the Pine Bluff Mechanical, Agricultural, and Normal School in Arkansas, Louise confronted the raw realities of the Jim Crow South, brought home by news of a lynching in Little Rock, only forty-five miles away. The experience brought back painful memories of the racist towns of Oregon and Nevada.[39] Looking for better prospects, she took a position at Hampton Institute in Virginia, a segregated faculty and facility. When students at Hampton went on strike, protesting the school's racist practices, Louise supported them. In 1928, longing to make her way to New York City, she left Hampton for Harlem, arriving keenly attuned to racial injustice.

That sensibility was about to blossom in 1930 when she closed the door on Mason. She was in effect leaving the Harlem Renaissance and entering the Red Harlem of the 1930s, which had become the center of radical Black thought.[40] The social networking and administrative skills that had landed her the position with Mason would continue to be assets in the next few years as she helped lay the groundwork for the Communist Party's expansive popular front even before it became official policy in 1935. By mid-decade, she would be the preeminent Black woman on the left.[41]

Thompson had a knack for recognizing how to seize the public's attention in order to make a strategic intervention. This ability, in combination with her aptitude for forging connections among people and struggles, was her brilliance as an organizer. It would be on full display in the 1933 march on Washington that she coordinated and in her leadership at the 1936 National Negro Congress, two among the many events she helped organize. These two were also occasions for her to publish feature stories in the CPUSA magazine the *Woman Today*. "And So We Marched!" (1933) and "Toward a Brighter Dawn" (1936) draw attention to the exploitation of Black women's domestic labor and to the life-arresting power of the state. A savvy organizer who developed extensive national and international relationships, Louise knew how to operate effectively and strategically behind the scenes and when to seize a platform out in front. Throughout the 1930s and for the next three decades, she pushed forward countless initiatives that brought together diverse constituencies. Her handful of publications demonstrate her skill in developing, conducting, and communicating these ideals to a broad public. She was not a grassroots activist; her talent was to think and act on a large scale as a convener of organizations and coordinator of events that addressed a range of related injustices and reached broad publics on local, national, or international stages. Invariably, she used these venues to bring women's issues into focus. The paid work she went on to do after leaving Mason fostered this talent and offered her opportunities to travel and expand her networks. It led her to join the Communist Party and to work on behalf of political prisoners, many of whom, like

William L. Patterson (whom she later married), were Communist Party leaders.

In 1933, the Scottsboro case would be her catalyst. Thompson displayed her incisive ability to seize the moment by organizing a march on Washington in support of Haywood Patterson, one of the Scottsboro Nine, who had received a second guilty verdict. The march brought five thousand people to the capital and became the basis of her article "And So We Marched!," in which she represents the event as "a landmark in the growing solidarity of the Negro and white people."[42] Her ingenious coordination of the event dramatically made this point by allying Black and white women workers brought together by the state's arresting power. Her essay "Toward a Brighter Dawn," published three years later, reports on the women's division of the National Negro Congress (NNC), an organization that would become the leading channel for implementing the CPUSA's popular front policy. Here Thompson spotlights Black women's domestic labor. Her relentless work on women's issues extended into the 1950s, when she helped found the militant Sojourners for Truth and Justice in 1951. Their manifesto, "A Call to Negro Women," and the delegation to Washington they organized had their roots in Thompson's strategic organizing of the 1930s, when her relationship to the Communist Party and the interventions she staged enacted forms of public pedagogy and an innovative and canny Black left feminism.

A month before her position with Mason ended, concerned at not having heard anything about the renewal of her one-year contract and needing a job, Thompson found a position with the American Interracial Seminar of the Congregational Church as assistant to the director of the Congregational Education Society (CES).[43] Here, at least, philanthropy was institutional and more fully directed toward labor and racial injustice. The society's focus on education and interracial understanding suited her. The extensive travel required for the position enabled her to form strategic connections for her increasingly left-leaning political activities. She worked for CES for over three years. During that time, she joined the National Committee for the Defense of Political Prisoners, which was actively involved in the Scottsboro case. In 1933, she left CES after finding a more stable job with the International Workers' Order (IWO), a Communist-supported organization. The IWO was a national fraternal insurance society operated by the party. Founded in 1930, in addition to insurance it offered community services to a diverse ethnic population. Its appeal for Thompson was that there was no patronage; instead, as she said, "It was people doing something for themselves."[44] Louise's vibrant energy made her perfect for the position. She suggested the organization reach out to African Americans because its insurance policies were far better than those of the infamous Metropolitan Life Insurance, which fleeced many of its Black policyholders.[45] She eventually became a field organizer and traveled widely to organize chapters, especially across the South. The work complemented her growing commitment to the party and her increasing involvement in a host of activities on behalf of those hemmed in by exploited labor and state repression.

Louise's political awakening was closely tied to a social life that spanned domestic and political spaces. An inveterate gatherer of people, she opened her New York apartment to organizing meetings, and many involved some facet of support for the Scottsboro defendants. She formed friendships with other freethinking so-called New Negro Women, who also smoked and enjoyed Harlem's social life. As a college graduate with no children then and with close connections to prominent Harlem leaders, she enjoyed a certain independence and cultural cachet. Because she did not pose a serious threat to middle-class Harlem society, she was an excellent liaison between its liberal members and the more radical Left.[46] She joined the Scottsboro Unity Defense Committee and worked on the dance benefit they held, which drew together an array of artists and jazz musicians for an audience of middle-class Black leaders. Events like this benefit expanded the party's political arena to entertainment spaces and liberal constituents and stretched it to engage more fully the culture and traditions of the Black community (McDuffie, 77).

Soon after her arrival in New York City, Louise had encountered Communists in many of the social gatherings she attended and among the friends she was making. She enrolled in the Workers' School in New York City and invited to her Harlem apartment intellectuals who discussed aspects of the Soviet Union's history and politics, Marxism, and Scottsboro. She coordinated the Friends of the Soviet Union, an organization that Marvel Cooke later joined.

In 1931, they held a presentation that drew over one hundred people. By the end of that year, she had aligned with the League of Struggle for Negro Rights, the party's national civil rights organization (76). In May 1932, she gave a speech at one of the party's several Scottsboro demonstrations in Harlem, this one sponsored by the National Committee for the Defense of Political Prisoners.

That June she helped coordinate a trip to the Soviet Union by a group of volunteers planning to make a film, among them her friend Langston Hughes. The experience would change her life (58).[47] She was inspired by what she learned, especially from women and from her encounters with the dark Uzbeks she met during the group's travel to central Asia.[48] She returned to New York in November, convinced "that only a new social order could remedy the American racial injustices I knew so well" and ready to commit to the party and its national campaign to support the Scottsboro Boys.[49]

In early 1933, her beloved Lulu succumbed to cancer. Knowing her mother would wish her to carry on with her political work, she plunged into the whirlwind surrounding the Scottsboro case. In the coming months, no young Black radical woman was more visible in building the Scottsboro support movement nationally than Louise Thompson (McDuffie, 77).[50] She accepted a position as assistant secretary of the National Committee for the Defense of Political Prisoners that was supporting the cause of the defendants. That spring, a stunning development took place in the case. Ruby Bates, one of the two women who had accused the young men of rape, claimed local officials had forced her to lie at the second trial of Haywood Patterson. She had gone into hiding and was living outside New York City. Unfortunately, her reversal was not enough to convince an Alabama all-white jury, and on April 9, they again delivered Patterson a guilty verdict. Louise immediately helped form the national Scottsboro Action Committee. As its executive secretary, she handled fundraising, outreach, and logistics and organized a string of public rallies.[51] In May, with the support of the committee and the ILD, she coordinated the Mother's Day march on Washington that brought people from across the country to the White House to deliver their petitions to President Franklin Roosevelt.

The event showcased Thompson's organizing skill and political ingenuity. She put women in the vanguard of a case that vividly encapsulated the lingering legacy of slavery in the South. The state's willing protection of white supremacy was on full display in the case of the criminalized Black defendants, and the white women's charge of rape made clear the power of gender and sexuality in reproducing white supremacy. The case confirmed that whiteness offered real and imaginary property and protection even to those women who owned nothing but their labor, and its advantages were forcefully guarded by the police and the courts. As several photographs of the march document, Louise used the event to intervene dramatically in that structure. In one, she appears in the front row next to Ruby Bates, and in another Bates is surrounded by Scottsboro mothers. Both tableaus capture a political intervention that exceeded the event's immediate aims.

Thompson makes this point in her piece "And So We Marched!" She represents Black women as the vanguard of a broad-based opposition to racial injustice that refused to comply with the racial and sexual policing that invited poor Black and white women to target each other. She places both Bates and Janie Patterson, Haywood's mother, in this vanguard as "the living symbol of the increasing unity" among men and women, white and Black, that the march represented. The scandalous joining of the mothers of the victims and their perpetrator represents Bates as having "come to realize the vicious frame up of the boys" and as now "willing to risk even her life" by going to court to free them. Thompson does not absolve Bates, however. Instead, she asks readers to see her as "a southern white worker" and to abandon the racialized sexual moral discourse being slung back and forth by all sides, a discourse that framed Bates as either an icon of innocent white womanhood or a whore.[52]

At the time of the arrest, Bates was seventeen, a migrant mill worker and sex worker, riding the rails dressed in overalls. Like Victoria Price, the other purported victim, Bates had reason to fear being charged under vagrancy laws and the Mann Act, which targeted sex workers.[53] Press coverage of the trial and the defense lawyers' statements represented her and Price as traveling "for immoral purposes."[54] Thompson's choreography of the march and her written account invite the public, and especially the Left, to see Bates differently. Placing her in relation to the young men's mothers made apparent that they shared a common struggle to survive

Mothers of some of the Scottsboro Boys posed here with Ruby Bates, May 1933. *Left to right*: Ida Norris, Janie Patterson, Ruby Bates, Mamie Williams Wilcox, and Viola Montgomery. AP Photo.

through low-paid, devalued labor as mill workers, sex workers, and mothers subject to the oppressive manipulations of a police state. Almost every line of Thompson's short essay makes this incisive point. In so doing, it reenacts the strategic use of public spectacle.

In her account, Thompson affirms that women were not merely symbolically on the front lines; rather, they made up the majority of the marchers, and the experience was instructive. As the caravan traveled from New York City through Philadelphia and Baltimore to the capital, women who joined "learned their lesson well," many testing their strength and realizing their power for the first time. Delegates brought to the capital two hundred thousand signed petitions for the release of the Scottsboro Nine, and they called for the government to comply with the Thirteenth,

Fourteenth, and Fifteenth Amendments to the Constitution. Although the president refused to see the delegation, Thompson's essay makes clear that the march had a broader aim. It set out to make "white workers see more clearly that the struggle for the Negro is also his fight for freedom from exploitation." Most important, Thompson concludes, "both are realizing that apart neither can be free."[55]

The following year, Thompson had her own brush with southern police brutality when fieldwork for the IWO took her into several southern states where she experienced it firsthand. In a visit to Birmingham, Alabama, she set out to meet with Elizabeth Lawson, editor of the *Southern Worker*, in order to learn more about a May Day demonstration and a series of strikes that had taken place there. Arriving at Lawson's apartment, she inadvertently walked into a police raid. Arrested along with several others, she was jailed in the same prison that had held some of the Scottsboro Boys. Du Bois agreed to publish her account of the event, the essay "Southern Terror," in the *Crisis*.[56] There she argues that a true program for Negro rights had to pursue the destruction of American capitalism.[57]

The previous month, the party had summoned Thompson to intervene in a turn of events that proved the mothers of the Scottsboro boys were continuing to play a key role in the party's political choreography of the case. Because almost all the defendants were teenagers, their mothers had to approve decisions regarding their legal representation. The lead defense attorney, Sam Liebowitz, was threatening to distance himself from the ILD and to recruit the Scottsboro mothers to press their sons to withdraw from the ILD's legal representation and proceed independently with him. The party called upon Thompson to persuade the mothers to stay with the ILD. She was assigned to pick up Ada Wright in Atlanta, Georgia, where she was working as a domestic in a wealthy section of the city, drive to meet Janie Patterson in Chattanooga, Tennessee, and bring them both to Montgomery, Alabama, where a demonstration was taking place. Janie Patterson was initially unwilling to go because she was caring for her granddaughter, but Louise managed to resolve the difficulty, and all three women ended up in the car.[58]

It is conceivable that one of Louise Thompson's most significant political encounters occurred while she was on the road with these women. If so, it is a story that is knowable only through oblique references in the official record. I want to think that the time the three women spent together gave Louise a chance, as car rides can do, to listen. I imagine her hearing Janie and Ada talk about their experiences as caretakers, mothers, and maids. Other moments like this car ride also occurred when Louise reached out to the mothers and won their trust. On several occasions, she welcomed Josephine Powell, Viola Montgomery, and Ida Norris as well as Janie Patterson and Ada Wright into her home in New York.[59] Perhaps some of the things they said in these encounters reminded her of Lulu. I want to think that their stories inspired her to foreground their labor in her work and confirmed her conviction that Black women are indeed the vanguard of the revolution.

What we do know is that in the next few years Thompson would pursue the struggles of Black women domestics. Her 1936 essay "Toward a Brighter Dawn" makes their case by drawing the reader into scenes that offer glimpses of their lived reality. The essay opens like the script of a play: "Early dawn on any Southern road. Shadowy figures emerge from the little painted wooden shacks alongside the road. There are Negro women trudging into town to the Big House to cook, to wash, to clean, to nurse children—all for two, three dollars for the whole week."[60] These figures in the dawn light are making their way to town to do day labor as domestics. The mention of the "Big House" they head toward casts the long shadow of slavery's history. Here, dawn marks the beginning of another day's work; by the essay's conclusion it also signals the potential brighter day of an organized political movement on behalf of domestic workers. Details of the domestic's working day enable readers to comprehend the extent of the labor and of the needs it meets, all for close to no remuneration. The resulting portrait dispels the myth of Aunt Jemima happily caring for white children while her own invisible family is left in the little wooden shack. Significantly, the narrator also mentions each woman's unmet need for rest, as she "must crowd into one day the care of her own large family" ("Toward a Brighter Dawn," 14).

As the essay unfolds, the drama shifts from workers at the "Big House" in town to early dawn on a plantation where dim figures "bend down in the fields to plant, to chop, to pick the cotton from which the great wealth of the South has come." The labor of the sharecropper's wife is in evidence here. Sardonically, the narrator comments, "She never has to worry about leisure time problems." Fieldworker by day, mother and homemaker by night, she scrubs the pine floors and boils the clothes in the big iron kettle in the yard. The scene then switches abruptly to dawn in the North, where in the Bronx women "emerge from the subway. Arranging the *Daily Mirror* and *Daily News* along a park bench, they sit and wait" (14). The passage goes on to convey their voices, signaled by the use of italics, addressing a prospective employer or calling upon a public: *"Here we are for sale for the day. Take our labor. Give us what you will"* (14). The narrator goes on to name the Bronx slave market as "a graphic monument to the bitter exploitation of this most exploited section of the American working population—the Negro woman." The term "triple exploitation" appears here, Erik McDuffie suggests, for what is perhaps the first time in print. It would become a signature concept for Claudia Jones and for Black feminist theorists in the 1970s (McDuffie, 112).

We eventually learn that this extensive dramatization of the low-paid and unpaid domestic labor of Black women across disparate regions is the backdrop for the essay's principle mission, which is to report on the meeting of the women's subsession of the National Negro Congress (NNC), a national federation of Black organizations whose convention was held in Chicago in February 1936. The lived reality of Black women's labor across regions was the basis for a resolution drafted by this gathering of women. It called on the NNC to prioritize Black women's domestic labor in a three-point program that promoted organizing domestic workers into unions to be associated with the American Federation of Labor (AFL), organizing housewives into leagues, and unionizing professional women. Of the three, only the last would come to fruition, evidence of the persistent devaluation of women's domestic labor even by the Left. It is noteworthy that the proposal to organize domestic workers also flew in the face of the AFL's notorious resistance to organizing unskilled labor.

The essay's message of Black–white unity was in keeping with the party's new popular front policy. During the popular front period after 1935, the party essentially broadened its base to form coalitions with unions, churches, and other political parties in an effort to enact practical reforms. Leaders began to recast the party's image as a responsible American institution allied with American liberalism. At that point, American Communism essentially abandoned its prior commitment to Negro self-determination, which had been supported by the League of Struggle for Negro Rights and its newspaper, the *Liberator,* and redirected its energies toward supporting the NNC (Naison, *Communists in Harlem,* 173). Although the NNC was not officially a Communist organization, the party played a significant role in its creation and initial meetings. Louise Thompson was one of the few women on the NNC's New York Sponsoring Committee, and like other party members, she played a significant though tempered role at the 1936 convention in Chicago (Naison, *Communists in Harlem,* 170–83).[61]

The fact that Thompson witnessed her mother's struggles no doubt influenced her commitment to women domestic laborers, and it also may have conditioned her own reluctance to be hemmed in by motherhood and marriage. She married William L. Patterson in her late thirties. Her pregnancy at age forty came as a surprise because she had had an abortion during the 1932 trip to Russia and thought her childbearing days were over. She was devoted to her daughter, Mary Louise, but she did not let motherhood keep her from a busy work and travel schedule for the ILD and other organizations. Ever the clever organizer, she recalled later that she opened their home at the famous 409 Edgecomb Avenue apartments to lots of people as a way to recruit babysitters.[62]

In 1951, Thompson Patterson launched an organization that would be one of her signal Black feminist achievements. At the time, Cold War terrorism led by Senator Joseph McCarthy was out to destroy American Communism and all it had accomplished in the previous two decades. Her husband, William Patterson, held top posts in the party, including as executive for the ILD and, in 1948, as head of the Council of African Affairs (CAA), an organization affiliated with the party that aimed to bring attention to the struggles of Africans.[63] Pat, as friends called him, soon became a target of the Red Scare unfolding across the United States. In 1950, as the national climate of repression intensified, he was summoned before the House Select Committee on Lobbying Activities, which demanded he provide the names of CAA members. When he refused, he was charged with contempt of court. Acquitted in 1951, he faced another charge in 1954, for failing to provide the Internal Revenue Service with a list of Civil Rights Congress donors. That charge sent him to federal prison, where he was one of a group of political prisoners that included Claudia Jones (McDuffie, 177).

By 1951, state repression of the radical Left was in full force, and state and vigilante violence against Black people was intensifying. W. E. B. Du Bois was indicted for failing to register as a foreign national, and the Red Scare became the pretext for indictments and arrests for all manner of trumped-up infractions. Louise Thompson Patterson was called to testify before the New York Supreme Court in a trial targeting the IWO as a Communist organization. During this time of expanding state repression, she and Beah Richards formed a committee that would become the Sojourners for Truth and Justice. As Thompson had done for many other organizations, she accepted the post of executive secretary. During the Sojourners' brief existence—from 1951 to 1952—they fostered a collective critical consciousness. Their manifesto of September 1951, "A Call to Negro Women," "stands as a landmark in twentieth century U.S. Black feminism"; it condemned Jim Crow, the lynching and raping of Black women, police brutality, Black poverty, and the political persecution of Black radicals (McDuffie, 175). Their efforts to forge ties with South African women anti-apartheid activists are evidence of Louise's long-standing commitment to fostering international partnerships (McDuffie, 178). Their call was directed to Black women, but the delegation they led to Washington that September delivered a message to all Black people in the United States, Africa, and Asia. The long list of demands they brought to politicians and cabinet officials as well as to President Harry S. Truman linked domestic civil rights, feminist, and international justice claims. Thompson Patterson's broad political perspective is evident in the connections the Sojourners drew between exploited and racialized wage labor, unpaid domestic labor, peonage, and state violence in the form of police brutality, poll taxes, lynching, and the confinement of political prisoners. Claudia Jones was a member of the Sojourners, but she was unable to join the delegation to Washington because she had been indicted under the Smith Act and was under house arrest.[64] However, she did send a telegram of support. Over the next decades, Thompson Patterson continued her work in support of political prisoners, most notably as the executive secretary of the New York Committee to Free Angela Davis, among whose many members were Ella Baker and Marvel Cooke (McDuffie, 198).[65] Erik McDuffie's history of the Sojourners points out that this little-known collective continued a long line of Black women's militant resistance, stretching from Sojourner Truth to the future Combahee River Collective and, we can now add, the Black Lives Matter movement (174).

In the last years of her life, Thompson Patterson was invited to participate in events honoring Zora Neale Hurston. Hurston's rediscovery by Alice Walker had led to a flurry of public attention to her work and life, including the first annual Zora Neale Hurston Festival of the Arts and Humanities, held in Eatonville, Florida, in 1990. In an oral history session, Thompson Patterson recounted her employment experience with Charlotte Osgood Mason and her brief history with Hurston. Her remarks pointed to "things that crippled" Hurston. "To know these things," she said, "is to know much better how to combat certain things that are still here. And because [Zora] was such an individualist, she tried to do it alone."[66] The "things" that can set a life course remained unnamed. Perhaps out of respect for the occasion honoring Hurston, Thompson Patterson did not develop her point. I want to think that reencountering Hurston at a time when Thompson Patterson was assembling her own life's memoirs may have reminded her of that pivotal day when she closed the door on Mason and set her own life on a different course toward fostering the collective endeavors of a Black left feminism.

Beyond Domestic Containment

The Elms at Morn

Barbed wire fence surrounds me
And the fog rolls slowly in
The elms stand tall and stately
And the maples crowd them in

The mops are on the porch my dear
And Frances sits beside me

Lois smokes a cigarette
I am in an awful net[67]

Claudia Jones composed this poem when she was in prison on Ellis Island under the Smith Act. Four years later, when she was sent to the federal Reformatory for Women in Alderson, West Virginia, she committed her poems to memory and only wrote them down after being released.[68] "The Elms at Morn," however, she enclosed in a letter to John Gates, the editor of the *Daily Worker*. I read it as a coded message.

Here, two four-line stanzas sparely and obliquely render an imprisoned speaker's complex affective experience of incarceration, but also something more. The first stanza's description sets up a tension between confinement and resistance that the remainder of the poem subtly unfolds. Barbed wire surrounds the speaker in the opening line, but it cannot keep the fog from rolling in, nor can it restrain the elms of the title. In a clever turn, their "stately" stance heralds the morning in sovereign defiance of the wire. The maples crowd the elms, but to be "crowded" is not the same as to be "confined." Indeed, a "crowd" can become a resistant force, as the second stanza obliquely hints. Here a voice that may or may not be the speaker's announces a pending domestic task, ending with a surprising endearment. If the line is spoken by a guard, that guard may be a prison worker, like Grace Campbell, and may even be part of the gathering on the porch. That mops are on a porch suggests a liminal space, a threshold to some outside world. Frances and Lois, their familiarity marked by the use of their first names, are close by. They sit and wait or smoke, their passivity conveying both the weight of prison time and their resistance to answering the summoning mops. The last line's jarring break from the poem's cadence is a clue to its coded message. If an "awful net" confines the speaker during her arrested experience, then this line's irruption of another temporality conveys a break, even a breakout, from the poem's confining rhythmic pattern punctuated by a call to mandatory domestic labor. Like barbed wire or a porch, a net is full of openings. The fact that the speaker, like the elms of the first stanza, is crowded by others hints of an unyielding collective that bears witness to a new day beyond awful confinement.

Thanks to Carole Boyce Davies's extensive recovery work, we

now know of Claudia Jones's poetry. Poetry was not the form she chose for most of her writing, but as Davies tells us, she turned her poetic sensibilities to the genre of prison blues as a form of creative resistance.[69] "The Elms at Morn" conveys in its coded form two central concerns of Claudia Jones's life's work: the link between women's domestic labor and the state's repressive power, and her vision of a better day achievable through Black women's networks and awesome leadership.

In the opening of her political biography of Claudia Jones, Davies announces the remarkable fact that Jones was "the only Black woman among Communists tried in the United States, sentenced for crimes against the state, incarcerated, and then deported."[70] Jones's FBI file reveals that what made her a public enemy was embracing Communism.[71] Imprisonment and deportation were the final acts in the state's relentless thirteen-year pursuit, which began with aggressive FBI surveillance in 1942.[72] Jones was arrested three times. The first was in 1948, when she was incarcerated on Ellis Island and threatened with deportation to Trinidad. She was not a U.S. citizen, and the State Department refused her 1940 application for citizenship because of her Communist affiliation.[73] The second arrest was in 1950, when she was found in violation of the McCarran Internal Security Act, suspected of engaging in subversive activities as a non–U.S. citizen who had joined the Communist Party. The third arrest was in 1951, again under the Smith Act, and in that year, she suffered a heart attack. When the Supreme Court rejected her appeal, along with appeals from sixteen other leading Communists, she was interned on Ellis Island, in a special McCarran wing, and was sentenced to one year and a day in federal prison to be followed by deportation. In poor health, she began her sentence in January 1955. At Alderson prison, she joined Elizabeth Gurley Flynn and Betty Gannett, also well-known Communist political prisoners, and the three became close friends and supporters.[74] Released from Alderson three months early for good behavior, Jones was deported to the United Kingdom in December 1955.[75]

Jones never argued for the overthrow of the U.S. government. She was targeted, arrested, and removed from the United States because she was a Black woman and an immigrant who advanced a political philosophy to address the exploitation of Black women,

Claudia Jones *(second from right)* in a police van at the Federal Courthouse in New York City, June 20, 1951, en route to the Women's House of Detention. *From left*: Elizabeth Gurley Flynn, Marion Bachrach, Claudia Jones, and Betty Gannett. AP Photo.

racism as a national domestic practice and state policy, and the spread of U.S. imperialism. In the McCarthy period of the 1940s and 1950s, this stance was grounds for imprisonment and deportation, especially when espoused by a Black immigrant woman calling for Black–white political unity.[76] Despite enormous pressure, Jones was undaunted in her commitment to historical materialism as a philosophy and practice that could speak to the situation of colonized people, and especially Black women, whose lived realities, she charged, had been neglected by democratic governments, the "free" press, and the Communist Party. As a party member for all her adult life and as a top-level party official, she was qualified to confront party members on this neglect. She did just that in "An

End to the Neglect of the Problems of the Negro Woman!," one of her most brilliant articulations of the political situation of Black women, which she published in the party's theoretical journal, *Political Affairs*, two years before her final arrest. I see this ground-breaking essay as a major contribution to feminist theories of life making. First, however, I turn to one of the consequences of Jones's arrest and deportation. Although the state imposed on her the "awful net" of imprisonment, it did not succeed in confining her political activities after deportation. It did, however, almost succeed in erasing her from history.

As Davies contends, the deportation of Claudia Jones effectively "deported the radical Black feminist subject from U.S. political consciousness."[77] In a sense, that was precisely the point. The U.S. domestic cold war on political dissent targeted Communists because they questioned the policies and rhetoric of postwar capitalism's economic boom and disclosed its dependence both domestically and abroad on a dispossessed cheap labor force. As a major voice of that position, Jones posed a significant threat. Less readily explained, except in the very terms that Jones named "neglect," is her invisibility in histories of the Left, including the feminist Left, where until recently she was also written out of history.[78] Davies ascribes this erasure to the general marginalization of Black women's radical thought.

As one of a group of Black intellectuals who recognized the far-reaching tentacles of the U.S. empire, Jones made clear that U.S. policies were recruiting formerly colonized people into new dependent labor markets. As a Caribbean migrant and a stateless person, she was all too familiar with the obstacles to life making that nation-states impose. Those obstacles continued after she arrived in the United Kingdom, where her temporary travel document was confiscated and was not extended to cover all of the British Commonwealth until 1962.[79]

Born Claudia Vera Cumberbatch in Belmont, Port of Spain, Trinidad, in 1915, she later adopted the name Jones as "self-protective disinformation," a choice that speaks to her early understanding of the need to navigate a treacherous public.[80] She and her three sisters migrated to the United States in 1924, joining their parents, who had come two years prior. Arriving in Harlem as an eight-year-old, she had only glancing contact with its

Renaissance. As part of the first wave of Caribbean immigrants to New York, her family confronted northern racism at every turn. At school, where her West Indian ways were mocked, Claudia faced a hostile environment. At home, her parents struggled to make a living. Her mother, Sibyl "Minnie Magdalene" Logan Cumberbatch, died in 1927 at the age of thirty-seven as a result of poor working conditions and overwork in the garment industry.[81] Her mother's death impressed on Claudia the life-eroding costs of sweatshop labor paid by immigrant women.[82] She remembers that her mother rejected Catholicism because of its hierarchical structure, a hint of Sibyl's independent spirit and critical mind.[83] Her father, Charles Bertrand Cumberbatch, had been editor of a West Indian newspaper in New York, and he often spoke to Claudia of their African ancestry. In the wake of the economic crash of 1929, he lost his job and became the supervisor of an apartment building on West 113th Street. The family lived in the janitor's small, dank apartment, which was damp from nearby sewage pipes. Possibly as a result, Claudia contracted tuberculosis in 1932 and had to leave high school for a year. After graduation, she found work in various low-paying jobs—in a laundry, a factory, a millinery, and a lingerie shop. Two of her sisters were domestic workers at some point in their lives.[84]

On her way to and from work or school, Claudia listened to the Harlem street-corner speakers. The cause of the Scottsboro Boys was often on their lips, and figures like Queen Mother Audley Moore connected it to the struggles of the Ethiopian people. Out of this vibrant politicized Harlem of the 1930s, Claudia's political awakening took place. From the middle of the decade on, she spent the most important parts of her youth in the party.[85] Inspired by its defense of the Scottsboro Boys, in 1936 she attended the National Negro Congress and joined the Young Communist League (YCL), the youth section of the party.[86] She began her party career as a journalist, becoming an associate editor and then editor of the YCL's *Weekly Review*. In 1937, she joined the editorial staff of the *Daily Worker*, where she was named editor for Negro affairs. Her column, Half the World, appeared through the early 1950s in the Woman Today section of that paper. In it, she publicized the Sojourners for Truth and Justice, and in this respect she was a major contributor to that group.[87]

Claudia Jones with a book by the American Communist leader William Z. Foster, National Communist headquarters, New York, January 26, 1948. Photographer: Keystone. Hulton Archive, Getty Images.

In her work for the party, Jones was involved in many organizations and quickly advanced through the ranks.[88] In 1945 she was appointed executive secretary of the party's National Negro Commission, and in that capacity she toured forty-three states over the next four years. In 1948, the year of her first arrest, she was elected to the CPUSA's National Committee.[89] The party gave Jones her theoretical orientation, but as Davies remarks, "If the Party made Jones she also made it."[90] She became the Communist Party's principle theorist on the woman question and the Negro question by advancing the concepts of gender and race as inseparable factors that contribute to exploitation. A generation later, Angela Davis's marxist–feminist politics could be traced to the thinking of Claudia Jones.[91]

Many of Jones's most significant contributions to Black left feminism are evident in her 1949 essay "An End to the Neglect of the Problems of the Negro Woman!" It is a major intervention into both the party's political practice and its theory. The essay is directed toward party members, whom Jones castigates for their inattention to Negro women.[92] She targets trade unions in particular for excluding Black women workers despite evidence of their strong support for the sharecroppers' and tobacco workers' strikes. Among the "crassest manifestations" Jones identifies of the neglect of Negro women by the trade unions is their failure to oppose Black women's relegation to menial work and their disinterest in organizing domestic workers.[93] Among the essay's theoretical interventions is her expansion of the meaning of "domestic" to span homebound labor and state policy. Jones highlights Black women's historical responsibility to care for the needs of the Black family and their efforts to shield it from an atmosphere of "lynch terror, segregation, and police brutality" ("End to the Neglect," 51). Notable in this history are the connections she draws between the devalued domestic's labor that nurtures life and the state's arresting oppression of Black people. She substantiates the relationship between home and the state by citing President Truman's hypocrisy in announcing love and reverence for all mothers of the land in a Mother's Day proclamation while not extending that love to the mothers of countless victims of lynch violence who dared to fight back (52).

Drawing upon U.S. Department of Labor statistics, she makes

clear that Black women, many of them heads of families, are also a majority of women in the paid workforce. Historically clustered in the lowest-paid domestic labor jobs, during the booming postwar economy they were once more being pushed back there. Confinement defines their "hemmed in" lives behind an "iron curtain" of low salaries, high rents, high prices, and high maternity and infant mortality rates (53). Jones's account discloses the "superexploitation" of Black women, who, as unpaid and underpaid workers, "are the most oppressed stratum of the whole population" (52). Like Louise Thompson, she dismantles the distinction in the party's separate woman and Negro questions by pointing to their inseparability in the lived reality of Black women.

Jones politicizes the private space of home when she demonstrates that it is a site for state-driven violence. She details the state's use of sexuality as an instrument of control leveraged with impunity against Black women, and thus she connects the notion of domestic violence, commonly understood as a private affair, to a very public state apparatus. Black women's unpaid and underpaid domestic labor emerges as valuable to capital precisely through a process of devaluation that is managed and compounded by the state's racist practices. State and capital thus make up twin agents of Black women's "superexploitation." She reminds readers that the "domestic" signifies not only the space of the home but also that of the homeland. Nation-state management of the devaluation of Black women's domestic labor stretches from its sanction of their labor's devaluation as enslaved women, mothers, Negroes, and immigrant workers to direct violence by state agents against their persons and their families. This amplification of the concept of the domestic is one of Jones's most incisive critical interventions.[94]

Furthermore, she discloses sexuality as an ideological weapon that has been used by the state not only to devalue Black women but also to divide Black and white women and to obscure their shared interests. She refers to the fact that police who jailed the first white suffragists placed them on cots next to Black prostitutes, confident that they would not link their struggles. And they did not. The fight for women's suffrage emphatically distanced itself from Black women's liberation struggles ("End to the Neglect," 63). It is out of this history that Jones claims, "A developing

consciousness on the woman question today, therefore, must recognize that the Negro question in the United States is prior to, not
equal to, the woman question" (63). Simply put, the point of "priority" here is that gender is always already racialized. Consequently,
Jones asserts, without the fight for racial equality, the struggle
for women as a group cannot advance because it would achieve
only partial rights. For this reason, "the Negro woman who com-
bines in her status the worker, the Negro, and the woman," is for
Jones the "vital link to heightened political consciousness" (63).
Significantly, it is not a single "identity" that places this woman in
the forefront of struggle for justice but, rather, her superexploitation through the compounded devaluations of race and gender.

   More than any of her contemporaries, Claudia Jones demystifies the notion of the domestic arena as a homebound place by disclosing how porous a space it actually is. As in her eloquent poem
"The Elms at Morn," she reveals the domestic as a realm of activity stretching from the mops on the prison porch to the national
and international ambitions of the carceral state. In her writing,
"domestic" becomes a term whose mystique accompanies the long
shadow of capital that has hemmed in Black women's lives, extending from profit extraction to prison confinement, from slavery to
the superexploitation of their care work and that of their sisters in
far-flung colonies. Like the elms of her poem, although stateless,
she remained stately and strong, persistently summoning community organizing and the power of the press to envision a better dawn.

You Can't Tell a Communist by Looking:
A Domestic Worker Speaks Out

Alice Childress (née Herndon) was probably only a year younger
than Claudia Jones. I say "probably" because there are several dates
on record for her birth, an indication, perhaps, that like Jones,
she or a family member may have practiced some self-protective
disinformation. Little Alice Herndon was only five, or perhaps
nine, when she came to Harlem from South Carolina to live with
her grandmother, Eliza Campbell, after her parents divorced.[95]
Also like Claudia, she loved the theater, and as a girl in junior high
school she joined several theater groups in Harlem. I imagine Alice

Alice Childress. Photographs and Prints Division, Schomberg Center for Research in Black Culture, New York Public Library.

crossing paths with Claudia Cumberbatch, perhaps unknowingly, when she and her grandmother or her Aunt Lorraine attended a performance in a Harlem church given by one of the theater troupes Claudia joined.[96] Growing up about a mile and a half from each other, they both attended the prestigious public Wadleigh

High School for Girls.[97] Alice was forced to drop out of Wadleigh after a year because her grandmother died, but during that year, Alice and Claudia may have encountered each other. I can see Alice in her first year learning about Claudia, the dynamic older student drawn to leadership and drama. Perhaps she admired her from afar, since Claudia was eventually chosen to be "mayor" of her class, and ironically, at graduation, she was awarded the Theodore Roosevelt Award for citizenship, even though she was not a U.S. citizen.

Like Claudia, Alice drew her life's work from a youth spent among the Harlem Left of the 1930s. In her reconstruction of Alice's life, Mary Helen Washington tracks the evidence of these affiliations in Childress's plays, novels, and journalism as inflected by the radical internationalism of the Harlem Left.[98] Although Childress was evasive about her left past, there is ample evidence in her FBI file and her work that she was involved with pursuits supported by the party. Many of those activities also drew Marvel Cooke, Louise Thompson Patterson, and Claudia Jones into networks of mutual support. Alice was one of the founding members of the Sojourners for Truth and Justice, and she was closely associated with the journals *Freedom, Freedomways,* and *Masses and Mainstream,* all founded by Communists.[99] She worked for *Freedom,* where she shared an office with Paul Robeson, Louis Burnham, and Lorraine Hansberry, an experience she later documented in an essay for *Freedomways.*[100]

Childress was aware of the state's intensifying repressive power against the radical Left as the Cold War years unfolded. She was active in resistance efforts and sheltered in her apartment at least one Communist who had gone underground.[101] She was involved in the Committee to Repeal the Smith Act when Claudia Jones was threatened with deportation—another indication that she knew of Jones.[102] As secretary of the Communist Party's National Women's Commission and as the highest-ranking Black woman in the CPUSA, Jones was a substantial presence in the Black left Harlem community. For this reason, Mary Helen Washington believes that Jones and Childress almost certainly knew each other.[103] In all probability, Childress had read "An End to the Neglect of the Problems of the Negro Woman!," which set off a firestorm among party members when it was published.[104]

Steeped in the theater and having worked briefly as a domestic, Childress knew well the canny art of performative masquerade. She studied drama in the American Negro Theater and devoted her life to the theater in the 1940s, sometimes taking odd jobs, including as a domestic, to support herself.[105] She became well known for her talent as an actor, most notably for her Broadway performance in the role of a prostitute in *Anna Lucasta*. One of her most remarkable creative contributions was her rendering of the fictional Mildred Johnson, bringing to life the lived experience of a domestic worker. In more than thirty monthly columns entitled Conversations from Life and published under her name in the newspaper *Freedom* (1950–55), Childress translated political theory and analysis into the language of popular education. In these columns, Mildred, an outspoken day-labor domestic worker, imparts detailed reports on her work and life. Mildred's stories of the contradictions in her employers' behavior are instructive and entertaining critical commentaries delivered through her generosity, wisdom, and warmth.[106] They are, in short, brilliant performances of public pedagogy.

Childress later revised and expanded these popular front columns into her 1956 novel *Like One of the Family*. Preserving the format of the columns, the novel likewise uses terms that an ordinary person in the community could understand and identify with.[107] Mildred's daily accounts of her life as a single woman in her thirties offer frank observations and validating depictions of the domestic laborer's working conditions. Proud of her housework, Mildred reports her varied strategies for refusing mistreatment or manipulation. Several of the columns drew from Childress's own experiences as a maid, while others were based on those of her Aunt Lorraine, who also worked as a domestic.[108] All bear the stamp of someone who has been there and is not to be messed with. As Trudier Harris describes her, Mildred "stood up straight and tall," much like the elms of Claudia Jones's poem.[109] She debunks old myths and takes no nonsense from her white employers when they try to trick her, demonstrate their distrust, or impose unearned efforts at friendship. She offers her militancy as a woman and a worker firmly centered in her abilities and in the dignity of her work.

Mildred's "conversations" with her best friend, Marge, are really monologues, because Marge is only indirectly audible, yet they bring to life a sustaining and precious friendship. We come to know their relationship as an essential lifeline for Mildred, a net that catches and supports her at the end of her day. This friendship is one of the most vibrant and tender depictions in literature of Black women's intimacy, rivaled to my mind only by Toni Morrison's *Sula*. The friendship between Mildred and Marge mostly takes place, as women's friendships often do, at the kitchen table, where all the ingredients of true love and companionship converge. Here the routine of daily conversation is punctuated by affectionate barbs, as when Mildred chides Marge, "No, I haven't forgotten my mind at all, but give me a chance." Or retorts, "No, I do not want to borrow anything or ask any favors."[110]

Written for an audience that can readily relate to Mildred, the novel also reaches out to readers open to reckoning with their own historical position, for Mildred is above all a fabulous teacher. Like much of Childress's political work, her teaching is artfully concealed in entertaining and engaging stories. One of my favorite stories is the chapter entitled "Hands," where Mildred urges Marge to use nail polish even though she, too, is a "house servant." At the mention of the phrase 'house servant,' Mildred starts thinking about how all of us are actually servants: "Now you just look at anything in the room or in this apartment and try to point out something that working people didn't have their hands in. . . . You can't name a solitary thing, be it cheap or expensive" (Childress, 62). This lesson on "the power and beauty of laboring hands" goes on with examples: the cotton in the tablecloth, the lettuce and tomato in the sandwich. Turning to objects in the room, Mildred urges Marge to see "the story behind" each, and in so doing she demystifies what Marx called the "commodity fetish." She ends her catalog of stories behind these objects with an assertion: "So you can see we are all servants and got a lot in common . . . and that's why folks need unions" (63). Navigating Marge's interruptions ("Oh hush, girl! . . . let's suppose"), she goes on to explain what Marx called the "theory of surplus value" without ever using that term. This is vintage popular education.

Many of Mildred's stories relate events from her work or her reflections on what took place there, and they often incisively lay bare the contradictions that race ideology conceals. To give one example: "The folks I work for are willin' to have me put my hands all over their chopped meat patties and yet ask me to hang my coat in the kitchen closet instead of in the hall with theirs" (108). Another of my favorite stories, near the end of the novel, is Mildred's version of the history of Harriet Tubman that she told to a dozen children who were visiting on a Saturday. The children's constant interruptions are part of the lesson as Mildred takes their questions seriously while also aiming to convince them that this story is not made up even though it is not in their history books. Part of the tale tells of Harriet arriving in Troy, New York, where she manages to free a man who has been captured by disguising herself as an old woman. The politics of performativity is one minilesson here. Tubman is also a well-chosen figure because she epitomizes the powerful life-saving ends of an undercover strategy. It may seem ironic, therefore, that the original publication of this novel went underground in the 1950s and its small printing was all too soon forgotten. But that is not the end of the story.

The recovery work of Trudier Harris, Mary Helen Washington, and a new generation of scholars has found Childress's work and made possible its republication. Tubman appears in the novel as a nod to Childress's own undercover strategy of keeping her Communist affiliations under wraps, an iconic example of the power of underground stories to teach. In this respect, Childress's undercover practice as a writer is coherent with the lessons she conveys through Mildred. Her tales from the front lines of domestic work are deeply and strategically attuned to Communist Harlem's restless history, which is seeable by those who can read the signs. Paul Robeson, for example, appears when one employer, noticing an ad for an upcoming concert by Robeson, warns Mildred, "He is the kind of man that gets his people in trouble." This not-very-veiled reference to Robeson's Red alliances and the power of the arresting state prompts Mildred to reply with a long history lesson whose point is *"I know who makes trouble for me!"* (122).

Childress found in the performative form of dramatic monologue a powerful medium whose potent critical lessons rest on the clandestine capacities of an art whose fictive form can carry a caustic political message through the masque of metaphor and character. Subterfuge was a classic Cold War tactic, and it was also one that the Black Left used to push back. It teaches those who, like me, were too young then to fully understand that to be undercover is not merely to be an agent of the state. It has also been a tactic to record history against the grain or other-wise by those who recognize that what is concealed remains legible by those who are able to see.

To different degrees, each of these four women writers from the 1930s navigated the murky waters of a reality premised on the equation between the visible and the seeable. That they used canny strategies for exposing the difference is perhaps not surprising. As Black women, they confronted every day the tyranny of the visible driving the commonsense insistence that race is an empirical, discernable, biological difference. In centering the life-making labor of Black domestics and its entanglement with a life-arresting state, their writings across multiple genres disclose another story behind this racecrafting. They enable their readers to see social relations obscured by the commonsensical and offer concepts for understanding them. They disclose the domestic as a broad arena of power and struggle, the arresting state as intimately involved in homelife, and Black women's domestic care labor, both paid and unpaid, as superexploited. Far from offering sanctuary from the world of work, the home appears in their writing surrounded, surveilled, and managed by menacing agents. In spotlighting the domestic worker, they contributed to a Communist popular front by questioning its assumptions. While they called for justice in the existing social system, they invariably aimed for more radical change. In the wake of the Cold War, their writings were suppressed and forgotten by many who were revamping a New Left. Yet here they are, still. Their centering of Black women's labor and the legacies of their lives remain extraordinary contributions to feminist thought, a rich archive for continuing struggles, guides to keep in sight capital's erosion of the reproduction of life across domestic and far-flung home fronts.

Land

Three
The Ground We Tread

As the fate of the planet hangs in the balance in the twenty-first century, the question of humans' relation to land and the place of that relation in the future calls for a reckoning. All who live on the earth, tread its ground, and call some patch of it home live in a relation to the land, the dependencies it sustains, the sustenance it provides, and the history that saturates and shapes it. So many of us, severed as we are from a life-making relation to the land, forget what we know of it as our home. Some remember, but it is often a remembering with a slanted relation to the truth. The writings of Josephine Herbst and Meridel Le Sueur are mostly forgotten now; to read them is to encounter that sort of remembering and two valiant efforts to reckon with it.

Herbst's and Le Sueur's novels and nonfiction from the 1930s through the late twentieth century approach the land as bound to the two great human stories of labor and desire and to women's reproductive bodies, minds, and care work.[1] Writing about them in 2021, I began to see their comprehension of the dependencies that cross the wide web of life making. Their rendering of that web's fraying during the difficult years of the Great Depression and the Cold War resonate with our contemporary struggles: the unemployment lines, evictions, and losses of Covid-19 that have affected people of color most profoundly, all of us under the cloud of global warming.

From the Depression years of the 1930s through the repressive years of the 1950s, Herbst and Le Sueur aimed in different ways to develop in their writing an expansive understanding of what it means to make and remake life. Their efforts speak to us precisely because they understand that continual process as an intimate dialectical relationship between humans and the land. Each of them came from families who settled in the Midwest. Herbst grew up in Iowa, where her parents had recently arrived from Pennsylvania with aspirations to climb out of poverty. Her father sold farm equipment, and her mother enriched their home adjacent to an endless, treeless horizon with stories of life "back East." Le Sueur's grandmother was the daughter of an Iroquois woman and a homesteader who claimed land in Oklahoma when the U.S. government offered it free to any citizen willing to improve it. Le Sueur spent childhood years there and, later, in Kansas and Minnesota. In her family's homes, Communist pamphlets and newsletters were read aloud or papered on the walls, Industrial Workers of the World (IWW) organizers were sheltered from vigilantes, and the radical socialist tradition of Eugene Debs was revered. Members of a younger generation with different ambitions than their parents, Herbst and Le Sueur left the heartland as young women eager to live in the big cities to the east and west, but the land soon drew them back. Fired up by the progressive spirit of the times, they tracked the impact of the Great Depression in the Midwest.

The intimacy with the natural world that they represent in their fiction and journalism has some of the modernist's lyricism, but they use it to call for more ample and tangible communal relations. The dependencies sheltered in human relations to the land appear in their writing from the 1930s, when an ecological consciousness made them outliers among Communist thinkers. Sometimes this ecology bursts through in their representations of women's attunement to their bodies, desires, and animal natures. Other times it appears in passages that relate the land to the value of human labor or that invite contemplation of embodied debts to the soil and its products. When they compare women's reproductive capacities to nature's or suggest that women's bodies, like the land, have become a form of property, their writing amplifies the literature of the Left. Beginning in the early 1930s, their alliance with workers' collective struggles went against the grain of the settler's fierce independence. Only later, in the 1950s, did they ponder the settler's relation to the dispossession of Indigenous peoples.

Then they attended to the land as a source of sustenance saturated with legacies of theft and violence, a contradiction at the heart of America that they placed adjacent to the confinements of gender and sexuality. In the process, they troubled common conceptions of property and rights. Ultimately, they approached a reckoning with their own settler history. In following them through that process, I discern their growing awareness of what we now understand as "whiteness." In all these respects, they insert a critical wedge into a national story and a feminist legacy.

Their dawning recognition of the costs of settler history is instructive precisely because it is belated, a consciousness awakened only later in life and then only partially or obliquely. Herbst and Le Sueur confronted their white settler history most directly only in their middle years, when they wrote through a dark chapter in American history. As for many writers of the 1930s, by the 1950s Cold War repression of Communists had made it impossible for them to publish their work. Writing that spoke to capitalism's erosion of the conditions for sustaining well-being for all but the rich was virtually banned as anti-Communist campaigns tightened their grip on cultural production in the United States. Throughout that decade, nonetheless, each held fast to her values and found ways to write books that could be published, books that encoded those values in histories that had been forgotten or repressed.

Herbst turned from creating quasi-autobiographical fiction to writing a biography of the eighteenth-century American botanist John Bartram. Le Sueur published several children's books, some featuring Indigenous peoples' history. In her middle years, she traveled to some of their communities where she lingered to learn more, and she confronted her family's and her own intimate and unsettling relationships with them in a memoir. To use Le Sueur's term, I think of these women's turn to history as a kind of "ripening." As a woman now past my own middle years, I find in their decision to keep writing, and to do so in a different key, evidence that even during a formidable fascist turn in the American homeland, life-affirming values can endure and continue to nurture the aspirations of those who tread its ground.

Both Herbst and Le Sueur sought in their writing to connect the everyday lives of individual women and their families to the social relations forming a nation. A strong historical impulse shapes their fiction and punctuates their reportage. "Reportage" is a term that has fallen out of use, but in the 1930s, it designated a form of advocacy journalism that allowed the writer to step out from behind the veil of objective documentary. That unveiled woman reporter is one of their interventions into a Left dominated by men. She was also a work in progress whose shape evolved with each writer's attention to her settler heritage. I read each of them, in chapters 4 and 5, respectively, for evidence of that critical perspective as it appears in certain patterns integral to her relation to the land.

One recurring pattern in Herbst's writing is her characteristic adjacent stance, a relationship always somewhat removed. This is the standpoint of an observer who lives close to the land but not too close, who is from the country but lives in town. In the 1950s, she finds a new shape for this removed standpoint in _New Green World,_ a tale of the land told through the lives of the eighteenth-century botanist John Bartram and his son William. After publishing this book, Herbst decided to write her memoirs. The project became an obsession, and she never completed it. Had the distance she cultivated created a knot at the heart of the material she confronted? Was she only able to come to terms with her history obliquely in fiction and through reporting on the lives of others? We see this mediated relationship most profoundly in her biography of the Bartrams. As Herbst's ancestors did, John Bartram settled in Pennsylvania. In his story, land, science, sexuality, and whiteness are entangled in events contemporaneous with her family's early colonial settlement. It is a history whose understory she touches but cannot fully represent, a dilemma I read as an allegory of the American postcolonial condition.

Meridel Le Sueur, late in her life, turned her political commitments from the 1930s to recovery narratives of Indigenous people and to family history in the lands of the Mid- and Southwest. Her historical project is an effort to re-member a fragmented legacy. I use the term "re-member" to convey a form of memory work that aims to reconnect relations that capitalism has dismembered. In her memoir, the embodied debts of whiteness appear in the form of parallel syntax that navigates a distance between settler and Indigenous that is never overcome. For both writers, intimate distance marks a limit that makes their writing compelling for the murky terrain of self-recognition it ventures into, where whiteness manifests in what is unsaid or spatially coded. It is precisely in those obscure places that they become luminous guides.

The Intimate Distance of Whiteness

What shaped the legacy of intimate distance that Herbst and Le Sueur inherited? When I first read Elizabeth Dillon's sweeping history of the seventeenth- and eighteenth-century Atlantic world, it struck me that here lay the answer.[2] As Dillon explains it, intimate distance manages the fundamental contradiction of the American colonial relation. That contradiction took place across two seemingly separate scenes: the extraction of land and labor in the colonies and the establishment of political liberty among men in Europe and, later, among whites in the Americas. In the European metropolis, despite intimate ties of trade and communication across the Atlantic, the fact that the colonies were far away helped keep the horrors of genocide and the brutality of slavery out of view—distant and dismissible.[3] In other words, the trans-Atlantic spatial dimension of the colonial relation enabled the ideological management of the contradiction between the scene of brutal extraction and the scene of liberty. That contradiction haunted the birth of democracy at the end of the eighteenth century, and it continues to this day in the overdeveloped sectors of global capital's democracies, where consumers remain unaware of the conditions endured by those who produce their goods and supply their services in fields, factories, and call centers far away.[4]

The spatial distance that managed England's relation to the American colonies was compounded by other intimate distances integral to the Western Enlightenment, distances that were shaping humanist culture: conceptions of nature, science, and aesthetics. The intimate distance encoded into these cultural forms also mediated social relations in colonial America, conditioning what was seeable and knowable and who could belong in the new commonwealth. In time, to be white meant appropriately, unconsciously, and habitually inhabiting these new spatial and epistemic orientations.

The concept of nature that is still most familiar to many of us also harbors this intimate distance. I want to stay with it for a bit, for it emerged out of the same historical developments propelling the entwined systems of capitalism and colonialism. Likewise, it had a formative impact on settler conceptions of the land. Across Europe between 1500 and 1700, the idea of nature accumulated layers of contradictory meanings.[5] On the one hand, nature came to be considered "out there," external to humans and human society, the raw material from which society is built. Yet another externality comprehends nature as transcendent, embodying or reflecting a distant yet intimate higher spirit, a conception commonly thought of, although not entirely accurately, as the Romantic tradition. On the other hand, humans considered themselves as intimately part of nature and as possessing a distinct and universal human nature. In short, two natures came to be—one outside and one that resides within. The internal–external duality of this humanist conception harbors a braided intimacy and distance. I grew up with this way of thinking, and it still rules the prevailing way of seeing the land as "out there," a resource available for use. This view enabled the settler's march into the New World. It legitimized their displacement of Indigenous people and dismissal of Indigenous epistemologies, which do not comprehend nature as external or internal to a human-centered perspective but, rather, center all relations in the web of life.

 The human-centered idea of nature was born in Europe and traveled across the Atlantic. Integral to the consolidation of capitalism in the early modern period, it produced a sweeping transformation in lived relations to the land as European peasants, Native Americans, and Africans were violently removed from the lands that had sustained them. Enclosure laws across Europe expelled peasants from their common lands and eventually forced them to survive by selling their capacity to labor in exchange for payment during a working day that produced a profit for the capitalist. The process of enclosure also waged war on women's relation to the land and the knowledge they had practiced as village midwives, medics, soothsayers, or sorcerers. As the commons were enclosed, women became the substitutes for the land lost to the enclosures, a communal good any man could appropriate and use at will.[6] The persecution of witches in the sixteenth and seventeenth centuries in both the Old and New Worlds paved the way for the new science that instilled a more instrumental relation to nature. New forms of consciousness distanced humans from nature and accompanied the abstraction of their labor into a commodity for exchange. They supplemented political upheavals at the same time as landowners were becoming free, possessive individuals while Black, Native, and female bodies, equated with external nature, were already being seen as ripe for appropriation.

By the late eighteenth century, nature had become "Nature," firmly objectified and associated with the feminine and savage other. As production for exchange developed into full-blown capitalism, the human relation to nature came to be based neither on the need for simple subsistence nor on the need for exchange in the form of trade but, rather, on the logic attached to the accumulation of profit. This is the logic of abstraction. Here is how it works: abstract value (that is, value understood as money) rests upon meeting life-making needs not through relations of labor to make useful things but through a collective forgetting or abstracting of these material relations into the price of commodities, the logic of the market. That forgetting legitimizes exploitation, making its injustice invisible and thus further enabling the accumulation of wealth by a few. It forestalls collective rebellion. As capitalism became global and, under the banner of discovery, swept before it all other modes of life making, human relations with nature no longer existed for the fulfillment of human and nonhuman needs. Rather, human relations with nature were merely for the fulfillment of one need: profit.[7] From that social relation emerged the ideology of nature, an inverted version of reality. Rooted in the interests of the social class that controlled the wealth, that ideology represents reality from their perspective and thus only in part. Behind the myth of universal nature, life forms were being socialized into resources for some to appropriate, a concept that denies women, people of color, the working class, and the land itself their history.

Earlier, in the mid-seventeenth century, when the brutal violence of the colonial relation was well underway, struggles for government by the people were beginning to take place in Europe. As Dillon points out, the execution of King Charles I in London in 1649 was a turning point when the English people began to acquire new representational authority and to debate the question of precisely who would comprise the new sovereign people. By the end of the eighteenth century, those debates would issue in four revolutions: a Glorious Revolution in England and bloodier revolutions in Haiti, France, and the United States. In the decades preceding, the intimate distance of the colonial relation for England and the colonies obscured the fact that "the people" of parliamentary government by the people did not actually consist of all the people. Forced labor in the New World enabled the enrichment of the empowered class in the British metropole, but it had to remain virtually forgotten in order not to threaten accounts of British liberty. Although representations of the New World were often being performed on the London stage, this "forgetting" nonetheless could be accomplished because the horror in the colonies was literally offstage in the colonies far away. In the colonies, however, the violence was intimately present. Although visible and embodied, it was at the same time unspeakable. This combination of intimacy and distance was central to the colonial relation.

While the contradiction between British liberty and colonial violence was reconciled in the metropolis by the fact of distance, in postcolonial America it was managed by the discourse of race. The idea of race justified the formation of a government by the people based on a way of life that commodified Black bodies as an enslaved labor force that worked the land and produced enormous profits. Race slavery in the eighteenth-century world was a form of enclosure in that it excluded portions of the population from the actual and political commons.[8] It imposed a symbolic and ideological distance between white settlers who mingled intimately with enslaved men, women, and children, and it suffused the conceptions of savagery that settlers applied to the Natives they lived among, whose lands they occupied, and whose claims to sovereignty they wanted to eradicate. That intimate distance became the architecture of whiteness. As settler colonialism transformed the colonies of North America into the white-identified nation of the United States, scenes of racialized oppression became politically unintelligible and thus "distant" even while they remained materially present in the intimacies of daily life.[9]

Josephine Herbst and Meridel Le Sueur both wrestled with the intimate distances that continued to underwrite the postcolonial cultural traditions of the American frontier. By forwarding a political consciousness that saw the land from the perspective of its relation to life making, they intervened into the East Coast Marxist establishment. Herbst did so from the intimate distance of a reporter returning to the Midwest already familiar with farmers, whom she knew as her father's customers. However, it was not until she traveled to Cuba's communal farmlands that, enabled by the peasant rebels she met there, she came to understand the landed and racialized history of global capital. I imagine that the significance of this trip germinated in her for a long time, even after its appearance in her 1939 novel, irrupting two decades later in *New Green World,* her biography of the Bartrams and a probing colonial history. Her allegorical representation here of an eighteenth-century settler's study of nature and his encounters with Indigenous people captures the colonial and postcolonial relation that would come to define the United States. As a frontline reporter, novelist, and biographer, Herbst attended to struggles over the land in her writing in tandem with the effort to reckon with her family's settler legacy and her own sexual agency. In all of this life writing, she maintained a relation to the land and its people that was both intimate and distant. Her formally curated adjacent stance, conditioned by her settler heritage, appears in her reportage, fiction, and memoir and especially in the life story of the Pennsylvania farmer-botanist John Bartram and his artist son who navigated the birth of appropriate whiteness.

In contrast, Meridel Le Sueur's representations of the land are more radical, which is to say, more rooted. Her dialectical sensibility intervenes in the ideology of nature. It suffuses her call to remember the web of life making and her attention to human labor as the linchpin in a relation between nature and humans. While she is not always consistent and at times seems to grant nature a universal agency, for the most part her lyrical prose discloses human dependency on the land as a metabolic relation in which labor intervenes, and she explores the costs to the reproduction of life when capitalist appropriation and accumulation organize that relation. Her lyricism is a formal device to convey this dialectical sensibility, a device through which she brings human relations to the land into focus. Thus, her writing circles around and through the ideology of nature. Neither essentially an external object nor a universal phenomenon, nature for her is saturated with the history of human socialization of land. Women's bodies as agents in social and biological reproduction come to life in her writing. She highlights the centrality of their devalued labor to capitalism's exchange economy. In addition, she understands that appropriation of Native lands was and remains a driver of capital accumulation through their conversion into farms, mines, or nuclear test sites. Not least of all, she comes to recognize that race as a cultural system of devaluation is integral to market relations and their colonial history, manifest both violently and subtly as white control over landed space. In her writing late in life, she wrestles directly with appropriate whiteness as a spatial relation, an effort that acknowledges both its intimacies and the distances it cannot bridge.

A Green and White Story

The writings of Herbst and Le Sueur appealed to me initially because I was looking for marxist feminist forebears, for a usable past. As I kept company with them during the Covid-19 lockdown, I recognized that I felt drawn to these two women because of a kinship that is familiar and white. Their stories as the daughters of Anglo settlers who came of age in the 1930s reminded me of my own mother, who lived her girlhood through the Depression in the care of her single mother, the grandmother we lived with when I was a child. I was also drawn to these writers from my own relationship to the lands they wrote about: Pennsylvania and Texas, Minnesota and New Jersey. I sensed in their writing patterns of intimate distance we shared.

I grew up in Philadelphia, a setting featured in several of Herbst's books. As a young adult, I lived for a time in Bucks County, Pennsylvania, very close to her home there. One of my daughters now lives in Le Sueur's beloved Twin Cities area. Before their late nineteenth-century journeys to North America, my ancestors came from Derbyshire and Nottinghamshire in England; Counties Tyrone and Cork in Ireland; and Germany's southwestern region. They worked with their hands as knitters and lace makers, servants, hostlers, wheelwrights, tailors, and farm laborers. Fleeing political unrest and famine in the late nineteenth century and eager for a fresh start and better wages, they entered the mills and ironworks, laundries, bakeries, and tailor shops of America. A few left families behind and went west, but most stayed close to the

East Coast. Later generations of men joined the military, became policemen and salesmen. Women with some schooling were book-keepers or musicians. As mother, daughter, or neighborhood mid-wife, they were caregivers. They settled in row houses in northwest Philadelphia on the banks of the Schuylkill River, a neighborhood called Manayunk (a Lenape word meaning "place to go to drink") nestled between the river and the forests of Fairmount Park.

Up the hill from Manayunk's crowded cobblestone streets, the expanding neighborhood of Roxborough runs on either side of Ridge Avenue. Originally the site of a Native American trail known as the Perkiomen Path, the ridge extended along the crested land between Wissahickon Creek to the east and the river to the west.[10] The street where I grew up turns off the ridge, dead-ending into land that had once been a farm. Decades earlier, the farmland's rolling hills had been sold to a rest home that bordered Fairmount Park. Its name, Fairmount Farms, and its expansive acreage conjured both its agrarian past and the forests of the park. "The Farms," as we called it, offered my sisters and me hours of out-door adventure. We were forbidden to play in this private prop-erty, and that made sneaking through the gate an enticing escape for the passage it offered to Fairmount Park and the Wissahickon.

Recorded history in that stretch of Wissahickon Creek goes back to the seventeenth century, when Johannes Kelpius and a group of followers established a monastery on the banks of the creek, named for its generous supply of catfish. "Hermit's cave" was the reputed location of the monastery, a place we found espe-cially mysterious and whose traces we recognized in local street names, Monastery Avenue and Hermitage Street. Land that be-came the park was part of William Penn's original tract and specu-lative venture. Absentee landholders in England and Ireland pur-chased portions of the land in the seventeenth century. In the Wissahickon sections of Fairmount Park over the next two hun-dred years, the creek offered power to mills along its banks.[11] In the mid-nineteenth century, the Fairmount Park Commission took ownership of the land and opened the area more fully to public rec-reation. In the 1930s, the Civilian Conservation Corps developed a bridal path and built retaining walls and guard stations along it.

When our father took us "back the crick" to feed the mallard ducks or to hike, he would regale us with stories of roaming these woods as a boy and tell us he knew them like the back of his hand. Our favorite hike was to the statue of Tedyuscung. Nestled in the trees on a rock high above the Wissahickon, this massive Indian still kneels, shielding his eyes and looking to the west. The statue was designed not to memorialize the well-known Lenape chief but, rather, to be a collective representation of the Indigenous people of the area looking to the western lands to which they were displaced. According to a local historian, as late as 1855 tribal members of the Lenape, who were by then both Moravians and Catholics, supposedly came to that spot, called Council Rock, on their yearly pilgrimage to St. Joseph's Church in Philadelphia. It may have been a resting place designated for discussion of tribal matters and close to nearby tribal burial mounds.[12] The Lenape, also known by the English name "Delaware," were a matrilineal society that had inhabited the forestlands of the Delaware River watershed for centuries. A tract of their land would become Roxborough-Manayunk after Penn purchased it from Lenape leaders in 1684. By the end of the eighteenth century, most of the Natives had been driven westward by broken treaties and the Indian Wars.[13]

When I was a child, however, they seemed to me to be still there in the deep woods of the Wissahickon. That this rock, earth, and water sheltered the people of Tedyuscung mattered in the strange temporality I gave to the Indians. It mattered, too, that the steep ferny cavern and majestic pines, sycamores, birches, and maples towering above the bridal path were public land. My sisters and I knew about private property, having been chased by the caretaker of Fairmount Farms when we sneaked into its grounds. We knew this place was not that. Even when we went to the creek unchaperoned, we understood that we were not trespassing. The scent of sodden earth and the sound of dripping springs were imprinting our lives, too, as we conjured on the path ahead of us the silent tread of the Lenape.

The fact is, of course, that the Lenape had never left. I do not know if their burial mounds were nearby, but I do know that we were treading on lands saturated with their history and presence. Many of the Lenape were driven out of the region they still call their homelands along the Delaware and Schuylkill Rivers. Today they control lands in Oklahoma, Wisconsin, and other parts of the United States and Canada. Some remained in Pennsylvania, however, where in the twenty-first century they still pursue land claims. After living in secret for more than two hundred years, in 2011 the Lenape of Pennsylvania decided to share their history publicly in a collaborative exhibit with the University of Pennsylvania Museum of Archeology and Anthropology.[14]

As a child and for years after, my relationship to this land on the edges of the city was also accompanied by another shadow. Our neighborhood was almost 100 percent white, the result of migration patterns and informal segregation practices in housing, hiring, schooling, and church life. They situated generations of Irish, German, Italian, and Polish immigrants in ethnic enclaves anchored by their respective churches in the neighborhoods along the banks of the Schuylkill. Beginning in the early nineteenth century, a canal system provided waterpower and transportation for the textile mills that would make Manayunk the Manchester of America. Growing up at the top of the hill and away from streets lined with row houses, I had access to the abandoned farm and forestlands farther to the east. When my grandparents bought their twin house in Roxborough in 1922, they literally moved up in the world from Manayunk. My grandmother was able to pay off the mortgage and own the property because of the life insurance she received after her young husband's premature death in 1929. He was a salesman for one of the mills owned by three brothers, his friends from the tight-knit Manayunk community. Their friendship extended into other networks, among them the American Legion. Those friends helped my grandmother through the Depression, providing her a job as bookkeeper in the office of their mill. She often told of the circumstances that enabled her to own the house we lived in. The story merged her relationship to property and our security with her escape from the fate of friends and family who lost their homes when the banks failed.

My awareness of home as concealing potential catastrophe became a facet of my wary confidence as a girl. Unlike my father, I was cautioned not to go into the woods alone, yet having access to the private lands across the street from our patch of lawn shaped my belief that I could move around in the wider world somewhat safely. I was aware that our house on this tree-lined street set me apart from schoolmates who lived in the lawnless blocks of houses in Manayunk. That immeasurable difference became a part of me inseparable from the fact that I lived on that particular verdant street.

In time, whiteness became the invisible canvas of my life, a given that shaped the femininity and intelligence I performed as an academic achiever. The Catholic girls' high school my sisters and I attended in the 1960s in center-city Philadelphia near Logan Circle and the Free Library was not strictly private but was supported by the parishes, a parallel system to the public schools in Philadelphia. Although the student body was almost 50 percent Black, only one or two Black students were in my academic-track classes. My encounters with Black classmates were shaped by our unofficially segregated coexistence and by the fact that I did not play a sport where we may have had a chance to make friends. At the University of Pennsylvania in 1968, I was assigned to share a room with Pat Butler, one of the handful of Black students admitted that year and the only Black girl on our floor. Coming from an all-Black high school and neighborhood in Pittsburgh, she was even more culture shocked than I was coming to Penn. At the time, the university was displacing people from the adjacent Black neighborhood of Powelton Village in order to build a new science center, and that fall students had taken over the administration building to protest the expansion. Neither Pat nor I had the vocabulary to talk about the protest across the foggy chasm that marked our time together. I spent nights studying in our room or hanging out with the other white girls in the suite; Pat did not. She had a cousin in Philadelphia who often visited, and they spent time in the lounge with a small group of Black friends. Inspired by a day-long event in Powelton Village aimed at raising awareness of racism, I did eventually talk about race with her. I remember it felt awkward but important. I vaguely recall that she had things to say about how hard the year had been for her. Then we went our separate ways.

It seems to me that despite all of the national discussion of race in 2020 and since, for white people there is a well of unfathomed comprehension of what whiteness actually entails, of how it saturates the geography of everyday life and is reproduced across the spaces we move through. I have no memories of learning in school how the city I lived in came to be so racially segregated or about the Indigenous people whose names mapped the rivers, creeks, and land in this corner of William Penn's woods. I did not ask why.

When I encountered the Lenape statue in the forest, I dreamed of Indians. Remembering that time now, a door opens onto a white landscape I struggle to see and name.

Whiteness is a slippery, shadowy substance for those who inhabit it.[15] Of the many scholars who have written about whiteness, I have found Linda Alcoff's approach especially helpful. Theoretically, she explains, whiteness is a complex identity formation, a "fluid amalgam" that is incoherent, historically evolving, produced in diverse locations, and constantly reinterpreted and contested.[16] Like other identities, whiteness is a material practice with variable and unstable borders. However, it can be empirically measured, a fact that is best understood in terms of geography: where one lives, attends school, works, retires; where one is permitted to go, and how one does so. It helps navigation of the social world. It also offers a descriptive narrative that connects individual and historical memory. That narrative is often not named "whiteness" per se even as it provides a purchase on patterns of social interaction and hierarchies of status that we witness and live every day (Alcoff, 46). It has a particular and varied relationship to historical events such as immigration from certain regions and to historical atrocities such as slavery or the genocide of Indigenous peoples (8).

Although the concept is a bit harder to grasp, whiteness is also imaginary in the sense that it shapes what is known and believed through images and mythologies that form a sense of self. It shapes a particular way of being in the world, what it means to be a certain kind of person experiencing and perceiving the social and natural environments (74). It produces a kind of "visual registry" that organizes social spaces and choreographs movement through them. It forms relations that become lived experiences and correlates with collective meanings, the "deep rules" and interpretive horizons that individual and group histories provide (49). In this respect, it consolidates "epistemic habits" or perceptual attunements and bodily comportments, whom to see, look at, and listen to. It affects what is seeable and what is not, the unconscious preferences and conceptions that help reproduce certain values and hierarchies (11).

Drawing upon a phrase from W. E. B. Du Bois, Shannon Sullivan characterizes this lived imaginary of whiteness as "unconscious habits." Feeling natural, they are anything but. They are social products, and they reproduce relations that structure the social world. They manifest in possessive relationships to place and to space that reap the economic, ontological, and psychological benefits of security and control.[17] These habits settle deep in the human affective register, conditioning what Sylvia Wynter has called the "psycho-affective field of normative sentiments."[18] As Wynter points out, feelings of what seems normal can reproduce an inequitable way of life. Manifest in behaviors that appropriate (take over) spaces large and small, whiteness carries with it traces of the colonial relation. Often unconscious, those traces motivate appropriating behaviors and distancing reflexes (e.g., disregard, silence, guilt, surprise) in encounters with devalued others. The scope and variety of the reflexes are worth careful reflection precisely because they are often subject to unconscious defenses that expel, project, or confess feelings rather than allow, decipher, and understand them.

My reading of Josephine Herbst and Meridel Le Sueur is an effort to address whiteness as it appears in their work, even when it is almost never marked as such and is discernable only indirectly. Their representation of the land, I found, reveals it. Their writing is aware that life making involves a web of relations binding humans to the land, and their white settler histories and habits are inscribed in that effort. Their reckoning with that history is an underrecognized feature of their Communist and feminist politics. It is also a process of coming to consciousness that is as edifying for its effort as for its limits. The past that lives on in both can illuminate the future.

In keeping with this braided temporality, I read their work from the 1930s for its imprint on their writing in the 1950s. The 1950s were years that Le Sueur called "the dark time." Her writings and Herbst's from that decade have received the least attention from scholars and critics, even during their brief recoveries when New Left feminists found them in the 1970s and discovered them again in the 1990s. Their writings from that Cold War decade are significant as reckonings with their settler heritage. They provide, as perhaps only works from a country's dark time can, reflections on a nation's history. Land was the battleground for many of the collective struggles of the farmers and miners that Herbst and Le Sueur reported on and joined from the 1930s on, but it was also more than that. If the land's Indigenous history only became fully evident to them in their later years, the seeds of that encounter were already there in the 1930s. Their decades-long accounting for it is as much a story for the present as is the Communism that drew them and that they elaborated into a communal sensibility awaiting fuller articulation. For us, survivors of a global pandemic, living amid a worsening climate crisis and the enduring devaluation of people of color, the limits and possibilities of that sensibility offer timely guidance toward rehabilitating a relationship to each other and to the ground we tread.

Four
Unsettling the Grass Roots

The Intimate Distance of Whiteness
in Josephine Herbst

Like other women writers from the 1930s, Josephine Herbst navigated a literary establishment run by men. Some, like Ernest Hemingway, were the golden boys of a literary men's club. They enjoyed the company of men, ran the show in the field abroad, and garnered resources, prizes, attentive publishers, and adoring fans at home. Herbst elbowed her way into that closed circle. She befriended many of the men, among them Hemingway and John Dos Passos, and she found ways to preserve her autonomy and to produce extraordinary reporting, often as an independent. She published three of her seven novels in the 1930s, each with a major New York publishing house, as well as scores of pieces in left-leaning and mainstream publications. In none of that work did she cloak her left politics. When anti-Communism spread like a virus across the United States during and after World War II, a new national consensus recoiled against the radical 1930s. American letters emerged from the 1940s embracing a virile late modernism that valued personality over social struggle, and Herbst's books fell out of print. By the time she died on January 29, 1969, her work and literary reputation were essentially forgotten along with their radical legacy.[1]

To its credit, the *New York Times* ran her obituary under a five-column headline. Reminding readers that she was best known for

Josephine Herbst passport photograph, 1922. Josephine Herbst Papers, Yale Collection of American Literature, Beinecke Rare Book and Manuscript Library.

the novels she published in the 1930s and that she enjoyed a "long and highly diverse literary career," it went on to mention her reporting on the American farmers' strikes and some of her "most spectacular journalistic feats." Among those named were her reports from abroad: from Cuba during the 1935 general strike, and the same year from Germany, when she wrote of Hitler's rise to power, and from Spain, where she was "one of the few women correspondents allowed to report from the front-line villages."[2]

The critical reception of Herbst since her death has remained sparse, and virtually none of it pays attention to her relationship to the land.[3] Sara Kosiba considers that she holds a complicated place in American literary and cultural history as a regional writer because she moved away from the Midwest yet continually returned to it in her writing.[4] Herbst's writing does indeed maintain such an intimate distance. I see this pattern as a feature of a more general ambivalence throughout her representation of the lands and loves that nurtured her. It is captured in "Feet in the Grass Roots," the report she wrote for *Scribner's Magazine* on the Iowa farmers' struggle in 1933. The report makes clear that both the 1930s farmers' movement and Herbst were grounded in the Midwest, even as her observations as a prodigal Iowa native situated her by then as both insider and outsider. As the returning city girl from the East, she was unlike the farmers she interviewed yet familiar enough to get them to speak openly with her.[5] She admired and endorsed their collective efforts to sustain lives working the land, yet she did so as an observer.

This insider/outsider relation to farmers and farmlands manifests in multiple other opposites over her lifetime.[6] Fierce commitment to the ideals of Communism inspired her writing in the 1930s, yet she never joined the party. This withholding did not spare her from state surveillance in the 1950s, however; nor did she escape blacklisting, which essentially ended her successful literary career. Her desire to flout convention was also ambivalent, at times out of tune with her resistance to change and longing for security. She pursued intimacies that defied the norms of monogamy and gender conformity, but when intimate relationships appear in her fiction adjacent to political plots, the transgressive details of her biography are concealed. She lived her writing and politics in tandem with passionate and often fraught love relationships, and she managed their adjacency through a keen facility for compartmentalizing.

In what follows, I trace Herbst's changing relationship to the land as it manifested in her life and loves, looking first at her Iowa childhood and then at her 1930s reporting on the strikes of midwestern farmers and her writing on a collective peasant experiment in Cuba's Oriente. Finally, I turn to her 1954 book *New Green World* as an allegorical reckoning with her white settler past and unnarrated sexuality, obliquely rendered through an eighteenth-century farmer's relationship to the land, its people, and the son he was unable to comprehend. Encoded across that writing are traces of the intimate distance that punctuated her relationship to the land and to her own life. Whiteness in all its unremarkableness appears here. As I discuss in chapter 3, that history manifests in the archive of postcolonial America between the lines, its traces spatially coded, most discernable in what is unsaid. I have found reading for this whiteness especially difficult because it means lingering with the commonplace, discerning in unconscious gestures of intimacy and distance a history of omissions. More than that, it has meant for me pondering my own uneasy identification with Herbst and discovering in her familiarity the landscape of my own white habits. Herbst became for me, in short, a grounded reference to discern the elusive shadows of whiteness and to speculate on the wayward paths they sometimes trace.

"I Was Already Somebody Else"

Josephine Herbst was born in Iowa where the Big Sioux and Floyd Rivers meet the grand Missouri on the edge of the tallgrass prairie of the North American Great Plains. The name of her birthplace, Sioux City, bears the imprint of its colonial history, "Sioux" being a French transcoding of Očhéthi Šakówiŋ, the name that members of the Seven Council Fires of the Dakota call themselves. The city sits on lands that had been home for Indigenous peoples even before the Sioux, as far back as AD 650, long before Europeans arrived as fur traders in the 1600s. Over the next generations, military conquest would be replaced by market relations administered by court decrees and then by leases, mortgages, and deeds. By the middle of the nineteenth century, Native tribes were being forced by U.S. government treaties to surrender their lands and tribal organization and divide their communal holdings into individual allotments. By 1848 most of the Sauk, Meskwaki, Winnebago, and Potawatomi people had been removed to reservations. Only the Sioux remained in their hunting grounds of the northwestern Great Plains.[7] The first white settlement in what would become Iowa was established in 1833, in defiance of the U.S. government's designation three years earlier of land west of the Mississippi as protected Indian territory. In two decades, that protection completely evaporated as settlers moved in and Iowa entered the union in 1854. By 1892, Sioux City boasted over forty thousand settler residents.

Mary Frey and William Benton Herbst, Josephine's parents, were part of the late nineteenth-century wave of settler migration to Sioux City. Respectable but poor easterners from Pennsylvania, they headed west in 1889, a year before the director of the U.S. census announced that the frontier had closed. Like so many others, they came looking for opportunity and a better life. William's people had been storekeepers in the Pennsylvania countryside near Harrisburg. Mary's were landowners closer to Allentown, cultivators of a claim said to have been granted around 1700 by William Penn himself.[8] The couple had lived in Pittsburgh and had made frequent stays in Vineland, New Jersey, where Mary's parents lived. The late 1880s were the golden era of Iowa, and Sioux City was rapidly growing into a town where the sale and resale of land was a topic on every potential settler's lips. For Bent, as Josephine's father was called, it was an opportune place to support his family by selling farm equipment.[9]

Josephine was the third of four girls, named for her mother's brother, Joe. He was a notorious figure in the family who would later appear in her trilogy, a charismatic ne'er-do-well who went south after the Civil War, made a fortune from shady dealings, and then fled west in pursuit of mining claims.[10] Josephine, nicknamed Josie, enjoyed working with her father, who "was a kind of family doctor" to the farmers' machinery "when it began limping in threshing season."[11] As a child, she drove all over the Iowa, Nebraska, and Dakota country with him, eating fried chicken and chewing corn on the cob. When the crops were in, they would take a team of horses and drive around "to see what cash he could pick up on old debts."[12] He would ask her to "keep office" when a big shipment of farm machinery to nearby towns arrived, and he introduced her to the farmers as "my office boy." She recalled that this job was much better than working in the kitchen, a place that, in spite of its delicious smells, could be a trap. "If you didn't watch your step," she remembers feeling, "you'd be in a little bungalow, beating eggs for keeps."[13]

Although her father opened the countryside to her, Josie's mother was the force in the family.[14] The Freys had emigrated from Zurich to Pennsylvania around 1700 when Josie's great-great-grandfather acquired a tract of land. Her maternal grandmother had been an indentured servant before being rescued, or rather bought, by Joshua Frey, Josie's maternal grandfather (*Starched Blue Sky*, 39–40). He was a surveyor of lands and roads and a member of the state legislature. Some land came to him through inheritance, and he speculated in more, accruing enough debt that when he died, he had nothing much left for his widow (40). Josie's grandmother took the children to Philadelphia, where she borrowed a sewing machine and made uniforms for Union soldiers, employing girls, among them her daughter Mary, who worked after school.[15]

In published excerpts from Herbst's memoir, the young Josie emerges as a child often situated at a remove from her environment and herself. From her office boy's perspective, she saw her father as both close to and remote from his customers. He "would be chatting with huge red-faced farmers whose legs in funnels of blue denim were as solid as the pistons of the big trains," his voice making him "a stranger among strangers" (*Starched Blue Sky*, 25). When hail crushed the crop, her father became the nemesis of families unable to pay what was due. Josie's relationship to the land was formed by her apprenticeship to her father's market relationship to farming, but it was compounded by her mother's desire for elsewhere. This desire shaped the map of the country Josie remembers having as a child in which Iowa lay between two borders—back East, where her parents came from, and out West, where Frey relatives fled beyond what she calls "our own barren middle ground" (3).

This detached perspective appears in "Magicians and Apprentices," a chapter of her memoir. The chapter begins with her memory of escaping Iowa as a six-year-old with her mother and sisters when they took the train to Oregon to visit Mary's brother, their Uncle Daniel, and his family. They sat all day with their noses pressed to the train window, which framed a vibrant panorama as "the land unwound itself" (*Starched Blue Sky*, 5). This signature moment in the development of her writerly relation to the land situates Josie as an engaged observer. The visit is also a telling beginning to a midwestern childhood, flavored by escape to Oregon trout streams, tumbling waterfalls, and salmon-filled pools. "The new things your hands and feet discovered" made that summer memorable for Josie precisely because being somewhere else wrapped the experience in "the glitter it offered of some distant beyond" (8).

Josie's Iowa discontent was soothed by her sister Helen, who was four years younger and her closest ally and friend. As the younger pair of the four sisters, Josie and Helen were almost in a separate family and delighted in being a world apart yet close to their mother, whom they wore "like an inner skin" (50). Mary's influence on her youngest girls was profound. Alienated from Sioux City and scornful of Iowa ways, she regaled them with vivid tales of the East. The distance that she placed between herself and her two worlds, encoded in the stories she told, shaped Josie's orientation as a writer and sealed her relationship to the land. The hundred-year-old farmhouse in Bucks County, Pennsylvania, that Herbst would live in for over forty years would be an effort to reclaim her mother's back-East past.

In her biography of Herbst, Elinor Langer paints the Sioux City of Josie's youth as a town of second-generation pioneers intent on denying their pioneer history. It was not a good place to be different, she concludes, a comment that captures the unease conditioning Herbst's emerging documentary stance, even toward her own body. The conclusion of "Magicians and Apprentices" illustrates her translation of that unease into a poignant portrait of the artist as a young woman. Significantly, it springs from Herbst's effort to process the experience of her first menstruation. "My body had spoken its first piece," she recalls thinking after her mother explained what the blood means. However, she wonders, "What had it said?" As if in answer, she remembers a night when she biked home with two other girls from picking cherries for a farmer who paid them a basketful for every four baskets they picked. The scene inscribes her "induction into womanhood" in an intimate and erotic description of girls perched in the "crotch" of cherry trees, "the scaly bark warm as a living arm . . . mouths and hands pink with the oxblood juice of the fruit, our gingham dresses stained as if we had knifed the throats of lambs and doves. . . . Pulled down from the bough, the pulp sucked free of its stone spurted its wild juice against the tongue" (*Starched Blue Sky*, 50).

The memoir winds to its conclusion as the girls ride their bicycles away from the farm, alone and adjacent in a little circle of lights. "Silently as robbers we skimmed the dark roads to arrive, taking the town by surprise," returning altered and confident from this luscious foray. The chapter's final paragraph presents Josie, the emergent witness: "But the scene was already detached from me as if I had been watching it slowly evolve in the depths of some crystal ball. On that first day of passing over to the adult side, I was already somebody else. I was shedding my skin and I could hear the old skin fall" (51). In growing that new skin, she will repeatedly flee the town and come back to the land.

Because his business was held hostage to the weather, her father was often unemployed, and so for Josie attending college was sporadic and supported by her own earnings. After high school, she attended the church-sponsored Morningside College and worked in her father's store. She saved her small earnings in order to escape the meager education there, and in 1912, she enrolled at the University of Iowa in Iowa City, the first state-supported coeducational university in the country where more than half the students were women. While she was at the university, her father's business failed, and for the rest of his life he worked for others for low wages. Josie consequently left school and accepted a teaching job in rural Iowa, only to realize that her dreams could never flower there. "'They aren't living, they are vegetating,'" she concluded, and wondered why they were all so *blonde*.[16]

In 1915, she moved to Seattle along with a high school friend, seeking a new life. While there, she underwent a painful induction into scientific abuse when both young women were drawn into a hideous experience. Unfortunately, it was not the last painful event she suffered in connection with her reproductive body. They sought treatment meant to cure menstrual cramps, and it led to gynecological surgeries to secure a "fallen womb," or retroverted uterus. It is not known what impact this treatment may have had on her childless future or on her sexual intimacies. The fact that the young women received exactly the same procedure suggests they may have been part of an experiment (Langer, 38).

After a brief return to Sioux City, Josie saved enough money for another escape, this time to California, where she enrolled at the University of California, Berkeley, to finish college (42). There, in a radical group centered in Oakland, she found like-minded friends who talked of resisting the war and of the revolution in Russia. It was in that circle that she began to feel comfortable as the intellectual equal of men (45). She graduated in 1918 at age twenty-six, eight years after starting college. She returned to Seattle in 1918, the year of the end of the war and of the influenza pandemic, and was there during Seattle's General Strike. Looking for more-promising opportunities, she moved on to San Francisco, and after a short stay, she finally headed east.

Josie's relation to her Iowa roots remained unsettled, however. Even if her father's work and her mother's eastern longings gave her an ambivalent relation to the farms surrounding her, those lands also shaped her membership in a community whose whiteness was remarkable for being unmentioned in her memoir of these years. An essential feature of a settler heritage that racialized space as white yet thought of it as neutral, whiteness appears in her memoir as an "unconscious habit," to use Shannon Sullivan's term. As the 1910 Iowa census reveals, race then was marked as three categories—white, Negro, or a conglomerate Indian, Chinese, Japanese, and all others, which was then further divided into native born (clearly not referring to Indigenous people) and foreign born, with the countries of origin listed being all western European. Where might this social stratification have conditioned Herbst's life? Would her mother's stories and discomfort in Iowa have resonated with another unspoken awareness of those "all others" who had been displaced? Did the young Josie see evidence of them, if only in Iowa City newspapers, even though the population of the state was by then overwhelmingly white?[17] I wonder if being white lent a veneer of security to her confidence as a girl or passable office boy who helped collect the farmers' debts and who was able to travel the surrounding country by bike or horse and wagon. The train that took her west as a child in 1895 was surely segregated, a fact unnoticed and unremembered by her. Seattle had a Black community that Louise Thompson and her mother joined, but it does not feature in Herbst's account of living there. Perhaps the gynecologist duplicated his hideous experiment on Black women, and if so maybe she and her friend shared waiting rooms with some of them. Whiteness is legible in Herbst's account of her youth only in what presumption can discern between the lines of her memories of the land. For many white writers, including myself, it is almost invariably and literally unremarkable, its absence a measure of the security it offers. For Herbst, awareness of this facet of her relation to the Iowa heartland would continue to germinate throughout the following decades.

Divided Heart

Josie arrived in New York City in October 1919, one of the most turbulent years in U.S. history and the year of the founding of the Communist Party in the United States. Interested in pursuing her writing and in further exploring the question of revolution, she joined friends, not in Harlem but in the bohemian neighborhood of Greenwich Village. Their basement apartment became a gathering place for writers and editors of the *Masses,* which was closely associated with the Communist Party. Cosmopolitan, international, intellectual, political—this was just the climate she longed for. In these circles, the Communist Party was welcoming and diverse.

In early 1920, Josie had a brief but passionate affair with the future playwright Maxwell Anderson. The experience was an induction into a sexual relationship and another jarring encounter with her own reproductive capacity. By summer, he had broken off with her, and she soon realized that she was pregnant. She found a doctor and had an abortion, recuperating from it alone in a hotel. That fall, Helen wrote to Josie distraught. She was married, unhappy, and pregnant. She desperately sought Josie's help in securing an abortion because doctors who would perform the procedure were difficult to find in Iowa. Distracted by her own new job with H. L. Mencken's magazine, and hundreds of miles away, Josie did all she could from New York except for telling Helen about her own recent abortion. Despairing, Helen went to a doctor whose reputation "was not of the best" (Langer, 64). She suffered an infection and died. Josie felt Helen's death was her fault and never forgave herself. The loss haunted her. Perhaps, coming so close on the heels of her own abortion, the loss of Helen melded feelings about her own abortion experience with guilt and grief over Helen. For the rest of her life, Elinor Langer concludes, Josie's most important relationships were efforts in one way or another to bring her sister back (66). That was true of her writing as well. In May 1922, Josie left New York for Europe and settled alone in Berlin. Here she wrote her first novel, an attempt to come to terms with Helen's death. It was never published, in part because it told the story of an abortion in explicit detail.

At the end of that trip, she stopped in Paris, and there in April 1924 met the man who would preoccupy her emotionally for the next decade and more. John Herrmann was twenty-three and Josie thirty-two, but having already shaved five years off her age, she told him she was twenty-seven. The son of a Michigan business-man, he had been studying art history in Munich but was more interested in becoming a writer himself (73). They made a vow to remain unmarried, a fact that may suggest Josie's desire to main-tain her reproductive and professional freedom and perhaps also their mutual interest in resisting the property relation of mar-riage. Ultimately, they both gave in to pressure from his parents, a concession that turned on property. John had asked his father for money to help in buying a house, and his father's approval was contingent on them marrying. They made up a fake license, but John's parents figured out their ploy and strong-armed them into actually marrying in September 1926. The newly married couple promptly tore up the license, but the money for the house did not appear. Nonetheless, John's father relented the following year and paid $2,500 for a small two-story farmhouse with electricity but no plumbing or central heating in the rural hamlet of Erwinna on the Delaware Canal in Bucks County. The house remained in John's father's name even after Josie and John divorced. For the rest of her life it was Josie's home, but she would never officially own it (84–86).

The 1930s began for her and John with an invitation to travel to the Soviet Union to attend the International Congress of Revo-lutionary Writers in Kharkov, which was then the capital of the Ukrainian Soviet Socialist Republic. Josie returned impressed and moved by what she saw but not a convert to Communism. She did join the National Committee for the Defense of Political Prisoners, an affiliate of the legal arm of the party, however, and like others of the Left, she supported the Scottsboro Boys. Her 1931 article in the *New Masses* on their trial notably represents it as a legal lynch-ing. The article is also striking for her extended quotation of Ada Wright, the widowed mother of two of the boys, who describes her family's efforts to survive after they were thrown off the land. Herbst would later "forget" this awareness of African American dispossession in her attention to Iowa farmers, Cuban peasants, and Native American removals, each with its own distinct politi-cal history. Not peculiar to her, the forgetting is one reminder of capitalism's fragmentation of ways of knowing, a destruction that continues to shape what and how we see.

In 1931, the effects of the Depression were settling on Bucks County, and John was increasingly involved with the dairy farmers there. As the price of milk sank, many small farmers were unable to pay their debts, and their houses and farms were being put up for auction. Local farmers began responding militantly to the threat of foreclosure and debated whether to call for a moratorium on debt as some midwestern farmers were doing. A few were Communists, and that year John joined the Communist Party (147, 117). The farming situation in Erwinna was part of an agricultural crisis unfolding across the country. Farmers were trapped in debt to the banks, bonded in peonage to landholders, and captive to the whims of weather and crop failure. The technological development of labor-efficient agricultural machines was also propelling many farmhands and tenants off the land. Those who stayed remained in the grip of mortgages and loans that could never be repaid. Most also assumed that the "free" land claimed by their homesteader predecessors was their rightful property and inheritance.

In the early 1930s, only a handful of Communist Party members were paying attention to agriculture.[18] In 1929, in its theoretical journal the *Communist,* the CPUSA ran a series of articles that focused on American farmlands and the impoverishment of small farmers owing to the rise of factory farms.[19] Although the party was never the leading force in the farm strikes that took place in the Midwest, it did enter the farmers' campaigns when the Farmers' Union and the Farmers' Holiday Association were the organized core of a Corn Belt rebellion in the early 1930s.[20] That movement confronted the agrarian crisis in the region with a withholding strategy that targeted the banks. If the banks could have a holiday, the farmers asked, why couldn't farmers keep milk and corn at home until the government and the public came to realize the importance of the people who tilled the soil?[21] Their aim was to combat falling prices by demanding that farmers, not the market, determine the value of the products of their labor.[22]

Among the Communist Party members active in this organizing effort were the notorious fiery speaker Ella Reeve Bloor, better known as Mother Bloor, and her son, Harold "Hal" Ware.[23] Bloor came to be called "Mother" because she brought motherhood, fam-

ily, and community into left politics.[24] In 1932, the party called
upon Ware and his colleague Lement Harris to build the agrarian wing of the proletarian movement in the United States. They
helped plan the mass demonstration in Sioux City that Herbst
would witness that September, and Ware went on to establish
the Farmers' National Committee for Action and Farm Research,
a Washington-based information bureau.[25] On August 11, 1932,
Sioux City was the focal point of a historic farmers' strike. Farmers blocked shipments from all directions and pickets spread like
wildfire across the grass roots of Iowa into Nebraska, Minnesota,
the Dakotas, and Wisconsin. The original aim of the strike was to
enable farmers to control the cost of production through legislation, but for the picketers the goal grew into keeping goods off the
market until prices went up. In the vanguard of the movement
were the dairy farmers, who delivered their milk to companies
that controlled the prices.[26] That fall, Herbst returned to Iowa to
cover the strike for Scribner's Magazine. Her article, "Feet in the
Grass Roots," was her first major contribution to the journalism
of the Depression, and it initiated a public identity for her (Langer,
133).[27]

Driving toward Sioux City from the east, she cast a critical eye
on the farm towns she passed through, where an emerging agribusiness accompanied by up-to-date homes suggested "a raw
method of getting and spending" and "industriously tilled soil
has brought trouble to the men who work it."[28] She arrived as an
outsider, but because she was from Iowa, she knew the lay of the
land and made that evident in her reporting by mentioning local
places—the Golden Slipper Dance Hall, the Big Sioux Bridge near
the picnic spot, or the dirt road leading to the rural school where
she once taught. In her account of the strike, she recalls "driving
all over this country" with her father as a child. Tutored by him
as he "would point out the fields quietly with his whip" when they
drove back "in the violet evening with the hills dark and lovely
and beneficent," she learned to observe ("Feet in the Grass Roots,"
46). These drives through the countryside instilled in her a way
of seeing as someone *from* the farmlands but not *of* them. The
distinction colors her descriptions of the people and places when
she returned years later. She writes of one night when she joined
the picketers around the fire at their blockade, witness to their

tableau. "When one talks the others listen," she remarks, "with a civilized courtesy that belongs to the stage, not to the town and its nervous, interrupted chatter. It is all orderly, like a play." Even "the night is set like a stage" (47). With the perspective of a returning daughter, she sees these young men with familiar yet fresh eyes. They "are big men, in overalls, stubbly faces, not so slack in the pants as the farmers I remember" (46). Only one of them, an "old man with a white mustache and fluffy white hair," "slides around" and tells her he remembers her father (47).

This Iowa trip inspired Herbst. Material from it would appear in the second novel of her trilogy, and she returned to Erwinna with renewed interest in the plight of local farmers (Langer, 150). She also returned completely smitten by a young woman she had met the previous summer at Yaddo, the writers' center in Saratoga Springs, New York. Marion Greenwood entered Josie's life like a whirlwind across the prairie. At twenty-three, she was considerably younger than Josie, who was then forty but passing for thirty-five. Marion was already a talented painter on the brink of a successful career as a muralist. Stunningly beautiful and dangerously reminiscent of Josie's sister Helen, she swept Josie off her feet into an intense infatuation. Somehow, Josie managed to keep her attention riveted on Marion even while covering the Iowa strike, and their passionate affair unfolded over the next year. True to her ambivalent form, she set out to have both Marion and John in her life. Before leaving Iowa, she invited Marion to come to Erwinna, telling her that she wanted John to know her (Langer, 132–34). At the time, Marion was involved with a married man, and she continued to have relationships with men, the details of which she often shared with Josie. For her part, Josie shared her intense feelings for Marion with John. In an ill-fated effort to resolve the tension that this sharing provoked, Josie suggested all three try living together that winter. On Christmas Eve, they crossed the Texas border into Nuevo Laredo, Mexico, and headed south to a house in a village near Taxco (139). By spring, it was clear that the arrangement was not working, and John left for Galveston. Josie felt she had to choose, and she chose John.

She saved her letters to and from Marion, however, in an envelope marked "Destroy" (128, 152). More evidence of her characteristic ambivalence, the profoundly mixed message speaks to this conflicted time in her life. Perhaps because Marion so reminded Josie of Helen or maybe because she met some of her sexual and emotional needs, Marion touched Josie deeply. The direction to others to do with the letters what Josie so easily could have done herself marks them as both scandalous and precious, with reservations about each. Preserving Marion in this way may also have offered Josie the solace of memorializing in writing a powerful intimate relationship she had otherwise concealed.

Herbst lived an intense, often tumultuous and transgressive personal life adjacent to her writing. Her ability to compartmentalize proved advantageous as her involvement in Communist political circles grew. Did Communism's critique of private property inform her awareness of the property relation embedded in her life's compartments? Did it heighten her understanding of marriage as an institution designed to control a woman's sexuality as property?[29] The little that is known about what transpired in those four months in Taxco is laden with secrets and betrayals as the three navigated the erotic desires and fears of an open marriage far away from the eastern farmhouse owned by John's overbearing father (Langer, 139–40). The Taxco house belonged to a Mexican official involved in a well-known "conspicuous circle of Mexican and American homosexuals," a fact that may have added to its allure (141). Josie would only indicate those relationships indirectly in the double plot of her novel *Rope of Gold,* in which Victoria's exit from a failing marriage parallels her involvement in struggles over land ownership in Cuba, the novel's fractured plots merely hinting at connections between marriage and the land.

With the affair with Marion ended, Josie and John struggled to make things work, and a reporting assignment she was offered on an issue he was deeply involved in seemed one way. In November 1933, she attended the Farmers' Second National Conference, in Chicago. The event marked her greatest identification with the Communist Party and the farmers of the Midwest. It was also the high point of the party's influence on rural protest. Over seven hundred farmers endorsed a radical program contesting the growing advance of market relations into the land. They demanded cancellation of debts, cash relief, and an end to evictions, and they called for other measures aimed at helping the "busted farmer." In her article on the conference, "Farmers Form a United Front," she recounts a year of intense agrarian organizing and notes the diverse organization the conference displayed. Black sharecroppers from the Deep South sat beside poor white farmers from Nebraska and the Dakotas, united by evictions and debts. They also found common cause in their opposition to the New Deal's price regulation plan, which required farmers to destroy surplus crops while sharecroppers' relief checks went to their creditors, the property owners, who deducted the farmers' running debts from their relief payments. Herbst notes that the delegation from her own locality in Pennsylvania aligned with farmers from across the nation who were demanding cancellation, not a moratorium, of debt they could never pay. Not only had these farmers grown more confident, but so had Herbst in her enthusiasm for their demands. Despite the high spirits of the event, however, the Communist Party would not go on to gain the full endorsement of the majority of farmers, its momentum undercut when the rise of fascism redirected the party's priorities.

The following September 1934, Josie returned to Iowa once more when Hal Ware's Farm Research Institute and the *New Masses* invited her to look at the impact of Franklin Roosevelt's farm policies and the status of rural protest throughout the farm belt. Earlier that year, Ware had invited John to work at his research center and John had moved to D.C.[30] The separation was meant to be a chance for Josie and John to recover what they could from their relationship. In this visit back home to Iowa, no nostalgia flavors Herbst's observations. Now the collective organizing of the 1932 pickets and the united front of 1933 are nowhere to be seen.[31] Evidence of impending disaster is everywhere. Drought scorches the land, and the air is thick with contradictory talk. The only common ground among the small farmers is the desire to get somewhere else. Herbst's article is full of numbers that tell a tale of debts and livestock whose market value is abstracted into units (a cow is a unit, a horse is a unit) that must be reduced if a farmer is to get relief. Small dirt farmers were being overtaken by big landowners and banks. Finally, Herbst is clear that homesteading is the root of the problem because "grazing land has been stripped of buffalo grass and cultivated to death" and now "dry hot withering winds blow on land that has been homesteaded to its last inch."[32] The very concept of the homestead, she explains, was built on a logic of colonial expansion and fraudulent misrepresentation of the land. The government had weather records going back years, she reminds readers. They knew that the homestead offer was for 160 acres of grassland soil that was never going to be "improved." Farming the prairie was doomed to failure. Teachers and clerks who had mortgaged the land to buy equipment, she reports, homesteaded most of the Dakotas, and they still had those mortgages. Her disenchantment goes only so far, however, focused as it is on farmers and their plight.

While Josie was in the farmlands, in Washington John was meeting the woman who would be his new wife, the diminutive, blonde Ruth Tate. Josie's marriage was essentially over, but she held on desperately. Meanwhile, that fall she published the second novel of her trilogy. It features material from her first Iowa trip, and two sisters are its main characters, one of whom dies while pregnant. Josie's reputation as a journalist also was at a high peak. When the *New Masses* invited her to go to Cuba to cover the brewing political situation there, she plunged into this dangerous assignment, her sights set on finding a way to visit communal farmlands in Cuba's wild east.

Realengo Witness

Herbst's Cuba experience turned out to be transformative. She arrived on the island in the midst of the 1933–35 revolution, a risky undertaking for a female foreign journalist traveling alone. Her personal life was in the throes of a painful transition she was unwilling to accept, and during her weeks in Havana she wrote obsessively to John. Her dexterity in keeping her emotions separate from her reporting, however, enabled her to focus on events on the ground and to save the parallel story of emotional upheaval for her next novel, *Rope of Gold*. In Cuba, Herbst saw international capital investment in land everywhere on full display on an island ruled by its most profitable crop, sugarcane. Being there brought into view the global colonial history she could not see in the farmers' struggles in the United States. In addition, her trip to Cuba's Oriente gave her a literal reorientation to the land and to agrarian resistance. Two of her three articles on Cuba give background on the impact of U.S. involvement and the reasons for the general strike.

She describes her five-day visit to the Oriente district of Realengo 18 as the first woman from outside Cuba to go there. Carved out of the Sierra Maestra in the island's easternmost province, in what Herbst would call a tiny soviet, a farming community was cultivating a communal experiment and understood its effort as part of a Pan American anti-imperialist revolutionary movement. The way of life she witnessed in her visit to Realengo 18 would introduce her to the possibility of an alternative relation to the land and reorient her relationship to marriage.

Herbst wrote her first article ten days after returning from Oriente to Havana, and we can see the impact of what she witnessed in her perspective on the strike. She explains that events in the eastern mountains "cannot be separated from the rest of the island" because hunger binds the people of the city and the country when "all must worship" cane.[33] Within a decade after Cuban independence from Spain, sugar companies had ramped up investment and planted every inch of the island they could with cane. By the time Herbst arrived, it was an island "sick with sugar."[34] Realengo 18 began as opposition to that sickness, a resistance effort threatened by the ring of sugar mills expanding like a cancer from the valley below its lush fields.

Oriente holds a contradictory place in the Cuban national imaginary. On one hand, colonial authorities subjected the region to racist derision because of the strong presence of Afro-Cubans there and its communal peasant traditions.[35] On the other hand, Oriente was, and still is, the most heroic of all places because of the region's history of strong political resistance. Here Fidel Castro was born, and the 26th of July Movement he led launched the final stage of the 1953–57 revolution. When Herbst visited, Oriente had the highest concentration of Afro-Cubans in all Cuba, and they equaled or outnumbered the white population. It also had a large campesino, or individual farmer, population, and the region was heir to historical precedents of Afro-Cuban political organization and interracial cooperation.[36] Women figured prominently in the region, and many were heads of households.[37]

On the road to Santiago de Cuba and then to Oriente, Herbst saw little land given to raising food crops until she reached Realengo 18, "a country the government forgot," perched "on top of the world . . . in the midst of steep cultivated mountains."[38] The government had not completely forgotten this place, however. The army came to spy, and the big sugar mills in the valley, owned by companies in Canada and the United States, were trying to claim the *realengos,* communal lands. These lands, she explains, originated in the old days when the rich were granted circular parcels of land. The interstices between the circles "belonged to the government, if anyone, and were known as *realengos.*"[39] After the War for Independence, soldiers were supposed to be rewarded with these leftover lands, but in most cases, squatters claimed them. Realengo 18 was one such area.[40] As her contact from the rebel underground led her to Santiago and then by horseback into the Sierra, Josie passed through mountainsides "so steep it seemed only flies could cultivate them." A stranger in overalls and a blue work shirt, she was welcomed warmly along the way into every hut where men wanted to know the news. Here, deep russet soil teemed with food, and she saw the land as an urban woman would: "Coffee and bananas patchwork the mountainsides in lines neat as machine stitching."[41]

Her initial encounters disclose other interpretive horizons she brought with her. Arrangements were made for her to meet with Leon Alvarez, the founder and leader of the fifteen thousand–member Associación de Productores Agricolas del Realengo 18 y Colandantes.[42] To avoid the army guards who were hunting him, he came under cover of night. Awaiting him, Josie talked with the wife of a comrade who had gone to Havana. "For a few minutes," she thinks, "we are two women, showing each other pictures of our absent husbands." She notes that the woman is white and her husband "a Negro," an observation that confirms for her "there is no race problem here," a detail that unwittingly discloses this otherwise perceptive outsider's blind spot. Herbst describes Alvarez as "a very Black Negro," but she does not seem to know that race in Oriente is more about politics than color.[43] Afro-Cuban resistance persistently and profoundly inflected the struggle over land. The *realenguistas* aligned their efforts with anti-imperialist and transnational struggles in Latin America and claimed solidarity with the assassinated revolutionary leaders Nicaraguan Augusto Sandino and Mexican Pancho Villa. She notices women's domestic activities as they rise to make coffee or offer orange-flavored drinks. In her report none of the women receive names, an omission that may suggest Herbst's unconscious effort to secure her authority as a woman professional. This distance is countered, however, by the trust she clearly developed with the group. It accompanies her own dawning consciousness of postcolonial America as she navigates the distance between the United States and neocolonial Cuba, between herself as an Anglo outsider and the *realenguistas* she comes to know. The intimate moment she has with another woman over photographs of their husbands and with men over news of the world are both crucial to that process.

By April, she was back in Havana reporting on the general strike that the U.S. embassy and General Fulgencio Batista had agreed would not happen. Triggered by people who had been terrorized and robbed of personal security, who demanded freedom of speech, assembly, and the press, it was, she affirms, "waged at base on a purely anti-imperialistic line."[44] These demands, so different in scope from those of the striking farmers in the United States, awakened her to the relationship between imperial ambitions and agrarian policy in and outside the homeland. The U.S. government pursued colonial intervention in Cuba after the Spanish ceded the island at the end of the Spanish–American War.[45] The war and occupation cleared the way for business investments via decrees annulling communal landholdings and initiating a latifundio system of large tracts more susceptible to being acquired as private property.[46] When Herbst arrived in Cuba, big business was in the hands of the Americans and the British, small farmers were being crowded out of the market, workers were being fired from the cane fields, and students, teachers, and doctors were demonstrating for equipment, supplies, and better wages.

The third article in her Cuba series is her best for its clear-eyed dramatization of the Realengo 18 farmers' awareness of these interests. It opens with a group gathered on the earthen floor of a hut where one of the men uses a stick to draw a map of Cuba. He shapes the island, "and we stare at its smallness" as "outlines of the United States, an ocean, Europe, and the Soviet Union appear."[47] The casual "we" in the scene enfolds the visitor and her readers into a circle of witnesses. Soon she becomes the center of attention when Jaime, a poet turned farmer, reveals that Herbst carries a passport with a visa from the Soviet Union. The passport goes from hand to hand slowly. Jaime says there ought to be a visa from

Realengo, and by that night, one has materialized, typed up and stamped by the *realenguistas*. When Herbst left the mountains, it went with her, an official document adjacent to her passport, evidence of a singular Caribbean soviet, a small transnational possibility of collective relation to land. The map scene captures the *realenguistas'* awareness of their place in a geopolitical network, dramatized in their gift of the visa, and it coalesces Herbst's expanding understanding of the land. Cuba is only a tiny island, and Realengo 18 is seemingly cut off from the outside world, but the members of this farming association "know too much to be alone" ("Passport," 11). They know that the labor they have given to the land is "the deep source that feeds their struggle to hold it," and the map captures the sizable threat they confront. They talk avidly about politics and history as immediate forces in their lives. Every person in the room has been "weighed down with the great bulk of the United States pressing from above on that map drawn upon the floor" (11). Cuba enables Herbst to see in sharp relief that capitalism depends upon the enclosure of the commons and the separation of production and consumption. That fact is starkly visible in the struggle of the *realenguistas* to keep the lands that sustain them in the face of foreign investment in a mono crop and consumer commodity that enriches a distant few.

Writing this article from her home in Pennsylvania weeks after leaving Cuba, Herbst renders what she witnessed there and its impact on her local experience. She remembers one Sunday afternoon in Realengo 18 when it was too dark to make maps and "we began singing, first the *Marseillaise* and then the *Internacionale*" (11). By May Day back in Bucks County, she was reporting that farmers were gathering on the courthouse lawn in Doylestown, testifying to their refusal to be evicted from the land. In closing, they sang "The Internationale." The international perspective Herbst gained in Cuba would lead her to Spain the following year, where she would be the only woman reporting from the front lines.

When the Cuba experience appears in her novel *Rope of Gold*, the fervor of Herbst's journalism is modified by the novel's form, which preserves an intimate distance from her past. The novel situates the farm strikes and Cuban struggles in adjacent plots that capture on a broad canvas the fragmented relations that span the Left's campaigns in Spain, the U.S. farmlands, and striking cities, here developed through a family saga loosely paralleling her own. In the story of her protagonist, Victoria Chance, the details of Herbst's fraught marriage and her relationship with Marion Greenwood that her reportage was unable to acknowledge appear in fiction's coded yet expansive form of life writing. Marion is transfigured into a man named Kurt Betcher, a leader of the antifascist German underground. The price of disrupting the heterosexual family as the anchor of property and the linchpin between capital and the state, a price Herbst actually paid, is barely hinted at, however, in Victoria's lingering affection for Betcher. More precisely, it is sequestered by the plot, which ultimately confines Betcher in a Brazilian prison.

As the novel ends, Victoria goes to Cuba as a reporter. Impatiently waiting in Havana for the contact who will take her to the mountains, she obsesses over the husband who has left her. Walking back to her hotel, she stops in a bar where a "lithograph of a Sidoney Indian girl looked down at her from among the bottles and fat little liquor jugs."[48] This painting is the only reference in all Herbst's writing on Cuba to the Indigenous people of the island. The Sitony were a Taíno group, part of the Arawak of the Caribbean and Florida. The most populous Indigenous people in Cuba at the time of Spanish conquest in 1511, they had disappeared as a distinct tribe by the end of the century, victims of smallpox, enslavement, and warfare brought by the Spanish.

The painting captures Victoria's awakening consciousness of the long history of colonization still being enacted in the Americas and of her own family's relation to it. "She would look up at the Sidoney girl, the very last of her lost race, stranded in a bar," and think of "her father's early conquests in business, their going West to the 'land of the free'" and of her grandfather "taking Swiss dairy farmers up the Mississippi to start little towns in the lush Wisconsin wilderness" (*Rope of Gold,* 362).[49] She thinks of Cortez coming to the shores of Cuba not to be a peasant but for gold, and she reflects that "men had been coming for gold ever since" (362). She thinks of the *realengo* mountain men whose labor had only brought upon them the covetousness of the big sugar companies in the valley "as if they signified the history of the human race" (362).

Victoria's reverie under the gaze of the Taíno painting is a powerful moment in Herbst's writing from the 1930s. It condenses into a representation of an Indigenous girl the arrival of capital in the New World armed with a new relation to the land. Aestheticized into a relic, the Indian girl conjures even as she obscures the extermination that spread like a virus from this small island to the Wisconsin wilderness. If the scene marks a moment of expanded awareness for Herbst, it does so through a strategy that so condenses and abstracts this history that it provokes a closer reading. The painting is an example of ekphrasis—the representation in a literary work of another work of art. The effect is to draw attention to the aesthetic as a representation of the social world it references. In this example, the referent is Cuba's history and Herbst's fictional-autobiographical rendering of it. The ekphrastic gesture adds one more layer of intimate distance to that history, a belated reminder of the disappearance of the Taíno people whose presence nonetheless remains. Like the Lenape of Pennsylvania, they were removed and annihilated, yet their relation to the land remains, surfacing here as a vestige of the colonial unconscious. The effect is underscored because the Sitony girl appears in a bar, a place where losses are anaesthetized and buried. Like a figure in a dream, she is encased in a nested series: in a painting inside a novel as seen by a character who is a fictionalized version of Herbst. As a cathected figure, she captures what narration can only enfold between the lines: the intimate distance of a historical relation Herbst is just beginning to crack open, a psychic seed that will take almost two decades to germinate.[50]

When Victoria leaves Cuba, her personal affairs have come to seem petty. "I won't forget them," she resolves as she travels north through Florida, remembering the people of Realengo 18 and the leader who "had looped his life to an entire world" (*Rope of Gold*, 406). She knows that she leaves many who had shed blood, not tears, and who "lay now in the prisons or in death," while "those that lived waited in silence to speak one day again" (406). Although she is changed, she remains a traveling observer much like the child Josie observing the midwestern landscape from a train window. As the bus carrying her home runs into daylight, she animates the land outside the window with qualified agency and hope: "The road and fields were solid ground and the objects of the earth like sleepy animals were rising to their knees" (406).

New Green World

Twenty years later Herbst brought her autobiographical bent to a new form of writing about the land that once more confronted American colonial history. Diving into extensive primary research on a time when the United States was still a British colony perched on the edge of a New World, she found a form to reckon with a relation to the land that by the mid-twentieth century had been all but lost to New World immigrants. Indigenous tribes in the Americas were still pursuing a balanced relation to that land, but their story is not hers to tell. Hers is the story of John Bartram, eighteenth-century Pennsylvania farmer and botanist. He has no place, however, in the title of the book, which is named instead for the land he encountered with wonder, whose soil he cultivated, and whose plants he collected and traded. But, you might ask: Why Bartram? Why does Herbst turn to his story when she does?

Aside from all the ways she may have identified with his Pennsylvania settler roots and his place in this new land as an insider-outsider, my best answer turns to *New Green World*'s narrative form. Herbst was not a formalist in the usual sense of that term. Her narratives were loose-knit family sagas in the realist mode, driven by national events and political struggles. Form for her was not about stylistic craft; it was a matter of finding a narrative cohesive and specific enough to render a sweeping epic through the daily dilemmas and desires of individuals. The life-writing form she finds for *New Green World* crystallizes the story of one man and his son into an allegory of American history and a reckoning with her own settler roots.

Herbst published *New Green World* in 1954, a time when the U.S. nation-state had begun menacing many of its citizens. The collective endeavors of the war years and the 1930s had disappeared, remnants of a way of life that was undergoing tremendous change. *New Green World* offered a history of land acquisition and commercialization at a time when the farmlands of Pennsylvania and New Jersey were being cleared for suburban Levittowns. The aspirations of the radical 1930s were not just receding underground by the mid-1950s; they were under attack by the federal government and were being actively crushed by an emerging postwar culture that championed capital development, consumption, individual ambition, and by an aggressive patriotism set against a Communist antagonist. In August 1951, the U.S. Department of State refused to renew Herbst's passport, and again in 1954 it denied her renewal request because she had once traveled to the Soviet Union, because John was a member of the Communist Party, and because she had supported various left causes in the 1930s.

The previous year, she once more met at Yaddo a brilliant and passionate woman, the poet Jean Garrigue, and another stormy relationship ensued. Fifteen years younger than the sixty-year-old Josie, Garrigue pursued men while they were together, and she eventually married one of them. Josie's life then was at a low ebb. She was desperately poor, and her work was all but forgotten. In 1952, FBI agents kept appearing at her door whenever anyone being investigated mentioned her name or John's. She claimed that writing *New Green World* "was a kind of rescue work" for herself (Langer, 287, 286). Even if it could not salvage Jean or the country, it was in part an allegorical diagnosis of both losses. *New Green World* maps the eighteenth-century emergence of what would become for the next three hundred years the cultural logic of the American settler's relation to the land. John Bartram's life enables her to represent that foundational pattern through the possibilities, contradictions, and limits of his wonder-filled love affair with the land. It is a tale with multiple layers whose principle actors are Bartram himself, his London agent and friend Peter Collinson, and Bartram's disappointing son William. While their story does not resolve Herbst's ambivalent stance toward the land, it does offer recognition of the history that shaped her settler legacy.

Between Bartram's birth in 1699 and his death in 1777, American culture was being born as a project of colonial settlement that would profoundly transform the web of life in the New World. In Europe and the Americas a shift was already occurring away from use of common lands for subsistence to the instrumental and abstract relations of profit from land extraction, speculation, and ownership. Herbst notes the tremendous historical transformation, remarking that "the enclosure of common land had been going on steadily since the Fifteenth Century," but "the face of England had begun to be really changed only after 1750 when a series of Enclosure Acts had gradually taken the land away from the common use." In fact, throughout the eighteenth century Parliament passed over two thousand acts of enclosure, privatizing the English commons.[51] While enclosure led to more-profitable use of land for those who controlled the acreage, it made the villager or small farmer who regularly accessed common lands landless, tossing him out to the cities "to sell his hands to the rising industries." This dispossession created "a great flux of displaced persons, with nowhere to go, who were already swelling the ranks of immigrants to the new world."[52]

Herbst charts this development through the life of Bartram, the grandson of a seventeenth-century immigrant. He was both an outlier and a leader in his time, pursuing his desire for closeness to the earth through farming while simultaneously cultivating the new science of botany and supporting development initiatives for the British king. Through the medium of scientific knowledge, he observed, named, collected, conserved, and traded plants, enamored by the New World's profuse vegetation and at the same time propelled by the scientist's dissection of it. The process placed him squarely in a contradiction. While he extracted from nature and commodified its bounty in trade, his impulse was not to make a profit but to preserve life forms before they were obliterated in the wake of the advancing development that funded his efforts. In the end, the botanist's impulse would become the agent of his failure. In narrating that flaw, Herbst allows us to see our own. John's son William was the living evidence of his father's limits, and he enters the narrative to point toward another possible path. Through him, Herbst offers a relation to the green world that is less driven by acquisitiveness, more vulnerable, one in which desire is oriented to know and respect those who came before, people who neither had to be antagonists nor had to be removed.

Allegory, as Fredric Jameson discusses it, is a second-order story—that is, a story about another story. As he understands it, allegory does not reveal the meaning of this other story; rather, it discloses the story's structure of multiple meanings. In this sense, although allegory's object is culture, it is akin to and yet different from scientific observation's distanced interest in patterns. The critical distance allegory affords lies in discernment of the coded imprint of history, including its secrets, in cultural texts, which are in turn agents in the web of life. Like other narrative forms, allegory is founded on relations—of one tale to another and of both to a history or histories conveyed through the material texture, the relational infrastructure if you will, of culture.

One of the more prevalent differentiating patterns in Western culture is a relation of opposition. We come to know the meaning of something or someone by way of what it is not. A farmer, for example, is not a nomad. Another type of negative relation is more passive—one thing is set against everything it is not. The farmer's cultivated lands are not the wilderness. In some forms, these differences are polarized, antagonistic: the cultivating farmer is opposed to and valued over the savage hunter. A complex of possible contrary and complementary relations are thus set in motion in a culture's signifying system. Narratives capture these relations of difference and opposition and the layers of individual and collective history they reproduce, as well as the possibility of their transgression or suspension. In this way, a culture's stories offer cognitive maps of the epistemic horizons that tell us where we stand, who we are or might be. These maps perform the ideological work of myth—the stories a society tells about itself in order to reproduce its prevailing relations. Myths and the relations they represent gain consent as common sense because they conceal their connection to the historical interests of the ruling group.[53] *New Green World*'s narrative of life in eighteenth-century America discloses a distant yet salient time and place, one that conditions an emerging national mythology whose layered tale enfolds and displays both the culture's desires and its secrets. That mythology's terms seep into Herbst's mid-twentieth-century present. And ours.

John Bartram's story is the tale of a man who lives on the cusp of a fast-transforming human relation to nature and adjacent to an emerging mythology of American settlement. "If man's divorce from Nature had begun," Herbst declares, "Bartram was not entirely the man to see it" (*New Green World,* 92). She contrasts him with his friend Benjamin Franklin. Their names top the list of founders of the Philosophical Society in Philadelphia. Both relied upon scientific fact, but they were otherwise unlike in their orientations. Franklin was practical, glorifying common sense and sacrificing sensibility; in this respect, he prepared the path for the nineteenth-century conquest of the machine (140, 93). Bartram's science was suffused with sensibility, what Herbst calls "wonder." Unlike the urbane Franklin, he was a farmer who lived close to the seeds that were his sustenance. Science gave him distance, the language of measurement and naming, and in that respect, he is like Herbst. He enters the uncharted lands of the New World from the grass roots as a colonial settler-farmer and awestruck observer set on mapping and cataloging the land and its flora.

For Herbst, he is a familiar figure, and she may have been drawn to Bartram for that reason. His close yet distant relation to the land echoes hers and her family's. Like the first Frey immigrant from Europe around 1700 who became a Pennsylvania landowner, Bartram's father settled in the East. The farm the young John Bartram developed was a scant thirty miles from Josie's Erwinna farmhouse. To read his story as allegory is not to see these details as merely similar to hers but to discern in their adjacency the space for reflection. The critical power of allegory lies in the distance it affords the reader to consider relations and their pertinence. As the past is illuminated, so is the reader's relation to his or her own present. The distance cannot repair an irrevocable separation from the lived reality of landed ancestors, but it can enable an unsettled relation to the land. Herbst explains in the book's foreword that *New Green World* is a counternarrative to the fragmented relations of a postwar consumer-driven twentieth century, and she describes Bartram's time as a pivotal one. "The centuries that followed the Renaissance had liberated the acquisitive impulses," she tells us, and had done so in the name of nature, severing "economic ethics from control by any comprehensive conception of the ultimate purpose of human living. The law of Nature became a sanction for the spoils of the world" (108).

The life of Bartram is Herbst's reckoning with the damage. That damage had already been hinted at by the brief appearance of the Indigenous girl in *Rope of Gold* as silent witness to genocide and forgetting. In *New Green World,* Herbst returns to the girl's hieroglyphic message, one that her farm reporting and fiction had not discerned. That she does so by way of the Bartrams offers a tale of two settlers' ambivalent place in that history. Their examples illustrate a human relation to nature undergoing massive transition, conditioned by an inherited dis-ease there was no vocabulary to diagnose.

When John Bartram encountered the Indigenous people in his travels, his reactions were initially favorable, but this favor had its limits and they were ominous. *New Green World* tracks his changing conception of the Native peoples as he eventually came to consider them a menacing obstacle to his activities as botanist and collector. They were in the end as incomprehensible to him as his son. In this respect, his tale is an allegory of the extraordinary yet failed potential of an American inhibited by a historical position he was powerless to change.

Farmer, Botanist, Trader John

John Bartram's grandfather came to America from Derbyshire, England, in 1682 before there was a single house in Philadelphia. His mother, Elizabeth Hunt, died in 1701 when he was two. His father remarried and moved to North Carolina, where he was killed by Indians, his wife and two children carried away and later ransomed. Little John, who had been left in Philadelphia, was raised by his grandparents. An uncle who was protective of the boy left his small farm to John's grandmother with the proviso that upon her death it be given to his nephew. John married a woman named Mary Maris, who died in 1727 during the epidemic then raging in Philadelphia. A widower with two children, he soon married again, to Ann Mendenhall. They would have ten children, six of whom survived, including a set of twins, Elizabeth and William. In a sheriff's sale, Bartram purchased a large tract of land around the farmhouse on the banks of the Schuylkill near Kingsessing, a Lenape word meaning "meadow." A year later, he expanded it with another two hundred acres and enlarged the house, cutting the stones himself. Scorning the excesses of the Philadelphia colonial elite and in keeping with his and Ann's Quaker background, they maintained a home that was all plainness. Unlike other settlers in the area, he had excellent farming methods, perfecting ingenious schemes to produce high yields from infertile soil. Grays Ferry and the nearby road gave him easy access to the city, where he went to transact business, visit the library of James Logan (William Penn's secretary and an avid collector of books), and attend meetings of the Philosophical Society.[54]

Botany came to Bartram "through his eyes and hands as he

ploughed a field or searched the woods for wild honey" (*New Green World,* 3). He was, in Herbst's words, "a farmer who never stopped farming," but his quick mind developed a deepened interest, handicapped only by a lack of funds (18). Botany let him through a door to nature, a door that was fast closing. It forced him away from home and "made him give up all dogmas," including the Quaker insistence that he recognize the Son of God (3). He was, Herbst concludes, what we might call a Deist who saw only one God reflected in all creation. She describes him as one of the men of the eighteenth century whose emotions were profoundly wrapped in wonder at nature's revelations and who felt it was their duty to "break through the thickets of superstition" and examine each specimen in its natural habitat (21). With a profound sense of mystery in the face of the tiny acorn that held a tree or the egg a bird, he cultivated a profound reverence that led to knowledge, a willingness to grasp all.

It was a time not yet given to boasting of human control over nature, Herbst informs us, and she walks beside the botanists observing this difference. For her, these men whose activities and natural habitats were sensuously and phenomenally related "seemed closer to stalks of growing grain in the field than we are" (2). She struggles for words to convey this intimate relation to the natural world. "You can call what they felt 'wonder.' You can call it 'love,'" she writes, but it is "an experience not even possible to transmit into words." She compares their enchantment by the world around them to "the deepest delight two human beings can take in each other." It was, moreover, a joy "geared to a profound respect for facts" (4).

Bartram did not attend school beyond the eleventh grade, but he kept gathering his facts from the books he borrowed from Logan's library. He was well-known among Franklin's set in Philadelphia and on the fringe of an international network of botanists at Oxford and in Sweden (23). Botanists, Bartram included, were collectors passionately driven by the desire for precision and accurate knowledge of hidden relationships. If Bartram discovered a new medicinal plant or herb, he didn't hoard the information like a miser but communicated it widely, and visitors came to marvel at his prize botanical garden (23).

Herbst follows the genealogy of plant knowledge in Bartram's world and concludes that the first botanical garden was probably made by a brotherhood of German mystics led by Johannes Kelpius who built their cloister in 1694 on the banks of the Wissahickon. Here they studied mathematics, experimented with alchemy, and planted gardens that ran down the glen "with a mainstay of herbs for medicinal purposes." Logan was another botanizer who also may have had specimens from Kelpius (61).

In order to collect more rarities in the wilderness surrounding him, Bartram traveled, organizing his trips around planting and harvest times on his farm. He journeyed to the source of the Schuylkill and by 1738 had gone as far as Lancaster County, Pennsylvania, and then across the Delaware River into Maryland and New Jersey. Although he would be sent to the Great Lakes and later to Florida on reconnaissance missions for the king, he never speculated on land or staked out a claim to seek a profit. He did trade what he found, however, and until the end of his life, Bartram would send a steady stream of plants and seeds to England. Herbst sees him as "forced to become something of a merchant," but without the typical merchant's interest in buying and selling. The prosperous London wool merchant and amateur botanist Peter Collinson had built up an exchange network of colonists who sent him specimens and in return would buy his woolens (7). Bartram became for him the ideal supplier: reliable, driven, and dedicated (19). They shared a sentiment and an interest, a common ground that would be the foundation of a business arrangement, correspondence, and friendship for over forty years. Collinson was a botanical agent for wealthy estate owners in England who were ornamenting their lands with exotics from the New World, and he also kept specimens for his own garden (19). The first substantial patron Collinson found for Bartram was Robert James, Baron Petre, who kept his nurseries stocked with plants and trees from afar.[55] After the baron's death from smallpox in 1742, Collinson found other patrons and requested many items for himself: terrapins and turtles as well as turtle eggs, fruit trees, and seeds that would be packaged in boxes or pouches in hopes they would survive the Atlantic trip. From 1735 until 1777, some 320 species of plants went to England from the colonies. The majority were from John Bartram (232).

A reluctant merchant, Bartram was also a contrary settler who saw other settlers as his antagonists. When he was finally appointed the king's botanist, a post he had much desired, he used it to fund trips that would beat other settlers into the wilderness, fearful that their cattle would chew the tender grasses under trees and eliminate some species forever (112). He did not see himself as one of them. He "knew that the country must be settled, the wilderness pushed back, opened up to homes and cultivated fields." At the same time, he feared the destruction of the thing he loved, not least of all because such destruction disrupted his mission. He wanted both "to run ahead of the pack and to gather first, and after that open up the pleasant land, build new waterways, make a great nation" (178). In his later years, Bartram was convinced that his explorations were not safe because of the Indians (132). Herbst's allegory maps the ambivalent cultural logic that conditions Bartram's relation to nature—scientific, orderly, distanced—yet relishing an awesome intimacy with it. His failing was to believe too stubbornly in his science, and it was also to refuse to recognize Indigenous knowledge and its intimate ties to the nonhuman world.

New Green World opens with Bartram's expedition to the Great Lakes region in July 1743. The trip was a mission for the British government to the Haudenosaunee, the tribes of the Six Nations, in the region of Lake Ontario.[56] It was politically delicate because the French and the British competed to control the fish and fur trade, and they had set the Haudenosaunee and the Lenape against each other in order to do so. The Society of Friends had the confidence of the Haudenosaunee, while the Lenape sided with the French. Bartram's aim was to negotiate with the northern tribes in order to assure tranquility at the frontier of Indian country, which settlers were already beginning to invade. He was to notice everything that grew and report to the king in the expectation that his findings would be useful for development of the region (*New Green World*, 8). Bartram's group was not out to conquer, nor did it intend to take land from anyone, hunt for gold, or stake a claim. They came in peace to Indigenous people and gave them the benefit of good intentions. Herbst speculates that Bartram was probably a useful pawn and did not know it.

The expedition included a cartographer, Lewis Evans, and an

interpreter, Conrad Weiser, who had lived for some years among the Native people. An "Indian" guide, Shicckalamy, and his son joined them on the tenth day. Shicckalamy was actually French; like other whites who had been captured and did not want to be liberated, he was adopted by the Oneida after being taken prisoner. The group passed through unmapped forestland so dense that at times it was totally dark at midday. When they encountered Haudenosaunee villages or Indigenous travelers on horseback, they would stop and eat together. Bartram notes in his journal the solemn song one of them sings in the night, and he admires the Natives' skill at snaring fish (32). The Indigenous would never be for him a source of fresh knowledge, however (38). In his journal, Bartram refers to them as "savages," although the word is tempered by a sense of their unjust treatment by scheming traders and encroaching settlers. Despite Bartram's conviction that he "had to measure up to the Indian conception of a friend," we do not see much evidence of friendship (39, 8). Herbst concedes that Bartram is "not the man to give himself over to an understanding of Indian life." On this trip, he "sees the Indian, but not quite" (41).

Ultimately, he came to resent the Indigenous as a treacherous foe because they stood in the way of his project (41). When in Bartram's later life the Indian Wars foreclosed his hope of exploring the lands of the Ohio and Mississippi Rivers, he blamed the Natives. For him, the Indian would "come at last to mean only another rattler" (135). Botany eventually so shaped his desire that the hunger to encounter more of nature hardened into a frustrated compulsion. This bitterness softened somewhat in his final trip to Florida, but it never entirely disappeared. Herbst notes that "the intricate tapestry of Indian life was invisible to the eyes of the colonists and rudely cutting through the multicolored web and weave, they were not even conscious of the extent of their destruction" (149–50). In the end, she concludes, "Bartram sided with the blind and ravenous vanguard." She speculates that perhaps his father's death was a stain that no Quaker upbringing could eliminate (149–50). It was John's shy, introverted son, with his rejection of the bustling hive, who gave himself up to a revealing study of Native tribes (41). Through him, *New Green World*'s allegory discloses its utopian possibility.

Utopian Maps: The Geography of Whiteness

William was John Bartram's "more sensitive, often difficult son" (5). I wonder if he favored his mother or his twin sister. It is difficult to know from *New Green World* since we learn nothing of them. I will return below to other details we learn little about in the utopian conclusion of *New Green World*. In considering William, Herbst is most interested in the ways he differed from his father, and she portrays him as unsettled for much of his life. This delinquency appeals to Herbst. Perhaps it is what leads her to romanticize William, as many of the readers of his *Travels* also would do, projecting a lost relation to the natural world onto him and the "no place" that he fabricated. "In an age when many men sought a Utopia," Herbst tells us, "William Bartram was one of the happy few" (260). Before he could render it in the published record of his travels in Florida, however, William himself was lost.

From his youth it was evident that Billy Bartram was not going to be the typical eighteenth-century man his father was (147). He was too much of an artist. From early on, he drew plants exquisitely and feverishly. Some of his drawings were sent to Collinson, who admired them immensely and sent orders for more. When Billy turned sixteen, his father felt it was time for him to propose some way to earn a living. John did not want his son to be a gentleman. The practical Franklin was consulted, and Bartram wrote to Collinson for suggestions. Father and son made some trips together to the Catskills and the Blue Mountains while waiting for a plan to materialize (141). However, every project Billy embarked on failed. He did not become an apprentice, a printer, or an engraver as Franklin had suggested. No surveying job opened up. "When John would put William on the spot and command a duty to be performed, William slipped from the noose and was nowhere" (181). He became apprentice to a Philadelphia merchant but ran away to his uncle's plantation in Cape Fear, North Carolina, where he borrowed money from his father to set up a mercantile shop to supply farmers and planters. He had been given this second chance, but his heart was not in it. Billy roamed the local woods to sketch birds and flowers and gather seeds instead of attending to business. He avoided writing home. He had become "poor Billy" and would remain so for the next ten years (147–48). Some might see him as the son of a prosperous man, indulged by the adults around him who worried and tried to help him find his way, even resorting to benign neglect. For Herbst, who sees him kindly, "he was a passive resister. . . . Getting ahead was not his line" (194).

In April 1765, King George III appointed John Bartram to be his botanist for East and West Florida, and the appointment funded a trip. John invited Billy to join him as assistant. The invitation was an intentional rescue operation. In October, they arrived in St. Augustine to explore the St. Johns River, East Florida's major waterway. This area of Florida had been transferred from Spain to Great Britain at the end of the Seven Years' War. When the Bartrams arrived, almost all the Spanish had gone to other Spanish provinces, most of them to Cuba.[57] On a whim at the end of the trip, William, by then twenty-eight years old, decided he would stay in Florida and become a planter. He secured a secluded hut on the St. Johns River thirty miles from St. Augustine.

Herbst offers scant details on the disastrous outcome of William's venture, again generously blaming his imaginative nature. "The young man behaved as if he were under an enchantment," she concludes. "And he was, but to be enchanted was not in fashion" (194). Collinson and Franklin repeatedly told William it was high time to marry and settle down. It was clear to them that what he needed was a virtuous and industrious wife. "They meant well," Herbst offers, "but they had no inkling of the young man's true nature or its complexities" (193–94). When no word from William arrived, John believed that the Indians had probably killed him. A little over a year later, however, William returned to his father's farm somewhat chastened. He rented himself out as a laborer to a neighbor in order to raise the funds to pay off his Carolina debts. In 1773, Dr. John Fothergill of London, a plant collector contact of Collinson's and a friend of Franklin's, rescued Billy Bartram and supplied the funding to support his solo return to Florida. He departed from the port of Philadelphia and arrived in Charleston, South Carolina; he would be gone for five years.

This trip would make William Bartram famous and provide the material for his travel book. Seventeen years later, it was published with the unwieldly title *Travels through North and South Carolina, Georgia, East and West Florida, the Cherokee Country, the*

*Extensive Territories of the Muscogules, or Creek Confederacy, and
the Country of the Choctaws, Containing an Account of the Soil and
Natural Productions of Those Regions, Together with Observations
on the Manner of the Indians.* It remains in print and has inspired
generations of readers. In Herbst's allegory, William redeems and
surpasses his father. Where John Bartram saw a single tree, she
tells us, William saw plants, birds, and Natives, too, in conjunction
with all life. A field was not just a spot of color for him but a hint of
the endless strength of the earth. He saw not things but relations
and everything in motion: "The leaves, the bark, the flowers lived
in a state of vitality" for him. "They breathed, they felt, they had
their immortality in fertility" (252). He was not afraid to touch, and
he was not afraid of the Indigenous. This pursuit of intimacy is his
distinction and escape hatch from the settler's prison. "He would
present the Indian to the world as he had found him during his five
years in the southern wilderness. He was no trader among them
but 'Puc-Puggy' the flower hunter" (249). He came close enough to
Indigenous bodies to observe the beautiful paintings on the skin
of their chiefs: "the sun, the moon, the planets upon the breast;
fanciful scrolls winding around the trunk, thighs, arms and legs,
divided the body into tablets of vision, each filled with innumer-
able figures, animals of the chase, bits of the landscape" (249). He
made a plea for (white) men to be sent to live among the Indigenous
to study their languages and become acquainted with their customs. The frontispiece of his *Travels*, a portrait of Mico Chlucco,
the Long Warrior, or King of the Seminoles, is testimony to his admiration and respect (247). Only those who attempted "to touch,
to see, to love, to *know*," he argued, could "assist in the formulation
of some judicious plan for the future of the Indian." In taking this
stand, he opposed most of the colonial world. One key word, here,
is "assist," and another is "future." For Herbst, William's failure
as a merchant is an admirable mark of resistance, his solo travels,
drawings, and encounters with the Cherokee, Choctaw, Chickasaw,
Creek, and Seminole evidence that another way in the New World
was possible. His notion of "judiciousness," however, also hints
of a future that is the planter's to control. Herbst predicts that it
included for the "white man more than he knew" (250). The same
could be said of the Natives.

Herbst closes the story abruptly. John Bartram died three months before William returned from Florida. For the next forty-six years, William never went on another journey. He lived a quiet life on the Bartram farm, sharing ownership with his brother. In 1782, the University of Pennsylvania offered William the chair of botany, and he declined. Thomas Jefferson urged him to accompany the Lewis and Clark Expedition, but he said no (194). Herbst closes *New Green World* with a report on William's death at age eighty-five: "It was July 22, 1823. He had never married" (267).

That final sentence pointedly rejects the classic ending of the bildungsroman in which marriage and property confirm the rightness of "settling down." It also hints that one of Josie's many investments in William Bartram may have been her own release from marriage and from ownership of a farmhouse that by then she had turned into a refuge for visiting writers. In her allegory, William embodies the utopian alternative to his settler father's acquisitive imagination. His story is also a reckoning for a prodigal Iowa daughter, yet one that takes certain presuppositions for granted. Looking for them exposes what is unsaid in her allegory and its utopian ending. William Bartram entered the wilderness to bear witness, but the facts he reported were not exactly the truth. What he was able to report was conditioned by his history. Like him, Herbst was an outlier in her own time. Trawling through available records to expose an uncharted tale of settler encounters before nature was thoroughly commodified, she navigated with the aid of familiar stars. She does not set out to question William's account, but she concedes in her conclusion that William's story is literally a familiar romantic one. His *Travels*, she asserts, would fire the imaginations of the poets she clearly admired: Samuel Taylor Coleridge, William Wordsworth, Henry David Thoreau, and François-René de Chateaubriand. It was also a fabrication.

To say that the ending of *New Green World* is a romantic fabrication does not negate the fact that it is also in part a counternarrative. John's wonder and William's relational sensibility do counter market logics and a prevailing conception of white masculine control. William can cherish the earth's strength, listen to animals communicating with each other, notice the leaves and flowers that are never still, feel everything in motion. This way of seeing and being is vulnerable to life and its imponderables; it interrupts the merchant's apprehension of things in isolation. It can lead to a willingness to speak openly on topics others ignore. What William Bartram and Josephine Herbst do not speak of, however, is also salient. Just as Josie is revealed in the Bartrams and the Bartrams in her, her allegory discloses what its own logic presupposes, and therein lies another lesson. While the ending of her allegory foregrounds William's resistance to settling down in marriage, with all the property relations of inheritance it would have secured, his romance with the land is also shadowed by a history that eludes his resisting temperament and discerning eye. Perhaps we can read these oversights as the effect of Bartram's "visual registry," his "epistemic habits" as a white man whose perceptual attunement, or, to use Silvia Wynter's phrase, "psycho-affective field of normative sentiments," shaped what was worth noting.[58] These habits of seeing may also have been conditioned by the labor force whose relation to the land was neither that of settler nor that of Native—a presence whose intimacy was so brutally at odds with human consciousness of a shared condition that it had to be forgotten by "free" men.

Many early "American farmers" were large landholders who were absent and far away for all or much of the year, their lands managed by agents, the labor of planting, harvesting, processing, and loading its bounty done by enslaved men and women. When William Bartram went to North Carolina to live with his uncle, he surely saw many enslaved people. During the Bartrams' travel in Florida, they visited several large plantations, and they were attended by enslaved people. Africans had been in Florida since the mid-sixteenth century when they arrived on Spanish slave ships. Some who were runaways or who had sheltered in Maroon communities were hunted down and captured or bought.[59] Others were granted freedom and land in return for defense of the Spanish Crown and remained in the area. By the seventeenth century, Black enslaved people made up well over half the population of South Carolina.[60] A hundred years later, colonial laws were designating Blacks as a different category of being, equating blackness with forced labor, and prohibiting Black assembly into anything like a commons.

The very fact of the Bartrams' ability to travel as researchers was premised on their social position as free men not bound by indentured servitude or enslavement. As English colonists who inherited land and Quaker community, they gained access to opportunity, education, property, and prosperity, supplemented by the recognition of influential white men who funded their avocations. John Bartram's botanical interest was supported by his paid subscription to Logan's library. The ability to secure the means and time to travel accompanied by time devoted to activities of the mind also had its geography—the valued stance of educated investigator, explorer, and recorder of observations, a stance implicitly reserved for rational white men. What goes without saying is the terrain of ideology, of common sense. Race in the eighteenth century was emerging as a naturalized, commonsense, human classification. It was already shaping a social-psychic-affective relation to the British metropolis and to a society simultaneously intimately encountering Native and enslaved persons as well as free Black Africans and forging a culture in which they disappeared into the margins. Marked indirectly in official and informal discourse, whiteness prescribed who was literate and seeable, who counted and mattered as human. Impossible to discern as a single phenomenon, it inflected so much. We can best track it in the relations it enabled and underscored, ghostly there in what is unsaid.

For example, Herbst tells her reader about William's disastrous year in a hovel on the St. Johns River by way of details provided by John's South Carolina planter friend Henry Laurens, who would later become president of the Continental Congress after John Hancock. We do not learn from Laurens how the young man was able to become a Florida planter, how he acquired the land or the seeds and farming tools or whether he had help with the labor. About all of that, there are so many unanswered questions. We learn from the historian Daniel Schafer, who retraced William's journey, located his farm, and read John Bartram's correspondence with his son, that Bartram supplied everything his son needed for farming: five hundred acres of land, goods sent by ship from Charleston—salted meat and other kitchen foods, garden seeds, cuttings, barrels of rice seeds, axes, shovels, cups, dishes, fishing line and hooks, and medical supplies—and six slaves.[61] Schafer does not note these advantages as having anything to do with William's whiteness, but how could they not? Laurens visited William and reported to John on his decline. Laurens was also one of the leading importers of slaves, a well-known fact that Herbst does not mention. She does tell us that the "kindly" Laurens saw poor Billy in a forlorn state stranded in a swamp without a wife or friend, companion or neighbor. "To be precise," she adds, not noting the slaves as legitimate companions, no less humans, "there isn't a human inhabitant within nine miles" (New Green World, 220–21). Although John was not comfortable with William's owning slaves, he nonetheless arranged for Laurens to select them. In a letter to William, John describes them with first names and the details of their height: Jack and his wife Siby; Jacob and Sam; Flora and her son Bacchus, who is three or five years old. Jacob's and Sam's height, at five feet and under, suggests they may have not yet been adults. Their description as "new Negroes" indicates they were recently arrived in America. Flora, who is designated a "croman-tee," may be, as Schafer suggests, the only one linked to a specific region of her homeland, probably the city known as Kormantse in modern-day Ghana.[62] Herbst briefly mentions the six Negroes as "helpers" on William's plantation. In her account, however, they have no names. We only learn that "two knew how to handle an ax, and one of these had been insolent" (New Green World, 239). No other record survives of William's relationship with them or their fate. He abandoned his settlement sometime in the autumn of 1766. The enslaved Africans may have been sold at auction, or they may have disappeared into the forest. Perhaps they joined the Creek Indians on the west side of the St. Johns River, as did other enslaved men and women who escaped from their British or Indigenous owners.[63] Some who escaped slavery formed fugitive communities in Florida, married Natives, became trusted inter-preters, and plotted revolt.

By 1773, when William returned south and arrived in Charles-ton, the city was a cosmopolitan hub in a Black-majority urban coastal area anxiously controlled by creole elites. Almost 40 per-cent of the enslaved Africans coming to the colonies were arriv-ing at its port. Unlike them, upon his arrival, William met with the friend of his patron, an eminent physician who referred him to "many of the worthy families of Carolina and Georgia" who would later host him at their plantations.[64]

Schafer's research on the East Florida of William Bartram's re-turn trip reveals that it would have been impossible for him not to see the many plantations located on the banks of the St. Johns

River as he sailed its length. He surely also must have noticed the work of slaves who tilled the endless rows of indigo and built dams and dikes for rice fields as well as wharves and fences along the river.[65] Freed Black landowners were also living next door to Spanish planters and running small businesses in the St. Augustine area. That William edited these details out of his *Travels,* Schafer suggests, indicates that he was fabricating from his memory of Florida an imaginative Eden, a nostalgic yearning for the "State of Nature." In short, his masterpiece—and much of Herbst's version of it—reconfigures the facts. That these facts seem to have escaped William's notice reveals the cultural relation of intimate distance that swirled around him. It lingered in the postcolonial culture that enthralled Herbst as well.[66] This imaginary Florida would remain a presupposition of her romantic allegory. The unsettled Africans nonetheless find their way into her story, an anonymous ghostly presence in Eden. The oversight by Herbst and by two expert observers, one of whom almost obsessively names and renders in flawless delicate detail every tree and plant he encounters, confirms the long-standing hold of the colonial relation.

Herbst concludes *New Green World* by situating William as a nature writer whose *Travels* fertilized the minds of the British and French Romantic poets who plucked from his descriptions of nature lush images and exotic figures for their imaginative escapes. It is a strange and disappointing conclusion, so out of step with the reckoning the book promised to be. In presenting William Bartram as a proto-Romantic, her allegory offers a utopian ending that translates the natural world and the people in it into an idealized "no place" evacuated of history. Such also were the modernists' readings of Coleridge's and Wordsworth's nature poetry. They were beginning to write during the same turbulent years when William Bartram drew up his account of the Indigenous peoples of the south and when postcolonial relations were shifting the contours of the intimate distance that conditioned the expropriation of bodies and lands in the Americas.

William's second trip to Florida took place during two adjacent bloody wars—the War of Independence, waged simultaneously with Indian Wars that lasted from 1774 to 1783. As Roxanne Dunbar-Ortiz's award-winning history of Indigenous peoples documents, during that time, settler-rangers violently attacked and destroyed Indigenous communities across the colonies and into Florida, with the goal of total subjugation or expulsion.[67] These wars were preceded by the Seven Years' War (1754–63), known in the colonies as the French and Indian War. Taking place in the Great Lakes region and in the Carolinas, it opened formerly Indigenous territory for settlers and set the stage for the independence of the settler population.[68] These are the Indian Wars that John Bartram resented for obstructing his travels westward. Native historians have outlined the history of the early 1770s as a time when terror against Indigenous people on the part of Anglo settlers increased in all the colonies.[69] It targeted entire communities, including non-combatants. The result was the destruction of thousands of homes and thousands of bushels of corn and other provisions.[70] Sale of these confiscated lands was the primary revenue source for the new government.[71] In the decades after William's return from the South, while he was writing up his travels, Indigenous genocide pursued what Patrick Wolfe has called "the logic of elimination."[72] From 1830 and through the 1840s, the seizure of lands and pillaging intensified. Natives in the Southeast were seized while working their fields or going along the road, their homes set on fire by looters who followed the U.S. soldiers. With the Natives eliminated from the land, it became privately owned and would be peopled with Black laborers to produce tobacco, turpentine, or cotton, the white gold of the Deep South.[73]

As settler colonial societies imposed their new homeland on Indigenous lands, the meaning of "land" became abstracted, made equivalent to the new nation as a "land of the free" or a "nation of immigrants."[74] Native scholars and activists have long contended that this systematic erasure and dispossession enacted material and cultural genocide. It robbed Indigenous people of their means of life making, supported as it was by land-based sustenance and relationships to their ancestral places. It violated a Native world-view that made no distinction between people and land.[75] By the early 1950s, when Herbst was writing *New Green World*, federal policy had turned from the mixed success of New Deal support for Indigenous autonomy to a new approach to Indigenous peoples, this time through a series of policy changes aimed at elimination through assimilation. These changes were formalized in a resolution passed by the U.S. House of Representatives and Senate in

1953, commonly referred to as the Termination Act. It aimed for the end of Native sovereignty, ended payments provided under federal treaties, called for the eventual end of reservation lands, and once more pressed to relocate Indigenous people with the goal of absorbing them into urban areas.[76] How much of this history was Herbst aware of as she conducted her historical research? It took me some time to realize that pursuing an answer was not the point. No factual account would address the unsaids in her narrative or do the more difficult work they invite.

Josephine Herbst was in many respects ahead of her time. Her characteristic adjacent relation to the land, her quasi-autobiographical fiction, and her turn to historical allegory capture an intimate distance at the heart of a national myth. That their forms also shelter a counternarrative to it remains a provocation. Even if the conclusion of *New Green World* weds Bartram's Native encounters to a romantic tradition that obscures a bloody history and its immeasurable human cost, that story's unsettling details nonetheless also beckon another reading. History's unfinished work surfaces in the loose threads of the narrative's texture. A sentence like the following offers one hint: "It began to be made clear," Herbst offers in the book's closing chapter, "that in the name of 'common sense' monstrous advantages were taken by practical men to entrench themselves far into the future" (*New Green World*, 248). Pulling on that thread leads to further reckoning. The celebration of Native culture that Bartram offered in his *Travels* when it was finally published in 1791 and in his ethnographic *Observations on the Creek and the Cherokee Indians*, published posthumously in 1853, is both prequel and sequel to genocide. It would be overtaken by the settler's mythology, obscuring the fact that wherever there was land to acquire, Native peoples would be removed. And yet they remain.

For me, the most compelling features of William's story are its least narrated, ghostly parts. I want to think of them as the dark seedbed of the sensibility that ultimately propelled him to become the antihero. These are the years when he was Elizabeth's twin brother and later a disappointment to his father, when he was "Poor Billy." We know little about that time except that his passive resistance kept him a queer son. An artist. What he saw and did in those years we can only imagine. In her history of this son and his father who know the land intimately yet not too closely, Josephine Herbst rendered the ineffable in between the lines of their lives. There, the epistemic horizon of a national condition comes into view. It harbors ungrieved losses, a sense of wonder propelled into farming, sketching, and reporting, but it also reveals something more in William, who veered wayward, who lingered and mingled with others before going his separate way.

Herbst titled her unfinished memoir *The Ground We Tread*. I want to think that this "we" encapsulates what she could never fully reckon and perhaps by the 1950s mourned: a collective that might untie the knot of intimate distance, vindicate a disappearing common wealth, and activate the potential encrypted in an unsettled relation to the land.

Five
The Radical Ecology of Meridel Le Sueur

O thunder of protein.
In the burning blaze in the autumnal air of sulphuric light
The green corn
The seed Corn
Rebellion.

—Meridel Le Sueur, "The Origins of Corn"

Meridel Le Sueur published the prose poem "The Origins of Corn" in her midseventies. A praise song to this signature plant of the Americas and the midwestern lands of the northern continent, it conveys the radical ecology she pursued in her writing. Condensed in corn is a web of dependent relations, from its genetic and molecular composition through the ancient soil, celestial energies, and Mayan hands that nurtured growth. Time, space, nonhuman and human biological life and death mingle in her rendering. She likens the golden pollen to a history "more ancient and fixed than the pyramids," and hears in it "the scream of fleeing Indians, germinal mirror of endurance, reflections of mothers of different yield." Older than the oldest human monuments, corn harbors generations of violence and resilience, changing and enduring ripenings. "The ancient women Gatherers, free wanderers loved the tiny grass," she tells us. Untethered, their brown hands pollinated the plants, a process Le Sueur calls "tendered," an interaction that

147

conveys the intimate labor of loving care. And so the energetic relations of dependency come full circle. Women inhabit the kernel and it mirrors them. It is not clear whether corn or women mother "different yields." What we have is an entangled relation. Here nature is not external to social life, an object to be dominated instrumentally by humans; rather, it is one agent in the relations of life making. The closing lines of the poem in the epigraph above capture the corn in its very form, suggesting that the labor of human writing as knowledge making joins the metabolic exchange embodied in the quintessential food source sprung from America's lands.[1]

Land as a source of life making is an embodied and palpable presence in Le Sueur's writing. Throughout her long writing career, its representation offers her readers a standpoint she describes as "dialectical," and it conveys her relational sensibility.[2] This is a way of knowing that centers the transfer of energy between the land and humans even as it arises from the voices of the working people whose talk fills her writing. If at times that talk seems to overtake her land-centered vision, be patient. Just when the people's voices appear to control the narrative, she returns her readers to the inseparable relations among life forms sustained by the soil of the earth.

These relations are implicit in her radical politics and are echoed in the twin meanings of "radical" and "radicle." The radicle is the embryonic part of a seed that will become the root. For Le Sueur, the word "roots" refers to many actors: plant life nurtured by the land and the people who love it as well as those who change, till, rape, or ruin it. Her radical politics aims to acknowledge them all without forfeiting her belief that life-sustaining common needs can be met justly. This breadth in her understanding of "radical" extends Ella Baker's connotation of a politics that looks for root causes to a deep understanding of the human place in the web of life. Le Sueur developed that pursuit from the 1930s into her last years.

Over a life of writing that spanned the twentieth century, she brought into view the dependencies that nurture human and nonhuman life. Her work discloses their dismemberment as one of the victims of capitalism and never forgets the dialectical relation that joins human life and the organic biosphere of which it is

Meridel Le Sueur, circa 1940. Meridel Le Sueur Papers, Minnesota Historical Society.

a part. In documenting the struggles that punctuate the history of the Americas, she persistently suggests an alternative relation to the land, one in which nature is neither objectified nor external to human life, neither idealized nor universalized. She recognizes that human activity is the linchpin in the metabolic connection between humans and the land. True to her Communist and socialist politics, she understands that this metabolism takes place through human labor that changes nature even as humans are in turn changed by nature. This attention to labor and to the productive force of nature distinguishes her radical ecology from the Romantic tradition and constitutes a major contribution to a materialist conception of life making across the web of life.[3]

From her earliest writings on the cusp of the early 1930s, Le Sueur conveys the sensibilities that bind people to the land and insists that women feel them distinctly. For her, women developed a sensory awareness of the personal and social body that is also earth consciousness. This sensibility pivots on an ancient figure for reproductive fertility that she summons to represent all life-making relations. Le Sueur's focus on the energetic labor of life making was not well received by the Left, however. Not until feminists recovered her work in the 1970s was it embraced as a liberating affirmation and an intervention into the patriarchal devaluation of women.[4] Although many feminists celebrated her recognition of woman's desires, sexuality, and corporeal sensations, some bristled at the seeming equation of woman with nature and the suggestion that women are "naturally" reduced to their biological reproductive capacity.[5] In the 1990s, marxist feminists recognized Le Sueur's understanding of women's reproductive labor as materially valuable to capital and as a stance that amplified the Left's radical traditions.[6] More recently, the environmental humanist scholar Stacy Alaimo has recovered Le Sueur once more and drawn attention to her depictions of bodies and lands as intertwined generative forces "with the potency of political struggle."[7] She emphasizes that Le Sueur represents women's embodied care labor as socially valuable and historically entangled in the reproduction of life across the relations of life making. Returning to Le Sueur from the second decade of the twenty-first century, I want to extend Alaimo's recognition of Le Sueur's thinking as a

forerunner of a materialist feminist ecocriticism and underscore
her deep roots in American Communism.

Before addressing Le Sueur's attention to women's bodies, I want
to pause to consider briefly the relation of the female reproductive
body to nature. Now more than ever, especially in overdeveloped
sectors, people understand female and male bodily differences
as shaped by gender formations that are social and changeable.
Because of developments in reproductive technology, the labor of
social and biological reproduction has become more flexible, although nature continues to impose certain constraints on it. In
some sectors of the world, capital has begun to accommodate a
gender system for the labor of *social* reproduction that is not biologically grounded. To date, however, female bodies are the only
ones to carry a fetus to term, and in this respect, capital continues
to depend on them for *biological* reproduction. As a social system
based in the accumulation of wealth, capitalism has historically
relied on bodies coded as masculine or feminine, man or woman,
and it still does. Most of all, however, it relies on a supply of bodies to produce children and populate the labor market. Whether
those who labor to nurture the social reproduction of life through
care work might someday be valued is another question entirely.
So long as the accumulation of wealth depends on devalued labor
within and outside the marketplace, capital will continue to invent
cultural categories that guarantee that relation.

When Le Sueur foregrounds women's contribution to the activities of social and biological reproduction, she ties that labor to
the land as a life-giving provider. Does this mean that she endorses
the terms that Western culture has used to devalue women by re-
ducing them to nature, an object for man's control and domination? Not at all. Aligning women's reproductive bodies and labor
with the land is her invitation to understand the human–nature
divide historically, materially, and dialectically, to disclose that
human and nonhuman capacities and dependencies coexist in a
reciprocal relation. Propelled by human labor, that relation depends on the nature that shapes it and that social history in turn
shapes. Thus, she opens for her readers a radical political ecology
of life making across the web of life.

Le Sueur's midwestern roots nurtured her attention to these

relations.[8] In her early writings from the 1930s, she figures the interdependence between women's bodies and the land, mindful of the temporality of reproductive labor and attuned to the reproductive rhythms of the earth. This writing from the 1930s was a seedbed for the dialectical sensibility that she pursued through the postwar years, when decades of industrialization had poisoned the land and the people. Although she documented the surveillance and fear that infected the country then, in 1945 she was nonetheless able to write a peoples' history that embraces both the known and the nameless life forms that strove to survive on the country's northern middle lands. Her work from the 1950s is especially interesting to me because it is then that whiteness comes into view for her as a relation to space and mobility that shapes conditions for life making. She traveled by bus in these years beyond her home in Minnesota and saw "upon the earth through the vent of cities, the people move in the dark of the American time."[9] She witnessed the impact of capitalism in the "cunning masks" of commodities and the "naked wars of aggression" encoded in racial differences that constrained who could move on the land, and where and how, and what they could do on it.[10] During this time of surveillance and collective anxiety, she became an unsettled race traitor.

Unlike Josephine Herbst, Le Sueur maintained the Midwest as her home, yet like Herbst, she made unsettling choices throughout her life. They manifested in her rejection of ways of being white that aligned whiteness with ownership and control over space. She refused to comply with the norms of middle-class white femininity, resisted marriage and the expectations of white heteronormative domestic life. She lived her unsettled ways through a relation to space and to the land that ripened as she aged into the nomadic practices of her later years. This nomadic relation to space and place appears in her work as a sensibility that resists the settler legacy, which she also to some degree embraced.

In her time of ripening, Le Sueur enacted her radical ecology in her writing through a process of re-membering. The seeds sown in Le Sueur's 1930s writings on women come to fruition when she researches the history of the Midwest and uncovers the embodied debts that capital accumulated through the erosion of people's bodies and of the land. In these years, she wrote more deliberately about Indigenous Americans, and she did so from the standpoint of a white woman struggling to do the work of betraying whiteness, in the sense both of disclosing its contours and of giving up some of its assurances. In her memoirs, she uses parallel syntax to represent the aspirations and limits of that political stance as she re-members wounded relationships between settler and Native women across losses and intimacies spanning space and time. She also developed then a new form of writing represented in the excerpt from "The Origins of Corn." With corn as a messenger, she imagines human and nonhuman dependencies that support the spiraling relationships among laboring bodies and landed places, their creatures and times. In the final decade of her life, still writing in her nineties, she launched what would become the collaboratively produced experimental novel *The Dread Road,* an expansive apocalyptic journey through the catastrophic violence against American land and life wrought by the colonizing thrust of capital accumulation. Against the tide of terrifying developments, her radical ecology's relational sensibility even here finds gifts. That attunement to the vestiges of possibility lodged in the metabolic relation of humans and the land, even when so much has been eroded, is the ground of her radical/radicle ecology, an insistence that it is never too late to nourish the seeds of life making's livelihood and rebellion.

"I Came Out of the Secret Pods of the Midwest. I Have Stayed Close and Paid Attention"

Born on February 22, 1900, in Murray, Iowa, and raised in Texas, Oklahoma, Kansas, and Minnesota, Meridel Le Sueur was shaped by a radical line of feminist and socialist dissent cultivated on those lands by her family.[11] Her mother, Marian Wharton (née Lucy), left her first husband, an itinerant preacher, when Meridel was ten, fleeing to Oklahoma with her three children from their home in San Antonio, Texas, because divorce in Texas meant a woman's children could be taken away. The divorce was eventually granted on the grounds that Marian had deserted her husband and read "dangerous literature."[12] Meridel and her two brothers lived in Oklahoma with their mother and Marian's mother, Antoinette Lucy, until Meridel was fourteen. Oklahoma then "was a wild region," Le Sueur later remembered, and "the first place I lived that was not primarily white and Protestant. My friends were Indians and I first felt in my bones the contradictions of American Midwestern life and also its hidden potential strength and beauty and, above all, the democratic traditions and history of the frontier people."[13]

The Native people opened for her an understanding of the contradictions of settler life, and in those years her mother also alerted her to others. A formidable influence, Marian was an ardent feminist who earned a living on the Chautauqua circuit lecturing on women's suffrage and reproductive rights. Along with other suffragists, she once chained herself to the White House fence, and she was tried in Kansas City, Missouri, for distributing birth-control information to a woman with fourteen children. In collaboration with Eugene Debs, Helen Keller, Charles Steinmetz, and Arthur Le Sueur, she helped found the People's College, an experimental working-class correspondence school in Fort Scott, Kansas.[14] As a member of the English department, Marian developed a popular education curriculum documented in the pamphlet *Plain English for the Education of the Workers by the Workers.* It was in Fort Scott that she met and married the socialist attorney Arthur Le Sueur. The son of immigrant farmers, Le Sueur graduated from the University of Michigan Law School and went on to become one of the primary organizers of the Socialist Party of North Dakota. He served as the mayor of Minot, North Dakota, before heading the Law Department of the People's College, of which he was later president. Many socialists and anarchists visited the Le Sueurs during their years at the college, among them the anarchist Alexander Berkman, who spent hours in conversation with the young Meridel. During World War I, antisocialist vigilantes destroyed the school and ran the Le Sueurs out of town. They moved to St. Paul, Minnesota, where for the next few years, Meridel lived in a home frequented by populists, Wobblies, war resisters, and members of the Farmer–Labor Party and the Nonpartisan League.[15] Arthur and Marian received many threats, and their children were ostracized at school, but they remained active socialists for years. Marian ran for state senate on the Progressive ticket in 1952 when she was seventy-five in order to protest the Korean War, and Arthur became a judge in Minneapolis.

As an adult, Meridel respected her parents' socialist politics, but she felt it lacked roots in the working class. She described her own political work as "moving deeper into, not away" from a socialist perspective.[16] Reflecting later on her life, she commented that the middle-class sexual repression that pervaded the atmosphere of her growing-up years had left her wounded. Her mother was clearly a force and may have been temperamentally different from Meridel. Her grandmother was what we might call straight-laced. A third-generation Puritan and deeply religious, Antoinette was an ardent campaigner for the Women's Christian Temperance League. "The only thing that saved me," Meridel once said, "was the earth."[17]

So did writing, which became the conduit for her sensitivity to the world. From childhood, she was an astute listener and recorder. "I truly began to write," she remembered, "when I was eight, I think, in Oklahoma where on market day I sat in the village square behind the water trough, although no 'nice' girl was supposed to do this—but then no 'nice' girl was supposed to write." Behind the water trough she discovered "the fabulous and strong remaking of the language by those who remake the earth," and she began to copy down the turns of phrase that "contained all the seeds of the old language as it was becoming a new one."[18] She became "a kind of village scribe," writing letters for people who could not write and in turn hearing their stories of "fabulous journeys, their frail rooted prairie existence, their homely search for word, song, testament."[19]

When Meridel was seventeen, her mother removed her from high school, perhaps fearing for her health and sexual safety, and sent her to Bernarr Macfadden's Physical Culture School in Chicago, a program that concentrated on physical movement and dance. Within a year or so, she left Chicago for New York City to attend the American Academy of Dramatic Arts. The distance from home and the vibrant New York City scene were liberating. She lived with Emma Goldman and Alexander Berkman in their well-known anarchist commune and earned wages working on the stage. In 1917, the United States was just entering World War I. Berkman and Goldman, both Jewish Russian immigrants, were organizing against the draft, claiming that America had to first make democracy safe at home. The previous year Goldman had been arrested under the Comstock Act of 1873 for distributing birth-control information. By June 1917, both she and Berkman would be arrested under the Espionage Act of 1917 and sent to prison. Le Sueur's brief time in their circle and on the stage must have been a heady experience, attuning her to an intensely committed radical Left, to her own body, and to women's bodies generally.[20] She remembered Goldman as the "only woman I knew who con-trolled her sexual life entirely."[21] Disenchanted by the discrimi-nation and objectification women faced in the New York theater world, she left for Hollywood, probably around 1917. She took jobs as an extra and a stunt girl in the silent film industry. Hollywood, however, turned out to be another professional disappointment. After one studio offered her a contract on the condition that she have surgery on her "Semitic" nose, she quit. Supporting her-self with work in restaurants and factories, she devoted her time to developing experimental theater projects in Berkeley and Sacramento. She may well have unknowingly crossed paths in San Francisco or Oakland with Josie Herbst or Louise Thompson.

The postwar decade from 1917 to 1927 was a time of political re-pression in the United States; socialists and pacifists, including Marian and Arthur Le Sueur, were persecuted, and hundreds of "foreigners," among them Goldman and Berkman, were deported. Departing from the progressive political views of her parents, Le Sueur joined the Communist Party and began writing regularly for the *Daily Worker*.[22] In 1927 she went to jail for protesting the exe-cutions of Nicola Sacco and Bartolomeo Vanzetti. At around that time, she married Harry Rice, born Yasha Rubonoff, a Russian im-migrant and a Marxist labor organizer she met in St. Paul.

— The last years of the 1920s were bleak. Meridel had no job and no money, but in the face of a world that seemed oppres-sive and deadly, she chose to have a child. She returned to Min-nesota and joined her extended family before Rachel was born in 1928. Less than two years later, she gave birth to a second daughter, Deborah. She and Rice divorced in the early thirties and Meridel then retook her maiden name.[23] When her daughters were young, she moved for a time to a small village north of St. Paul on the banks of the St. Croix River, an area she would later write about in *North Star Country*. The Twin Cities remained Le Sueur's home base for most of the rest of her life. During the Depression, she and other women and children lived in an abandoned warehouse in St. Paul, an experience that became the basis for the final section of her novel *The Girl*.[24]

In the challenging decade of the 1930s, Le Sueur blossomed as a writer. She had published her first story, "Persephone," in the prestigious literary magazine *The Dial* in 1927, but by then her political interests and commitments were already drawing her and her writing further to the Left. She joined the staff of the *New Masses,* which was closely associated with the Communist Party, and frequently published there and in other party venues, among them the *Anvil* and the *Daily Worker.* She joined the Workers Alliance of America, a popular front organization that mobilized the unemployed, and she wrote for their newspaper. She was involved in all kinds of Communist Party activities—reporting from strikes, writing leaflets, working in the bookstore of the Workers Alliance, and holding offices in the party's local organizations. One organization that she described as especially nourishing for her work was the Chicago branch of the John Reed Clubs, a literary organization with branches across the country established by the Communist Party to support young writers. Through the club she met other writers, and when it became the League of American Writers, she was one of those who signed the call for the 1935 American Writers' Congress.[25]

This event summoned American writers to stand up for a political goal that now seems unfathomable: to "recognize the necessity of personally helping to accelerate the destruction of capitalism."[26] The Congress established a League of American Writers committed to fighting fascism, imperialist war, white chauvinism, all forms of discrimination and persecution against Negroes and other minority groups, and the imprisonment of revolutionary writers. It also called for solidarity with colonized people in their struggle for liberation. The event brought together a large number of prominent writers, among them Theodore Dreiser, Langston Hughes, Nathanael West, Tillie Olsen (then Tillie Lerner), and Josephine Herbst. Le Sueur played a prominent role at the congress. Sharing a stage with the literary theorist Kenneth Burke, who was also a member of the Communist Party, she made a case for the "phalange on the prairie" as being in the forefront of revolutionary culture. She spoke out for the farmers who love the land and for whom it has not been completely claimed by capitalism. Following through on her position, immediately after the congress, she and Dale Kramer founded *Midwest Magazine*.[27] The next year, she helped organize a Midwest Writers Conference that aimed to foster regional cooperative publication networks and a regional audience. This effort grew out of Le Sueur's deep personal commitment to developing a progressive midwestern community of writers committed to a socially and politically conscious literature of place.[28]

During the 1930s, she published over two dozen pieces of reportage, almost thirty short stories, some poems and miscellaneous articles, and a writing manual for workers based on the classes she taught under the auspices of the Federal Writers' Project.[29] Many of her stories from that decade remain unpublished, however, as do her journals, which span the years from 1917 to 1994 and include over 140 volumes. Communist Party support probably aided Le Sueur's survival as a woman writer, even though her attention to women was contrary to the party's direction.[30] She had long-standing friends and acquaintances among other women on the left who gathered around the party, among them Josephine Herbst, Muriel Rukeyser, Grace Lumpkin, Sanora Babb, Agnes Smedley, and Mary Heaton Vorse. Like many of them, she was critical of the party's male-dominated leadership, and some male party members criticized her writing as "undisciplined."[31]

In pursuing her commitment to the party, she was actually provoking it to expand its political horizons and address the exploitation of women and the land, a provocation it wouldn't recognize for another generation.[32] She remained in the party nonetheless, even if, as she put it, "a maverick" and in practice a feminist.[33] In her later years, she was the mainstay of the Communist Party Bookstore on Twenty-Second and Hennepin Streets in Minneapolis, walking there every morning to open it.[34] Elaine Hedges quotes Le Sueur as saying that she "dropped feminism and identified with those below," a comment Hedges interprets as Le Sueur's retort to her mother and grandmother, for whom, as Meridel saw it, feminism meant achieving such middle-class goals as women's rights or the vote.[35] I would say, however, that until the 1970s when she embraced a New Left feminist movement, Le Sueur lived a

politics of feminism from below, fed by Communism's understanding of capitalism as a system of accumulation based in exploited
labor and women's reproductive care work. Hers was a grassroots
feminism inflected by the progressive and populist socialism bred
in the Midwest, one that listened to the talk of the people of the
prairie, especially the women, and revealed their lives with profound tenderness.

"I Know the Slow Time of Growing"

Meridel Le Sueur was consistently attuned to the cyclical temporality of reproduction, a temporal sensibility that she unabashedly
claims women especially live and feel. From her earliest novel,
I Hear Men Talking, modeled on the Greek myth of Persephone
and her mother Demeter as figures for seasonal growth, harvest,
and death, to the experimental novel *The Dread Road* that she was
writing in her late eighties, women and the land are entangled
agents of relational life making. Land is "the haven of women, the
great beloved woman of my country,"[36] she asserted in midcentury;
they "carry life upon them like the bee does pollen."[37] These life-
giving relations were difficult to discern, however, in the urban
spaces of the Great Depression. In her reporting on the economic
crisis of the 1930s, when Le Sueur looked for women, she confronted the startling fact that they seemed to have disappeared.
"There are not many women in the bread line," she reports, "and
there are no flop houses for women as there are for men."[38] She set
out to find them and catalogued where they were—in attic rooms
and condemned buildings, eating a cracker a day and quiet as a
mouse.[39] In "Women on the Breadlines" (1932) she describes the
toll of the Depression on women's bodies and does so in terms that
conjure the times of seasonal regeneration.[40] One such time is the
time of waiting, made unnatural in this alienated period of unmet
need. In the domestic employment bureau, women come every day
to wait for a job, and there are no jobs. Girls who had been machine
operators, pressers, trimmers, or button sewers are now out of
work. Hour after hour they sit, "always before them the pit of the
future."[41] There are only a few more days of summer, and they are
anxious to "lay up something for that long siege of bitter cold."[42]
"Dreading that knowledge," she writes, sitting among them, "we

look away from each other. We look at the floor. It's too terrible to see this animal terror in each other's eyes."[43] This empty time of waiting that irrupts when the structures of production and circulation fall into crisis is the complement of capital's abstract time by which wages are calculated. This time is not generative; it only multiplies need, breeding a "city hunger," as she calls it, "like the beak of a terrible bird at the vitals."[44]

From the stories she hears and the desperation she sees written on the hungry faces of women and girls, Le Sueur makes visible the bodies of those for whom there are no statistics, and she draws a gendered history of the ravages of abstract labor time on bending backs and water-soaked hands. Migration from the land to the cities leads to years of toil yielding only loss, propelling men to go away to hunt for work, not find it, and drift on, leaving women to struggle alone, feeding many mouths, starving silently. Many, like Mrs. Gray, wash and scrub their whole lives and never earn any security. Their bodies absorb the cost. Bernice, a "large Polish woman of 35," has been working in people's kitchens for fifteen years or more. "She is slightly deaf from hanging out clothes in winter," and she "suffers from loneliness and lack of talk."[45] There is Ellen, who shows her legs in the alley to men who give her food and small coins. However, as Le Sueur points out, like every commodity, the body is difficult to sell in hard times.[46] A few bold girls become hobos riding the rails across the land, and Le Sueur interviews them, too. "They arm themselves alone," she writes. Some "keep away from men and marriage," swapping reproduction's slow and laborious time for a more immediately gratifying one. "I'll drink when I like it and have a time," they say, "but no guys for me." They are on strike, Le Sueur concludes; "they don't like the terms so they aren't having any of it, and it will make a difference to our living for a long time."[47]

In her fiction, Le Sueur pursues this slow time of life making as gestation, which she sets against the abstract labor time of capital. The narrator of her often-anthologized short story "Annunciation" (1935) is a woman whose body is too pregnant to work for wages. She stays home alone in a one-room flat all day while Karl looks for work. Ever since she knew that she was having a child, she has been writing on scraps of paper. Her writing draws out, preserves, and values an embodied time. She gives up trying to locate past events in clock time: "I don't know how long it was," she says, "for I hadn't any time except the nine months I was counting off."[48] She remembers the hard times of looking for work punctuated by this other time of the body in the early weeks of pregnancy. Then, lying in bed, she was "nauseated by the smell of the foul walls." In an alleyway when she "must give it up with the people all looking," Karl was angry, walking away so they would not think he was with her ("Annunciation," 126). She savors the memory of one night when they rode on a riverboat to get out of the cold and she charted her child's future with wishes that might bind it to other earthly life forms. She hears the scurrying of tiny animals on the shore, and their little breathings seem to be all around. "I think of them, wild, carrying their young now," she says, "crouched in the dark underbrush with the fruit-scented land wind in their delicate nostrils, and they are looking out at the moon and the fast clouds. Silent, alive, they sit in the dark shadow of the greedy world. There is something wild about us, too. . . . We, too, are at the mercy of many hunters" (128). Perhaps because of this shared precarity with other creatures, she wishes the child to "come glistening with life power . . . a warrior and fierce for change, so all can live" (128). Her musing integrates this future time with a "life power" that also courses through other life forms on the land, a common vulnerable energy that hints of another possible way of living.

One of these life forms is a pear tree beyond the porch that becomes the central vehicle in the story. It propels the narrator's reflection on the transformative time of regeneration that occurs when "everything is dead and closed" and "suddenly everything comes alive," as it has for her. At the same time she wonders if she may "have a hard time remembering this time at all" (128–29). So she writes it down. Her meditation conjures a counterchronology to clock time, a season when light is falling upon darkness, closed spaces are opening, and still things are moving. The time she plots in her writing is not an aesthetic escape to a romanticized ideal, although it has a utopian dimension. Its expansive potential "of moving kernels, expanding flesh" is the kind of activity "that makes a new world." Nature's potential linked to human potential becomes the fuel of radical desires. This new world is one to be made and remade together. "For us," she tells her child, "many kinds of hunger, for us a deep rebellion" (131).

The woman in this story sees through her window activities in the house next door that contribute to reproducing life. Several involve the body's need for rest and renewal: a young man sleeping, a young girl making a bed from which she had just arisen, an old woman rocking who "scratches herself, cleans her nails, picks her teeth" (129). Other actions highlight the embodied capacity building of learning, feeding, and care: a boy leans over a table reading a book; a woman who has been nursing a child "comes out and hangs clothes on the line, her dress in front wet with milk" (129). By throwing into relief these socially necessary activities, each embodied and contributing to the reproduction of corporeal life, the narrator reorients abstract time into the time of life making. "My child," she writes, "may be looked at in this way as if it suddenly existed . . . but I know the slow time of making. The pear tree knows" (131). The child she imagines will be born from the life of the land, arriving "from a far seed blowing from last year's rich and revolutionary dead" (131). Nature is politicized not as external to human life but as an integral relational force. The narrator is aware that the "wondrous opening out of everything" will fade and the moments of openness will be sealed up by hard times, in part because history does not authorize her story. "It is hard to write so it will mean anything," she says. "I've never heard anything about how a woman feels who is going to have a child" (131).

Le Sueur pursued that topic in her novel *The Girl*, which she completed in 1939 but was unable to publish until 1978. We learn in the opening paragraphs that its unnamed narrator is surviving through sex work, dodging plainclothes men and police matrons "who will pick you up . . . and sterilize you and give you tests or send you to the women's prison."[49] The closing pages pursue the insertion of women's reproductive labor into historical time in a scene of social unrest reminiscent of the food demonstrations during the 1934 Minneapolis Teamsters' strike. The word "remembering" marks time here like a drumbeat, as women's reproductive capacities and embodied temporalities punctuate their demands for fresh milk. "We got to remember," announces Amelia, the organizer from the Workers' Alliance, adding her injunction to "remember the breasts of your mothers" (*The Girl*, 175). In a reflection of Le Sueur's own life, in the novel women and children are living in an abandoned warehouse. Several of the women abort pregnancies; others resist forced sterilization. The narrative interpolates all of them into its re-membering work, as the "strange timing" of the girl's childbirth takes over, and Amelia, now become midwife, marks birthing's time with her instruction to the girl to "wait— push—stop—breathe" (181). Together the women generate collective agency sprung from their time-consuming labor to sustain life. It becomes the basis for a public demonstration demanding milk, an action that thrusts into political discourse social reproduction as embodied, generative, necessary labor and a well of unmet need.

"From the Bloodiest Year Some Survive to Outfox the Frost"

In her memoir, *Crusaders* (1955), Le Sueur attributes her education in communal sensibility to the radical legacy of her extended family. Her parents were the children of settlers who became regional leaders and democratic socialists who "in the slow, tortuous movement of the agrarian struggle . . . were moving toward Marxism, aware that sharper instruments must be had for the stronger struggles."[50] In the decades following the 1930s, Le Sueur was increasingly drawn to using those tools to account for her settler and Native roots. "My family came from all the great migrations," she asserts: "the Black Irish fleeing the famine of '48," others forcibly dislocated and traveling "the Trail of Tears from seized tribal and ancient and deeded lands" (*Crusaders*, 6). Her great-grandmother was Iroquois and married an Irishman. Her grandmother, Antoinette Lucy, was an independent woman who "sat in her buggy on the line of the Indian Territory of Oklahoma, when the stolen land was opened as a state. With her shotgun over her knees, she made the run and held the land until the claim was filed" (7).[51] The tensions represented by these grandmothers straddle several disjointed times, which Le Sueur set out to account for in the radical ecology she pursued in the wake of World War II.

In the mid-1940s, during the war, which she supported, and with a Rockefeller Historical Research Fellowship in hand, she wrote a people's history of the North Star country. With Minnesota as its hub, she announces, the northern Midwest "occupies the exact geographical center of North America and has three great drainage systems flowing in divergent directions through the wide valleys of glacial loess."[52] Land is more than a backdrop here; it is one actor in an epic drama of people and places, ancient and new, that spans a history of love and abuse. *North Star Country*'s story opens with ancient remains dating from somewhere between eight and twelve thousand years ago being unearthed from deep in the land. They include the body of a young woman with an ax through her head, a pit of workmen, interglacial plants, and the teeth of chaetopods, small worms, and elephants, all "witness to the tide of frost and northern lights" (*North Star Country*, 4). From them, as Le Sueur tells it, a nation is born. We are not encouraged to celebrate this nation, for we learn early on that it is shaped by those who arrived with a disturbing new relation to the land. The prairie then, she tells us, was a network of trails connecting the territories of the Ojibwe and the capital of one of the great nations of the earth, the Nation of the Buffalo: the Sioux. She recounts stories of famous Sioux chiefs, of their courage and fatal terror of annihilation in the face of the relentless onslaught of the whites and their deceptive government. The "Indians did not know why the white man wanted to kill off the animals," she writes, but "this is how the animals disappeared from the country" (58). She goes on to document the enormous numbers of skins—of beaver, fox, otter, mink—that the white men took. Stark details follow of the fortune amassed by John Jacob Astor through his American Fur Company, which artfully gave whiskey and rum to the Indians in exchange for furs from trapping (58).

The newcomers also brought with them other migrants in the form of seeds "sewed up in the full petticoat, hidden in the hide of a trunk, secreted in a sun bonnet, or shaken out of an old hat." Corn was already here, however, and Le Sueur lingers on it. "The Ojibwe called it Mon-da-min," spirit grain, and they grew it in forests and on the plains. She tells of Native rituals for growing corn and of its passage into the hands and memories of the settlers. The companies of Cyrus McCormick and John Deere became the reaper kings, ruling the fields, while others, like the grassroots farmers' movement, the Granges, fought them (61).[53] The settlers' landed story is also a tale of trees turned into timber and railroads, of the immigrant tycoons Frederick Weyerhäuser and James J. Hill, who worked together on that gigantic enterprise. Le Sueur's assessments confront layers of contradiction. She credits Hill with loving the land and warning of its doom from lack of care even as he stripped the forests when he drove the railroad to the coast with the labor of competing Celts and Chinese, a destructive path to progress the Indians tried in vain to stop (163–65). Other robber barons—Andrew Carnegie, the Rockefellers, Henry Clay Frick, and J. P. Morgan—entered the North Star country contending for mineral resources and breaking the political supremacy of agriculture. She calls them visionaries of modernization but goes on to declare that it was "the unnamed workers who created this great empire." Those workers made their relation to the earth the theater for struggle on Minnesota's Mesabi Iron Range when the IWW with Big Bill Haywood arrived in the mines to declare war on U.S. Steel.

There is so much more to this story, and Le Sueur serves it up as a skilled storyteller with a keen eye for detail and a listening ear attuned to the voices of the people. By any measure, this is a remarkable regional history and an outlier among U.S. histories of the time for its renarration of the myth of U.S. exceptionalism that was the order of the day after World War II. Le Sueur devotes multiple chapters to Native people, their rich history, genocide, and displacement by land-greedy speculators in league with a treacherous government. In the end, the immigrants drive the narrative; however, most of them are nameless, looking not to accumulate but to survive on the land. Plowing up the prairie, they produced destruction, sometimes unwittingly. She remarks on the sign of that ruin visible by the 1930s, when "the corpse is the very earth," the bald prairie without a blade of grass, "the grasshoppers ticking like clocks" (238). "It fills you with terror," she remembers, "as something invisible does . . . like the flu terror" (265).

Passages like these still resonate. Others make me wonder how much Le Sueur was tempering her critical standpoint, perhaps mindful of the Rockefeller Foundation that funded the research or a readership no longer receptive to a radical history. This accommodating stance is evident in the conclusion, where she gives over to the land's natural cycles the responsibility for redemption, conceding in the closing paragraph that "some of the grain will be good, some of the crop will be saved" and that "from the bloodiest year some [will] survive to outfox the frost" (321).

By the end of the 1940s, the survivors in her writing are witnesses to ruin. Among the most remarkable are the people she meets when reporting in 1948 on the organizing efforts of the Congress of Industrial Organization (CIO). One is a miner on the Mesabi Iron Range in northeastern Minnesota; another is a mother in the lead and zinc mines of Oklahoma. In each article, Le Sueur foregrounds the women as principle interlocutors who greet their visitor warmly. She opens each story with details of domestic labor—the meal made ready for a son, the bread baked, the "white, very white curtains" of the tiny wooden house or the loose swinging door of the company shack.[54] In "Iron Country," the Croatian wife of Mr. Julius tells us that her husband is sick and the CIO union has been taking pictures of his lungs. Her report conveys the dignity of Mr. Julius as a man proud of his forty years as a miner, reluctant to blame the company because they "give me work for forty years" and in denial now about how sick he is. Ever since 1933, when he had "worked in mine so dusty and steamy so couldn't see partner," he felt bad and lost weight, but no company doctor on the range would ever say the dread word "silicosis" ("Iron Country," 58). With his silicosis far gone, Mr. Julius can barely breathe. "It's murder," Le Sueur exclaims to the CIO organizer, and he replies, "But the murderer is a big guy" (53).

In her report of her visit to the lead and zinc mines of Oklahoma the principle witness is also a woman from a mining family, herself an exhausted survivor who recounts the neglectful poisoning of the land and the people. The narrator of "Eroded Woman," clearly Le Sueur, does not reveal why or how she happens to arrive at a shanty in the lead mine district. We only know that being there conjures in her a feeling of melancholy. She traces it to her childhood growing up in Oklahoma amid "the bare duned countryside, the tough thin herb stains of men and women, from the Indians of the Five Tribes to the lean migrants from Valley Forge."[55] She is afraid to see this woman from a union family whom she has been directed to meet, perhaps because the devastation evident everywhere conjures ungrieved and ungrievable loss. The woman appears at the door dressed in a kind of flour sack with a hole cut out for her head. Inside the house, everything is coated with dust from the zinc mine. It covers every inch outside as well, and nothing will grow. "Seems like you're getting sludge in your blood," the woman comments. Without knowledge of the concept of commodity, she knows that the land has become just that. "The

Quapaws owned this land," she says, "but the big oil scared them and they signed it over for ninety-nine years" ("Eroded Woman," 226). When her son arrives from the strike where the CIO is supporting a new union at the mine, he speaks passionately of the organizing effort—reporting that the Klan came in to suppress it and that the Communists help you and "ain't afeared" of beatings. He remembers seeing his father die from years in the mine, "his lungs turned to stone" (227). We learn they are on the border of northern Oklahoma and Kansas, having migrated there from farming in Kentucky and then Arkansas.

The woman tells of her growing-up years, when she and her mother and brother worked in the mills. All her teeth were gone by her fourth baby, she says. Le Sueur sees her deep exhaustion and sorrow wakened by unaccustomed talking, like soil stirred. The sorrow of its ruin is in her, the human and the land "interlocked like doomed lovers" (230). She invites her visitor to stay the night. Lying beside her, Meridel is wakeful, thinking of human waste and injury and of this woman who, like the land, has been worn away, undermined. The final paragraph is one of Le Sueur's eloquent renderings of that loss and its cost: "All over America now lamplight reveals the old earth," it begins, "the vast spider network of us all in the womb of history, looking fearful, not knowing at this moment the strength, doubting the strength, often fearful of giant menace, fearful of peculiar strains and wild boar power and small eyes of the fox. The lower continent underlying all, speaks below us, the gulf, the Black old land" (230).

The narrator apprehends the broad reach of a giant menace threatening to obliterate any awareness of collective strength and yet hears the Black old land.[56] The lead mined in the area was used for bullets in World War II. It turned out that the tons of waste piled up all over town severely affected environmental health in the area, contaminating the groundwater and exposing residents to toxic chemicals everywhere they went. Kids rode their bikes through it and used it in sandboxes. In 1983, the federal government declared the Tar Creek area of over a thousand square miles a Superfund site. A decade later, many children were found to be suffering from lead poisoning.[57]

The arrival of the Cold War in the United States ushered in another form of state-supported killing in what Le Sueur called "the dark of the time." During that period of political repression, the Left was forced underground. Le Sueur's parents were hounded out of the Farmer–Labor Party for being too far left. To support themselves they ran a boardinghouse. The decade was personally tough too. Arthur died in 1950. Bob Brown, the artist who had been Meridel's partner for twenty-five years, died in 1954, the same year as her mother. Unlike other writers during the 1950s, Le Sueur never left the Communist Party, and she endured the painful consequences. During the anti-Communist campaigns led by Senator Joseph McCarthy, mainstream publishing houses cut her off, and she was only able to publish in left magazines. From 1947 until the 1970s, almost all her writing was published only in Communist Party journals.[58] She had the memoir of her parents privately printed. She resorted to writing children's books, but even some of them were banished from school libraries. She was under constant surveillance by the FBI, who tapped her phone. When she used her parents' boardinghouse as a source of income, her lodgers were harassed. The students in her creative writing correspondence courses were discouraged from taking her classes or quit out of fear, and she was fired from a series of waitressing jobs. By the end of that decade, in order to support herself she resorted to working in garment factories, chauffeuring a disabled woman, and, as a volunteer, attending to women in a state asylum.[59] The House Un-American Activities Committee issued a subpoena for her to appear before them in 1954, but they could not find her.

Perhaps in part because of her youthful travel to the East and West Coasts and her experiences in the commune of Emma Goldman and living with Minneapolis squatters, Meridel resisted many of the norms that prescribe middle-class white women's relationships to domestic spaces. Letters from her close friend, Irene Paull, suggest that she was what we might call a housework dissenter.[60] She did not embrace or even pursue domestic order and routine, expectations of white settler women that were increasingly organized efficiently as "home economics."[61] Paull's poignant admiration of her beloved friend acknowledges that Meridel's refusal of housework made her both extraordinary and frustrating. There is extensive evidence in Le Sueur's journals and in other letters that she loved her daughters fiercely. Interviews with family members attest to her diligence in attending to order regard-

ing the tools of intellectual life—her books and time for writing—
and to her creativity in managing to satisfy both the requirements
of that life and the needs of her daughters. If Rachel and Deborah
learned not to disturb their mother while she was writing or other
women sometimes took care of them for stretches, perhaps that is
the way it should be in a world that values dependency. As someone who juggled childcare and writing for many years, I know the
challenge well, and I remain in awe of any single mother who can
manage to make the time for writing, political activities, and children. If Le Sueur's noncompliance with the expectations of the
middle-class white mother were unsettling for her friend, perhaps
that was the point.

"'What Turns,' She Said, 'Returns'"

The late 1940s and the 1950s proved to be a turning time for Le Sueur.
She began to travel by bus as a reporter and social historian on
trips that took her through and beyond the northern Midwest.
She also began to come to terms more directly with her heritage
as the granddaughter of white settlers. Although she may not have
put it this way, from a twenty-first-century perspective we might
say that she became more attuned to whiteness, especially as it is
lived through a relation to space. In her book *Revealing Whiteness,*
Shannon Sullivan considers space to be racialized, a fact that is
often invisible because space is thought of as neutral.[62] Bodies become racialized, Sullivan explains, through their unconscious habits of lived spatiality. One of the characteristics specific to whiteness is what Sullivan calls an "appropriate" relation to the earth
and to the people and things that are part of it. Here "appropriate"
connotes "appropriation," as in taking something without permission. Failure to embody this appropriate relation to space marks
one as improper or inappropriate—that is, as not legitimately in a
position to own or control property. Nonwhite. Sullivan's example
of the Roma, or so-called Gypsies, illustrates how their unsettled
relation to space and to property ownership is racially coded as
inappropriate.

    We might think of this spatial coding as an example of the logic
of exchange extended into cultural formations when social identities become consolidated and commodified, their histories erased,

naturalized. Racial coding, often most intensely reproduced out-side the marketplace, pursues the logic of exchange by inscribing on bodies values that help guarantee their present or future value as labor power in the form of wages. Many factors contribute to that valuation, of course, but race remains a powerful one. The positive value of whiteness as a spatial relation manifests in vari-ous scales of what Sullivan calls an "ontological expansiveness." It underlies the American settler's rightful claim to "free" land from first encounter through the twenty-first century. Whiteness as a spatial relation also appears in everyday white habits of exercising control over environments or making rules that nonwhite people are forced to accept.[63] It manifests in the persistence of Jim Crow laws and customs that regulate space through gerrymandering or redlining. Consider also less formal habits that code certain spaces as dangerous or welcoming. Sullivan emphasizes that the habits of ontological expansiveness are unconscious for white people. Consequently, they are difficult to recognize and even more dif-ficult to change. Because they are learned, however, they can be unlearned and altered. The task is to use the social fact of being white or considered white to counter racism by mindfully and trai-torously inhabiting space rather than acting "whitely."

In the mid-twentieth century, Le Sueur became more attuned to whiteness as a spatial relation in this sense. That awareness ap-pears in her writing in striking examples of spatial navigation that display the difference between acting whitely and being white. Here we see her practice what it means to be a race traitor. Her own life grew more unsettled spatially as these years unfolded. She took over her parents' boardinghouse for a time; house-sat in Santa Fe, New Mexico, and Iowa; and lived for several years in a condemned bus in New Mexico. In the 1970s, she traveled to Mexico and wrote about its revolution and Indigenous history. She visited the extensive mounds that ancient peoples built across the face of the American continent and wrote a book about them.[64] She spent time working and living among Native people in northern Minnesota, South Dakota, Arizona, and New Mexico.[65]

During a bus trip in the 1950s to Elizabethtown, Kentucky, to do research for her children's book on Nancy Hanks Lincoln, the mother of Abraham Lincoln, Le Sueur witnessed white control of public urban lands in the segregated spaces of Kentucky and Washington, D.C., where police descended on Black men.[66] Her narrative of that trip, "American Bus" (1953), conveys racialized relations to space that she also discerned in the talk of the people on the bus as it traveled across the country. One day, two of the men, Pee Wee and Butch, discuss the pressure to get ahead, to climb higher, to go the extra mile. Without the narrator saying so, we know that the expansive extra mile they refer to is white. Another man, hand over mouth, tells her he is a refugee. He is afraid to reveal everything, he says, because someone might be listening, but he discloses, "I got out of Germany just in time. I'm a Jew." A Mexican woman in the restroom nursing her baby "is glad to spill some of the pressure of her long trek after working in beets, wheat, peas, corn." She tells how she and the other migrant workers "came in trucks standing tight like cattle, the driver getting fifteen dollars a head for each one arriving alive."[67] In each instance, race becomes legible through a body's relation to landed spaces that have been abstracted into the logic of exchange. The extra mile alludes to the promise that hard work leads to success, and implicitly the road is marked "whites only." The metaphor also maps the migration of Jews and Mexicans on the highways the bus travels, many of them state-funded postwar development projects. As the next two bus scenarios disclose, travel on these U.S. highways was often fearful for nonwhites, exposing them to harassment or state policing.

The most dramatic example unfolds in the closing scene when "in the middle of the afternoon an awful thing happens" ("American Bus," 137). A "handsome Negro woman with a crippled child on her arm" boards the bus as they "get into the sloping hills of the Missouri tobacco country." There is only one empty seat, beside a cattleman in a big hat. Seeing this woman, he "spread himself across the empty seat and said in a loud voice, 'in mah part of the country we know what to do with niggers. What you Yankees need is what we got there—a Jim Crow and a poll tax'" (137). In her representation of what ensues, Le Sueur captures her own and the other travelers' halting responses as they navigate what had been openly declared a white space. The narrator offers the woman her seat and holds the child. She reports her visceral response: "I can feel the pulse in my own body and the weight of every person on the bus suddenly alive in a horrible world of guilt and before us the Negro stands looking straight into nothing" (137).

As she offers the woman her seat, "to my horror," she reports, "she looks at me and sees the menacing white face." No one moves. Standing in anguish in the aisle and "ashamed of being white," the narrator realizes that the pressure of her body in the aisle almost forces the woman into the seat. The man, casting a lascivious eye, offers the narrator his empty seat, to which she responds, "I wouldn't care to sit beside you" (138). The bus is silent. The man gets off at the next stop. The driver says, "Good for you," and then everyone speaks at once for or against the cattleman (138). When the woman with the child gets off the bus, a farm woman says in a stern voice, "Did you ever stop to think that the Blacks outnumber us?" A terrible silence follows in the bus "as if something sick or dead is lying in it" (138).

Race as a spatial relation is conveyed powerfully here through the narrator's attunement to the bodies and atmosphere in this crowded space and through her own awkward effort to escape collective assent to white control. She wants to be not-whitely. Her apprehension of the response she receives from trying, however, blocks her desire, and that is unsettling. Literally. Her attention to the "Negro woman's" refusal to be thankful reveals an awareness of her desire for recognition from the other as an insidious instance of unconscious whitely emotional control that propels and lingers in the wake of good intentions.[68] I especially appreciate her representation of the discomfort provoked by the cattleman's enactment of an appropriating whiteness, an exercise of spatial control that is supposed to remain unremarkable. Notable, too, is the narrator's refusal of the white seat he had claimed, an act that ushers into the narrow space of the bus a momentary paralyzing affective response. She takes up the collective burden, naming it "a third face of guilt among us" that shatters unremarkable whiteness. The farm woman's whitely announcement echoes the cattleman and reclaims the bus as white space. That both cattleman and farm woman are figures associated with the land is an intervention into pastoral farm and ranch morality, which often inflects a racism that ultimately serves only ruling-class interests. The scene ends with the narrator powerless, able only to diagnose a lethal pathology. It is a small traitorous gesture, metaphorically naming white supremacy as a deadly American disease. From her childhood, Le Sueur leaned toward that treachery. She felt an affinity with Native communities, and those ties unsettled her white heritage even as they nourished her Native one. When Meridel was growing up, she spent time in Indian camps. In her later years, she lived months of each year among Native communities, and these alliances spilled into extended family ties. Her daughter Rachel's husband, Ken Tilsen, was lead defense attorney for the American Indian Movement (AIM) participants in the Wounded Knee occupation and attorney for AIM leaders Dennis Banks and Russell Means.[69] All of Rachel and Ken's family became involved in the struggle; one of their sons, Mark, chose to leave high school and join full time, later marrying a Pine Ridge Native woman.[70] One of the children's books Le Sueur published, *Sparrow Hawk* (1950), is the story of a Sauk boy and his settler friend. It was reissued in 1987 with illustrations by the Indigenous activist Robert DesJarlait (Red Lake Anishinaabe) and an admiring foreword by Native scholar Vine Deloria Jr. (Standing Rock Sioux). Another manuscript, "Zapata!," unpublished but probably written in the late 1950s or early 1960s when Le Sueur traveled often to Mexico, is a story of the Indigenous struggle over land and liberty led by Emiliano Zapata in the Mexican Revolution.[71]

In 1950, she also published "The Dakotas Look Back on a Trail of Broken Treaties," a report on her visit to Native communities after a harsh winter at a time when the Indian Termination Act I referred to in chapter 4 was well underway. She tells of her encounters with Native grandmothers taking care of children whose parents have gone to the cities looking for work and with Native farmers in the valley who had to rent their lands for pasture. She meets a mother who, barring the door, saw Le Sueur as the white oppressor. "I was in misery," she writes, "unable to tell her [that] I had no land" and that "some of my grandfathers were Indians who married Irishmen, too, and were chased west straight over the rim of the horizon, until with their backs to the sun they had to combine and turn to fight."[72] A decade later, she published a piece in the magazine *Mainstream* that even more directly draws the reader into "a tale of the American Indian's fight for his land." Entitled "The First Farmers' Revolt," it begins with a twist, framing the first farm revolts in the Midwest as the Indian uprisings when the Dakotas and the Anishinaabe of Minnesota attempted to get their land back in 1862.[73] The statement is a surprise for any reader who understands the farm revolts as a chapter of settler history from the 1930s, a chapter that Josephine Herbst, among others, reported on. When the narrator asserts, "I was a young'un then but I remember it like it was yesterday," the reader is again turned around. This is not reportage, you realize, but creative nonfiction or fiction, and the speaker here is not Le Sueur.

The narrative then opens onto a story from the vantage point of a nineteenth-century white settler, a man who was the child of German radical freethinkers, abolitionists who believed the homesteader and the Indian would have gotten along if not for the traders and the merchants. Like Le Sueur, as a child he went to the Indian camps and saw the Indians "dancing, living deep in the land. The land was their mother" ("First Farmers' Revolt," 21). "I have thought about it all my life," the man adds. "I have thought about my part in it. I have thought about it on many surfaces and directions" (21). What follows is his eyewitness account of the New Ulm Massacre, when the Dakotas rose up after years of frustration and settler land hunger. About fifty-five civilians and over four hundred Indians were killed in that uprising. Angry settlers called for vengeance, and three hundred Indians were put on trial in Mankato, Minnesota, and condemned to death. Chief Little Crow was scalped and his corpse dragged through the streets. Some say his body was taken by a medical fraternity and embalmed in Philadelphia. The narrative ends with an indirect invitation to renarrate a history that had become an infamous tale of innocent settlers brutally murdered by savage Indians: "I wake up now sometimes with the same foreboding," the narrator concludes. "What did we do? Upon whose heart is the guilt fallen?" (26).

Le Sueur's relationship to her settler and Native history was always somewhat unsettled, and it became increasingly so in her seventies. At that time, she wrote a history of the Native American mound builders and a memoir, "The Ancient People and the Newly Come." She represents the history of Native losses as counter to and at times entangled in the history of Midwest settlers, farmers, and workers, some of whom, like her parents, "stood against the kings of power in the vast new empire" (*Crusaders*, 55). Evident in these representations is a consciousness of the claims and lives of Native people, a claim that haunts the hearts of white settlers, especially the radical ones. Le Sueur surpasses the limits of Marxism in her attention to women's labor and to a deeply relational ecological sensibility; here she expands that critical scope to acknowledge settlement's debt to the Indian people it annihilated and displaced and whose lands it appropriated. "I had been conceived in the riotous summer," she writes,

> and fattened on light and stars that fell on my underground roots, and every herb, corn plant, cricket, beaver, red fox leaped in me in the old Indian dark. Crouching together on Indian land in the long winters, we grew in sights and understanding. The severity of the seasons and the strangeness of the new land, with those whose land had been stolen looking in our windows, created a tension of guilt and a tightening of sin.[74]

Le Sueur recognizes the gaps punctuating settler relations to time and space when she asserts that growth in "sights and understanding" became for her felt knowledge of the fractured relations of settler life. She concedes that at a time "in the beginning of the century [when] the Indian smoke still mingled with ours," her grandmother "probably did not consider that the house she built as a homesteader was squared off on an ancient land of mounds and pyramids and cones, land that had not been plowed in a million years. Neither did she think the land had been monstrously taken from Native people" ("Ancient People," 39, 50). Le Sueur also admits, however, that "the design and beauty" of her grandmother's house moved her, "and when I see its abandoned replica on the plains," she adds, "I weep," for it was "a haven against the wild menace of the time" (50). Recurring acknowledgments like this one offer a complex historical memory that speaks from settler heritage while also disclosing the relations it so violently severed. Le Sueur's lifelong political commitments take the form of such a dialectical sensibility, a re-membering that refuses to ignore the comforting elements of a settler past and the ancient inhabitants it so brutally uprooted and removed.

Native people appear in her narratives not as icons or props but as actors and generators of knowledge. That she most often represents them through a strategy I am calling "parallel syntax" is a feature of Le Sueur's multifaceted handling of space and time. Parallel syntax conveys the gaps, silences, and contradictions in the daily lives of midwestern settlers who lived side by side with Native people. It has the effect of capturing the silences that punctuated the times and spaces that defined their lives. We see this parallel syntax in the marking of seasonal time in her historical narratives. In recounting the autumn years of her youth in Minnesota, for example, Le Sueur lyrically recalls annual activities that entwined farmers who showed their crops and beasts in great fairs with Natives clustered nearby in their summer campground. As the days grew shorter, a dark wind would flow down from the lands of the Mandan people and the Indians would slowly move out of the camp to return to the reservation. Then "Aries, buck of the sky, leaps to the outer rim and mates with earth. Root and seed turn into flesh. We turn back to each other in the dark together, in the shortest days, in the dangerous cold, on the rim of a perpetual wilderness" (42). As each group returned to its winter places, a summer mingling, or perhaps merely a parallel coexistence, would leave its trace in shared ancient maps of sky and harvest. Whether "we" represents members of each community singly or together is left unclear, even as the season's fertilizing cycle is written in the heavens and saved in seeds that bound them "in the dark" to one another.

The unsaids embedded in this parallel form shelter both the clashing aspirations and firm allegiances of the women in this region. The summer when Meridel was twelve was a significant season of budding awareness of these divergent and entangled histories. She situates it in a time line of international sovereign struggle and violence: "fourteen years from the Spanish American War, twenty-two years from the Ghost Dance and the Battle of Wounded Knee, and four years until World War I would change the agrarian world" (42). In the wake of this martial imperial history, her relational sensibility was being nurtured in "the maternal forest" of the "three fertile and giant prairie women" who reared her (42–43). They were her mixed-race grandmother and mother and the Mandan Native woman "we called Zona" (50). They "strode across my horizon," she announces, "in fierce attitudes of planting, reaping, childbearing and tender care of the seed," their influence organic and nurturing. "As a pear ripens in the chemical presence of other pears, I throve on their just and benevolent love"; yet, she declares, they lived "a subjected and parallel life" (42). These "puritan and Indian women" seemed to her "similar, unweighed, even unknown, the totemic power of birth and place, earth and flesh" palpable as they "listened to each other and the horror of their tales" (42). Their stories traverse a fractured ruthless history: how the Iroquois fled the assassins of her grandmother's village; her mother escaped from Texas law; and Zona's mother ran to her death in the battle of Wounded Knee.

It was Zona, "tall and strong like many of the Plains Indians," who sealed for the young Meridel a relational sensibility (44). She lived in the grove with the Indians who came to work in the fields, and she helped the settler women at canning time. Le Sueur remembers that she sneaked out with Zona frequently to "go through the pale spring night to the Indian fires, where the Indian workers drummed until the village seemed to sink away and something fierce was thrust up on the old land" (44). Zona would tell the girl stories of how the grass once moved in the wind "before the terrible steel plow put its ravenous teeth in her," and she took Meridel to Mandan to show her "the great mounded grass-covered excavations with no windows except the top" (44). Zona told of the many animals who lived upon the plains that in the spring "seethed with the roaring of mating buffalo" (44). She told of the warriors who hunted them in summer to provide meat for the winter when the Mandan in their mounded cathedrals would tell stories of the mountains and the sea to the west (44). She told of a relation to the land that was not for taking nor to be divided into squares, and she prophesized the earth's response to this violence.

> She said the earth would give back a terrible holocaust to the white people for being assaulted, plowed up, and polluted. She swept her sacred feature around the horizon, to show the open fan of the wilderness and how it all returned: mortgaged land, broken treaties—all opened among the gleaming feathers like a warm breasted bird turning into the turning light of moon and sun, with the grandmother earth turning, turning. What turns, she said, returns. When she said this, I could believe it. (43)

Zona's cyclical ecological time prefigures the earth's vindica-
tion even as it is rooted in the metabolic time-space of growth and
regeneration. In this respect, it differs from the time of the Ghost
Dance that she recounts. One summer day when the women all sat
together on the porch, Zona spoke sadly of the Ghost Dance and of
her inability to believe the dancing would bring the land and the
buffalo back. Zona's husband had died of grief because the buffalo did not return and because, after the ruthless massacre at
Wounded Knee, the government had suppressed their societies.
Her story ends, however, with the affirmation made by so many
peoples: "We have to keep things alive for the children" (46). At
this point, the narrative stitches its parallel syntax. The young
Meridel's "mother and grandmother nodded. They knew this. They
had made long treks to farms they lost to the same enemies" (44).
The grandmother sings "her own ceremonial and prophetic song,
'We shall come rejoicing, bringing in the sheaves.'" Meridel, however, picks up Zona's visionary warning: "I look out now along the
bluffs of the Mississippi where Zona's prophesies of pollution have
been fulfilled in worse ways than she could dream. Be aware, she
had cried once. Be afraid. Be careful. Be fierce. She had seen the
female power of the earth immense and angry, that could strike
back at its polluters and conquerors" (48). Le Sueur weaves the stories that bind and distinguish these women into evidence neither
of settler triumph nor of a dying Native people but of embodied
debts. While they record fragmented parallel temporalities and
spaces, they also offer a critical perspective that is layered and
wide-ranging. From the labor and ecology of women emerges a
dialectical knowledge indebted to both the ancient people and
the newly come.

Time in Zona's prophetic vision leaps out of the past to fore-
tell a dire future that counters clock time: what turns, Zona says,
returns. In Native culture, this cyclical time has a material existence and efficacy. It renders for the young Meridel both the earth's
warning and "the benevolence of the entire cosmos" (47). In her
memoir, the lessons of Native people remain a potent parallel heritage to the "prairie agrarian prophets" that conclude "The Ancient
People and the Newly Come" (62). Here Le Sueur remembers being
present as a young girl at a speech given by Eugene Debs, founder
of the IWW and the great champion of workers, a charismatic man

who conveyed for her "a new kind of tenderness" (62). Although his voice gets the last word, in Le Sueur's retelling, his cry "All we want is the earth for the people!" echoes a Native demand and vision as the narrator concludes, "These prairie agrarian prophets, these sages of the people still rise in the nitrogen of the roots, still live in the protein" (62). Here in an expansive rendering of ecological time and space, the dead return, a presence in the land, to collaborate and usher in new ways of living.

"The Earth Is Not Sleeping, She Is Violated and Furious"

In 1991 Le Sueur published her third novel, *The Dread Road,* when she was ninety-one years old. It is a daring tour de force. I say "daring" because it is a radical departure from realist fiction in substance and form. The vision is apocalyptic, the setting her beloved Southwest. In its substance, this experiment is a coherent outgrowth of the dialectical sensibility she had been nurturing since the 1930s. The core narrative is based on an actual event, a bus trip Le Sueur once took from Albuquerque, New Mexico, to Denver, Colorado, on which she encountered a woman who carried in a suitcase the dead baby she had delivered in the restroom of the bus station. The story of the journey is told in three adjacent columns. Parallel syntax characterizes its formal structure as the two bookending columns frame a core narrative. The logic of their relationship is intuitive and expansive, fanning out from a journey across three states and two hundred years, eliciting weblike connections and breaks. On the left are excerpts from the stories of Edgar Allan Poe. They read like prophetic commentaries on America and remind us of the night terrors deeply embedded in the white American grain. On the right are passages from Le Sueur's journal. They are printed in italics and punctuated with ellipses that conjure the pauses of the breath. At times these breaks register anxiety, at other times merely silence. They speak from a voice that may be that of the woman narrator of the core story or unidentified fragments of a national consciousness. This voice bears witness to a wide net of destruction: unending government lies, uranium mines among the Laguna, grandmothers dying of the poisons sprayed on insects, mothers bursting out of mass graves in the overturned earth. This voice is also witness to the night chant of the Navajo, the "I can do this," the moving forward, as an old woman claims the dead child as ushering in a new race from the rejects and the strontium, from the kernel taking root. As the title suggests, *The Dread Road* is a passage through terror in America. Literally buried in the past, the dread seeps into the present. Toxic and violent, it permeates the land, air, and genetic material of human and nonhuman relations. The consequences are lethal and ominous. The main actors of the core narrative are the narrator, who is an old woman who boards the bus in Albuquerque, and the young Mexican fieldworker with the dead baby, whom she meets in the bus station. Two other figures serve as foils: a nosy and aggressively inquisitive white woman passenger and the bus driver. The bus's route parallels the current Interstate 25, traveling from El Paso, Texas, to Albuquerque and Santa Fe, New Mexico, and then on to Trinidad, Pueblo, and Denver, Colorado.[75] The journey passes through Ludlow, Colorado, the site of a 1914 massacre, an event to which the young woman is connected in some way and in which the narrator's grandfather died.

Around 1910, the United Mine Workers began to organize immigrant miners in Colorado. In September 1913, the miners went on strike demanding better working conditions, shorter hours, better pay, and company compliance with state labor laws. When they walked out, they abandoned the shacks the company had provided and built tent colonies near each of the mining communities. The Ludlow colony alone housed over a thousand men, women, and children.[76] On April 20, state-supported militia arrived armed with rifles and machine guns and attacked the miners, some of whom hid in pits under the campsite.

Meridel was a teenager when the massacre occurred, and she heard the story from the workers themselves when they visited the People's College later that year and organized a parade in commemoration of the victims.[77] She remembered seeing "the bodies bearing the mark of their oppression, of their stolen labor, and now their holy dead. Their bodies were hieroglyphs of their exploitation, . . . their lungs turned to silica stone, a strange and terrible sadness and even humiliation in them but also something else, a terrible fire and grief" (*Crusaders*, xvii).[78] The narrative weaves together the history of that massacre with the story of the nuclear testing that took place nearby. The testing materialized in the atom bomb and in the contamination of the web of life by U.S. military-industrial power. The children of these two women bear the evidence. The narrator is traveling to Denver to see her son, who was born with one eye lying down on his cheek; his feet never grew, and his hands curled into broken buds.[79] "I hid him there after he was born, too early, not early enough to be dead," she tells us. She was a young pregnant wife when they carried out the test "that killed the sheep and the fish and the foliage . . . changed the genes, the seed forever" (*Dread Road*, 1). She used to take tranquilizers when she visited her son, "going through the dread road north through the injured earth" (1). She knows that Louis Tikas, a Greek immigrant who was one of the leaders of the Ludlow strike, was riddled with eighty-five bullets "as he tried to protect the children underground in the cave beneath the tent" (1).

Slow violence hangs over the journey like a zombie. It materializes in ghostly presences along the road as the bus approaches Ludlow, *"the desperate dead untethered"* (16). The state appears as a killing agent throughout, coordinator of the massacre and the nuclear testing. The young Mexican woman with the baby in her zipper bag had been on the bus from El Paso. On that leg of the trip, the bus picked up several other Mexican passengers, some of them undocumented workers, and "at regular intervals police went through the bus, armed to the teeth" (2). Surveillance enters the bus in a more subtle fashion in the person of the prying white passenger, probably a social worker, seated behind the old woman and the girl with the baby. Her suspicions about the girl eventually prompt her to call the police when the bus arrives in Denver.

One of the few hopeful messages in this dreadful novel lies in its production. Le Sueur explains in an author's note that the work is "a communal creation, using the collective experience of a number of people." Patricia Clark Smith, a Poe scholar, went over the Poe material and suggested its placement in the text. Le Sueur's daughter Rachel Tilsen, John Crawford (Le Sueur's longtime publisher at Westview Press), and Patricia Smith edited the draft. Le Sueur and Rachel then reviewed the editing. Meridel's daughter Deborah Le Sueur did the cover photography, images taken from the United Mine Workers' monument to the dead workers in Ludlow. Le Sueur suggests that the collective authorship also includes "the woman and the dead child she carried from the fields."

The narrative lifts her story "from personal and private grief" and extends the collaborative process to include the reader, who is also "not private but part of a collective consciousness."[80] True to Le Sueur's relational sensibility, in the midst of dread and terror she manages to apprehend that life nonetheless insists, and that insistence is rooted in the dependent relations of people and land.

In the end, there is no resolution to the core story, only hints of openings, cracks in the tales of these events. When the bus arrives in Denver and the prying white woman calls the police, the girl with the baby disappears. The narrator searches for her for a week but fails to find her. On the seventh day, the narrator notices a newspaper story, *"small as if it had been a fantasy . . . could not have happened. A young woman had stood up in the capitol and held a dead baby up to the pure golden dome as if a sacrifice"* (*Dread Road*, 47). Here the small "as if" captures the space between fantasy and fact, the frail capacity of metaphor to relate and repair. The material of imagination. The story may or may not have appeared in the paper. The narrator may get her son out of the institution, or she may not. There was a trial about the Nevada nuclear tests, she tells us. Some families got recompense. The government knew the danger of the fallout but lied. The earth is still rolling in agony. Bones remain pulverized on the dread road.

The last words of each of the columns read like fragments of Le Sueur's life's work. The Poe quotations in the first column end with an excerpt from his story "MS. Found in a Bottle." A tale written in journal entries, it evokes Le Sueur's journals, which are excerpted in the third column and surface here like messages in a bottle. The core story of the second column ends with the narrator, dreamlike, settling her attention on woman's reproductive body—the signature figure of Le Sueur's work and emblem of the wounded earth. She notices that the front page of the newspaper had pictures of women all over the world holding their dead babies on their knees. This international figure, she affirms, "was deep in us all" (47).

The voice of the third column gets the last few words, an imperative to join an uprising from the cornfields and wheat fields as they burst into bread. *"Hide and embrace the guerillas"* it commands. *"They are rising in their flesh of necessity, simple hunger . . . They are there"* (47). This voice then turns to confront once more the nagging situation of the settler of the Americas, as if it will have a bearing on any alliance with uprising. I imagine Le Sueur pondering this last paragraph, possibly aware that these might be her last published words and considering what to leave as her final declaration on the heritage that had so defined her life as the great-granddaughter of an encounter between Native and colonizer. It is a profound moment for her, and she begins with an annunciation. Part wish and part confession, it spills into a small fantasy of the possible. *"It is a love affair . . . with my country,"* she begins. *". . . the wonderful earth of the middle country . . . inheritance pirated."* The breathy voice goes on to imagine what it would mean to *"go to origins that are pure . . . without theft . . . with only gifts"* (47). It is an intriguing concept to emerge here, punctuated by the elliptical breathing. We might ask: What pure origins? What gifts can possibly reconcile the terror and genocide deep in the heart of America, get to the root of the white settler's situation?

Shannon Sullivan's study of whiteness offers one answer. She turns once more to W. E. B. Du Bois to understand the relation of race to the gift. In his 1924 book *The Gift of Black Folk,* Du Bois offers the concept of the gift to rename a history of embodied debt embedded in what has unfortunately come to be called "white privilege." For me the power of the concept of the gift is that it recasts this now-popular term. The problem with that phrase, as I see it, is that "privilege" allows moral censure to provide an escape hatch from confronting the persistent lived history of race. Ever an insightful guide, Du Bois explains that the white habit of appropriation and control is lived consciously and unconsciously as ownership of the earth and of people and things.[81] What underlies this appropriating standpoint is the land of Native Americans and the exploited labor of Black slaves that made the (white) United States. By turning his attention from "theft" to "gift," Du Bois shifts the standpoint for comprehending whiteness from the agency of whites to the activities of those populations who remain the source of accumulated wealth. The bodies of Black folk—and we can add the lands of Native people as well—are gifts to whiteness in a very material sense.

Appropriated "free" Native land and slave bodies entered into the market as commodities ripe for planting, breeding, and speculation. By the nineteenth century, Black slaves had become the most valuable commodity on the U.S. market. Long after the official end of slavery, race as a cultural mark of difference continues to reproduce surplus value through the economic, political, and cultural devaluation of those bodies whose labor enables sizable profit margins. While Du Bois does not stress this point, their disposability is a source of value. It continues to enable an array of social structures that maintain white control and suppress any threat nonwhite people pose to real and imaginary political power and capital accumulation. The hypervaluation of European and American whites as entitled to dominate the earth enabled the settler to declare rightful access to "free" Native lands, transforming them into real estate, and to commodify Africans as "free" labor. The process persists as the neocolonial axis of the capitalist enterprise, in which "race" as a cultural formation is integral to the market relations that extend over the web of life.[82] The commodification of land into an object for exchange and speculation enabled "free" land to be claimed from Natives, whose resistance meant they simply had to be exterminated. Consolidated by agribusiness, the land continues to be worked by the exorbitantly profitable cheap labor of a disposable population of renters and undocumented workers, whose continued devaluation remains essential to the U.S. economy.

Du Bois's concept of the forgotten gift is rooted in these relations of devaluation as a source of value, relations that make race an integral fixture in the cultural levers of capital accumulation. If we follow the trail of the gift's logic, we find it lodged in the freedoms encoded in the so-called privilege of whiteness, gifts that continue to be given. For the wealthy few, these gifts materialize in the freedom to appropriate land as vast stretches of real estate that accumulate enormous profits through unpaid labor and speculation. For most whites who control little or no wealth, these gifts manifest in the freedom of ontological expansiveness, unpoliced mobility, control over everyday spaces, a psychic state of security, and the satisfaction of unconscious desires. These are smaller, less tangible gifts that actually function to sanction the big ones. As contemporary events in the United States make all too clear, many white people, some of us the great-great-grandchildren of settlers, are only beginning to recognize and investigate the source of the value accorded to whiteness and to comprehend its relation to the gifts of those whose devaluation enable it.

There is another legacy of gift giving that this scene conjures, one rooted in Native ontologies of survivance. "Survivance" is a word that means more than mere survival. It connotes all the relations that a way of life entails. Native scholar Jodi Byrd (Chickasaw) refers to survivance as a reciprocal relation to nature, a sovereignty that is not possessive. For her, this is a sovereignty grounded in motion or transit, "to be active presence in a world of relational movements and counter movements." To be in transit, she explains, "is to exist relationally, multiply."[83] Rauna Kuokkanen (Sami) underscores that this relational way of being is fundamental to Indigenous epistemes and is represented in the gift. In her long chapter "The Gift" she explains that in Native knowledge, the gift is not a medium of exchange. Indeed, understanding its meaning requires a radical shift in perspective from the logic of exchange so basic to Western thought and market capitalism. As Robin Wall Kimmerer (Potawatomi) explains, "A gift asks something of you. To take care of it. And something more."[84] That "something more" is a "pact of mutual responsibility to sustain those who sustain us." Water, earth, and air. Gifts to pass on. As Kuokkanen explains, in Indigenous philosophies, "the gift is part of a worldview in which social ties apply to everyone and everything, including the land, which is considered a living, conscious entity" that gives to people provided they treat it with respect and gratitude. The gift is the manifestation of permeable boundaries of reciprocity across the web of life. It reflects a bond of intimacy, interrelatedness, and dependency from which responsibilities emerge.[85]

By ending this last novel with a brief meditation on the Indigenous gift, Le Sueur offers that concept as an opening to reimagine the settler's story. She introduces the explorer Álvar Núñez Cabeza de Vaca. Beginning in 1527, he spent eight years traveling through Texas and the Southwest on orders from the king of Spain, later documenting his meetings with the Native people living there. Le Sueur imagines these encounters as if a *"nakedness always beyond the robber . . . nakedness to nakedness"* took place, a scenario in which Cabeza de Vaca is neither conqueror nor settler, for *"the conqueror can never be naked."* "Nakedness" conveys the vulnerable animal body, the "flesh of necessity" and "simple hunger" that joins humans to one another and to other living creatures. That naked need and its exposure, she announces, the man who has power never touches. She imagines this encounter as *"pure . . . without theft . . . with only gifts, as they gave Cabeza de Vaca."* Significantly, as she re-members it, what occurs is not an exchange. Only the Indigenous give gifts, and the narrator concedes that they continue doing so, for she reveals, *"They met me as they did him, with the gifts of their naked bodies, robbed of everything but their basic root . . . down to the root"* (*Dread Road*, 47). The gift lies in the relation and its lesson. It arrives in the next and final sentence, a surprise and a parable. *"Root hog or die,"* it instructs.

The shift is at first confounding. It turns out, though, that the hog has a mixed history in the Americas. Hogs were immigrants from Europe. Spanish explorers and settlers introduced most of them. Some of those pigs, like the Spanish, brought diseases that wiped out entire regional native populations. Many, but not all, Indigenous people domesticated them for meat.[86] In turning unexpectedly from humans to the humble pig who feeds on waste and roots in the land, this surprising instruction invites the reader to consider humans as if they are another animal who likewise unsettles the land, laboring in search of food, some bringing destruction in their path, some provision and sustenance. Le Sueur's dialectical sensibility is evident here, connecting settler and Native, human and nonhuman, animal and cornfield, their common needs rooted in sustaining life, perhaps even in survivance, the mutual dependency of life making.

Returning to the story of Cabeza de Vaca, the explorer who humbly meets the Indigenous in his nakedness, a newcomer like the pig, we can discern in this extraordinary concluding paragraph echoes of the strange image in the core story, the newspaper account of a woman in the capitol building holding up her dead baby, a story the narrator tells us is *"small as if it had been a fantasy."* As if. I think of these two words as Le Sueur may have considered them: seeds that harbor a seeming impossible possibility, the stuff of imagination. As some of us struggle in the twenty-first century to comprehend and reimagine what it means to relate to the land, to be unsettled settlers, white without theft, the image seems right. Meridel Le Sueur's encounters are instructive "as if" moments. She pursued them in the places where ordinary people

converge—bus trips and bus stations like the ones in this story—
because they offered opportunities she relished, chances to watch
and listen to the talk, as she once did in the Oklahoma City bus station for two days, huddled with the heroin users, sex workers, and
other transients.[87] In these situations, she risked being vulnerable
and awkward. No doubt she made mistakes. At times, perhaps, felt
guilty. Yet she kept showing up, lingering, in small acts of attention and imagination, remembering and bearing witness. There
is much to be said for such behavior when at a loss for how to act
"as if" and feeling inappropriate . . . vulnerable . . . naked. As white
people, we can never transcend our "appropriate" whiteness nor
our settler heritage. We can only recognize our whitely behavior
again and again on the way to relinquishing control, to becoming
otherwise. On that journey we may find ourselves humbled and
exposed, and perhaps as a result better equipped to join the guer-
rillas who are "rising in their flesh of necessity" against the systematic erosion of so much life by a killing state in league with the
greedy few.

As Zona predicted, devalued life is pushing back in the form of
floods and fires, drought and extinction. By the time Le Sueur was
in her seventh decade, she was witnessing the prophecy unfold. "In
75 years this rich land has been corned out, poisoned with chemicals, over plowed, eroded, the homestead gone back to the banker
and the land now subjected to corporate funds." For her, however,
there is always more than ruin. As she tells it in her life story, the
film *My People Are My Home,* potential remains in a relationship
with the land that she renders here as an intimacy of the sort one
might only have in her seventies. Clear-eyed, returning to a familiar old body, tallying the parts, the scars, imagining the traces of
others there:

O prairie I know all your little trees. I have watched them far
and bud and the pools of winter frozen over, your tracked roads
footprints of fleeing people going where.
In the country now a sense of ruin and desolation. I can
never leave you.
I have stayed with you, being in love with you, bent upon
understanding you, bringing you to life.
For your life is my life and your death is mine also.[88]

The energy of life making that rises in the nitrogen and lives in the protein cannot prevail unaided against the ravaging drive to accumulate wealth and appropriate the earth's resources. Nonetheless, the capacity to nurture relationships that renew and sustain across the web of life lies in the hands and hearts of humans. It pulses in the human power to remember collective dependence on one another, on the earth, and its creatures. It surges in the capacity to listen and act other-wise, to imagine impossible possibility. To rise up.

Time is running out. Nature has long ago been thoroughly socialized. There is no turning back that clock, no return to the garden. Humans have placed themselves in the center, and from there we must now act. The question is not whether we can or should control nature but how to find a new relation. One that is not socialized for profit. Such an ecology requires a political economy not driven by the appropriation of land and laboring bodies, the accumulation of wealth by and for the few, or "appropriate" whiteness. It re-members human accountability to the web of life, to the earth, and to each other. For that task, Meridel Le Sueur's dialectical and relational sensibility is an untimely resource. We might even say it is a gift.

Love

Six
Particles of Intense Life

Muriel Rukeyser was one of the most politically committed twentieth-century writers. A major figure of American letters, she is best known as a poet, but she wrote in other forms as well, creating, among other works, three major biographies, a cross-genre musical about the illusionist Harry Houdini, a memoir, a novel, numerous film scripts and translations, children's books, a nonfiction account of the Irish festival of Puck Fair, and many essays.[1] She assembled an expansive archive in preparation for a biography of the anthropologist Franz Boas; although never completed, the project took her to visit and live with the Kwakwaka'wakw people of Vancouver Island and to think through the legacies of Indigenous thought.[2] Adrienne Rich called her "as much an American classic as Melville, Whitman, Dickenson, W. E. B. Du Bois, or Zora Neale Hurston." She was courageous and unapologetic, "a big woman, alive in mind and body, capable of violence and despair and also of desire."[3] For Rukeyser, poetry is an exchange of energy, a system of relationships. This definition also applies to her work in other genres, and it might well characterize her as a materialist. Her materialism does not comply with orthodox Communism; nonetheless, her early affiliations with the party shaped what would become her radical interventions into its political scope.

Rukeyser brought to the progressive Left's discourse on race her attunement to the exchange of energy in the form of the life-making resource Eros.[4] As Audre Lorde puts it, Eros is "rooted in the power of our unexpressed or unrecognized feeling."[5] Its energy

Muriel Rukeyser, 1937. Photograph by Nancy Naumburg.
Courtesy of Margie Goldsmith and William L. Rukeyser.

is felt in the body's neurons before the brain can produce the
words to name it. It is, moreover, an intensity in the positive, life-
enhancing register that stimulates and enlivens as it is transferred
between bodies; it infuses an environment, transmits enthusiasm, pleasure, affinity, or joy. Uncontained, it can defy and exceed
available categories. Socially and historically organized, it gets contained by conventional distinctions and ideological distortions. In
Western culture, the sanctioned forms that Eros takes tend to be
confined in discourses that help reproduce the relations of capital-

ism. (Think, for example, of heteronormativity or romance.) It can and does spill beyond those discourses, however, into unruly sensations and energy exchanges. Its truth resembles the truth of imagination or intuition that passionately pursues the unthinkable and impossible, what is censored or forgotten. Rukeyser understood this bodily intensity as the catalyst and effect of the creative process. "One writes in order to feel," she asserts in *The Life of Poetry*, and that mandate animated her poetry as well as her biographies.[6] For her, life writing is not an effort to convey the details of a figure's personal life. Rather, it engages the reader in what she called "unverifiable facts" disclosed through traces and analogues that draw these traces into a felt relation to a subject. The effect is a reorientation in the reader's own life.

The life-giving energies of this ancient form of Eros suffuse her political commitments as well as her poetic imagination. As Eric Keenaghan asserts, this affective dimension actually "helps remap what we mean by the term 'the political.'"[7] Rukeyser tracks these affective energies in the aspirations and incompletions of U.S. history and modern invention and in the conventional distinctions of sexuality and race that she confronts and interrupts. Elisabeth Däumer warns readers that Rukeyser "is not a safe subject."[8] Indeed, I discovered, she is not. Her pursuit of the subversive, reflexive energy of Eros across public and intimate environments is one reason why.

Rukeyser's attention to the transmission of energy appears in her writing from the 1930s and recurs throughout the next three decades in her works on science and history, poetics and politics, biography and anthropology, drama and film. Repeatedly, she breaks open conventional forms to account for material reproduced and organized across multiple environments, including the social struggles in which she actively participated and on which she reported. As she delineates the brutal power of capitalist relations in the harvesting of water and land, in the laboring bodies of miners, migrants, and the mothers who care for them, she also recognizes the life-giving energies that shape the collaborative powers of imagination, technological development, and collective action. During the 1930s and 1940s she brought these interests to several collective campaigns led by the Communist Party's popular front, among them its international support for the Scottsboro Boys and for the victims of a West Virginia mining disaster.

Her biography of the physical chemist Josiah Willard Gibbs, which she was completing in the final years of the 1930s, is a stunning example of her life writing and a fascinating history of unattended material relations.[9] It is an eccentric biography, breaking away from the conventional form to bring into focus unexpected relations. As several critics have remarked, it anticipates her poetic manifesto, *The Life of Poetry,* in claiming that the world of the poet is also the scientist's.[10] An approach to life writing that refuses the singularity of the personal, it opts instead to foreground the energetic relations traversing science, literature, historical events, and physical processes that conditioned Gibbs's discoveries and the dream of progress that unfolded from them across the buried devastation of America.

Gibbs was one of the greatest scientists of the twentieth century. The founder of physical chemistry, his work brought together two fields, physics and chemistry, that had not been on speaking terms, yet he remains unknown by the general public. His research was instrumental in accelerating modern industrial development throughout the twentieth century, ushering in what has come to be known as the "chemical regimes of living."[11] While a professor of mathematical physics at Yale in 1876, he formulated the phase rule in his paper "On the Equilibrium of Heterogeneous Systems," which maps the roles of entropy and energy in the theory of thermodynamics. "Phase" refers to the composition and thermodynamic state of a body without regard to its quantity or form. Bodies that differ in composition or state are different phases of matter. Phases that can coexist are considered to be in equilibrium. The most familiar example of different phases is ice water versus salt water, where water and ice or salt as vapor coexist in a glass. Gibbs was interested in calculating the transformation of matter from one phase to another, and he set down the formula for that calculation as the phase rule. Represented in mathematical terms, the rule states that if F is the number of variables of a system if you change the pressure or the temperature, C is the number of component parts, and P is the number of phases, then $F = C - P + 2$.

Into the tale of Gibbs's inventions and modest life, Rukeyser enfolds a history of national ambitions punctuated by unacknowledged relations. Beginning in the biography's first chapter, she counters the fragmentation of science and history by introducing Gibbs's birth year with the arrival of the slave ship *La Amistad* in the port of New York City. Chance intimacies bind two white New England families to the enslaved Africans who had taken control of the ship after it set sail from Cuba in 1839. The elder Josiah Willard Gibbs, then a professor of theology and sacred literature at Yale, had devoted his studies to comparative languages. That year, soon after his son and namesake was born, he was summoned to aid in the preparation for the trial of the *La Amistad* Africans, tasked with finding an interpreter for them. Rushing off from New Haven to the docks of New York City, he did. Their case would go to the U.S. Supreme Court, where former U.S. president John Quincy Adams would be their lead counsel. Rukeyser pursues the relationships between the Adams and Gibbs families. That story, she writes, "swings through the history of the United States like a mystery saga, in which the clues are laid down by one generation which forgets and dies, until the traces are picked up unconsciously by their children and grand-children."[12] The covert intimacies of these two families would shape the phases of a national history over the next hundred years. In Rukeyser's telling, they run like a baseline through the biography, amplifying the very meaning of life writing into a new form.

"The lines of families," she writes in the biography's penultimate chapter, are like those of Gibbs's formulas or the culture of nations; they "mark the recurrence of energies . . . which may by analogy apply to any natural form." The analogy, she continues, "is as sensitive here as if itself were another form of life, delicate, vulnerable, and precious" (*Willard Gibbs*, 403). If John Quincy Adams met the elder Josiah Gibbs the day he came from New Haven to see the *La Amistad* prisoners, he left no record, nor did Gibbs. It took the next generation to make the connection. Henry Adams, the grandson of John Quincy Adams, would apply the younger Gibbs's rule to history, drawing out a relation between changes in physical and historical phases "with the daring of a fortune-teller or an inspired analogist" (411). The fusion of science and history that Adams proposed met with disagreement and even failure, and Rukeyser recognizes such obstacles as ingrained in the creative process. Indeed, the equilibrium of failure and luck, she announces, is the formula for invention. For her, luck is "a possibility word," a term that turns failure not toward increased effort but toward an encounter with unlooked-for relations. Such luck is the effect of "induced sensitization" and "a deftness in using good fortune" (421). Good fortune in her sense is nothing more than one's own prepared awareness. For Rukeyser, this awareness is lodged in "the hidden life of the senses, the vivid, speculative life of the mind" (1). The energy of imagination is thus suffused with the relational life-giving material of Eros, a "sensitization" that guides intuition and conditions invention (421).

The sensitivity of analogy as a form of representation and "itself another form of life" is a feature of Rukeyser's poetics and politics related to her interest in Eros. What she calls analogy's sensitivity is in essence affective attunement. I think about it this way: two things are analogous because they are similar but not the same—in other words, different yet related. In this sense, analogy is the linguistic equivalent of relational dependencies of many sorts: social and natural interactions, the making of meaning, and the naming of unnamable intensities. As a "form of life," analogy captures the relationality that enables survival: relations of labor from which a way of life is produced and a system of differences and similarities through which meaning takes place. Relations are the essential material structure of life making—at the molecular level, at economic and political levels, and as meaning-making systems. The recurring energies that traverse these relations are what in a broad sense we might call the transcorporeal forms of erotic "life energy," agents in the project of mutually dependent survival. This conception of analogy as a relational sensitivity is another name for the formal infrastructure of what Rukeyser later designates "ecology," or "the study of interrelations of living things" (390). She tracks analogies that span nonhuman and human phases, physical and historical phases in relations vital to life making, where "particles of intense life" are transmitted across multiple intimate environments (325). Some make up unattended relations, like "the hidden life of the senses" that accompanies the "speculative life of the mind" (1). Others "swing through history like a mystery saga," and Rukeyser tracks them in her biography of Gibbs as she pursues "the clues . . . laid down by one generation which forgets and dies, until the traces are picked up unconsciously" later.

That she understands this ecology of interrelations as deeply
entangled in the history of modernity is evident in her life of
Gibbs, where she acknowledges that "in a real and terrible sense
the world has become a Gibbs laboratory" (424). Precisely because of the multiple wondrous and awful monsters that his work
spawned, Gibbs is for her a monumental twentieth-century figure
at a time when "ecology—the study of interrelations of living things
and their environments was passing from the hands of botanists
to become a science of regions" and their physio-chemical groupings. The ecologist deals with the "biosphere," she explains, "the
space occupied by living things, that is the whole ocean, the earth
to some yards deep, and the air at some height.... This is a science
of mutually dependent survival, and Gibbs's work is used here"
(390–91). Gibbs's great paper on the phase rule laid the groundwork
for capital investment in the biosphere, what would become the
bioeconomy fueled by industrial chemical synthesis. It features
still in the science that enables the extraction of oil from coal, the
development of ammonium nitrate explosives, the production of
metal alloys and new forms of cement and ceramics. Agricultural
chemists use Gibbs's phase rule as a guide to augmenting soils. In
the early twentieth century, industrial chemistry was already in
the hands of global conglomerates, among them Union Carbide,
with its alloy plants in West Virginia. DuPont was developing synthetic polymers then, as was the German-based IG Farben. By the
mid-1920s, Farben was the largest chemical and pharmaceutical company in the world. Its scientists discovered the first anti-
biotic and were the first to produce agricultural pesticides. Farben
bought the patent for the pesticide Zyklon B, which was used to
disinfect the clothing of Mexican immigrants to the United States
and to kill over two million Jews, Roma, and homosexuals in the
gas chambers of Nazi Germany. Rukeyser connects Gibbs's legacy
to "the double history of democracy" in which invention is de-
ployed for life enhancement as well as destruction (424–25). She
sees the tendency of modern history to these dual ends as analogous to the relation of acceleration to entropy. Significantly, she
finds in Gibbs's discovery of the drive to dynamic acceleration in-
cremental reductions in the entropy that leads to nothingness. In
that process, a degree of freedom remains from which change in a
system is possible—a vulnerable and precious analogy. In writing

the life of Gibbs, she looks for dynamic equilibrium and finds in its analogues incompletion: two great New England families brought together by Africans whose sojourn falls into the background even as it refuses to go away.

"It is the poet's claim to ask these questions about a great scientist," Rukeyser announces in the biography's introduction: "What was his work and life? What kind of love produced them?" (11). To these questions of a master of science she brings the poet's passion for analogy and recasts it, transposing love onto new ground. "What the love, what the desires did, that led to these researches," she writes of Gibbs, was in some sense the material of entropy's reduction. It brought "a delicate and enormous human expansion" that "might grow and grow in the imagination, filling thought . . . enlarging the capacity of those who see the images, indeed enlarging their desire, until new gifts arrive" (382). Such sensitized imagination for Rukeyser can "bring a fuller life to a desperate time." Its power is the capacity to respond with love to the wishes of history, "however disguised, however premature and dark" (2).

Rukeyser calls her audacity as a woman and as a writer of poems who undertakes writing the life of a scientist "a presumption." As Däumer notes, her venture as a poet (and as a woman and a Jew) into highly specialized fields like science is egregiously presumptuous.[13] For a poet to ask about a great scientist, What was his work and life? What kind of love produced them?, is an audacious presumption because it defies the poet's training. It lets prescribed kinds of knowledge fall away from each other (*Willard Gibbs,* 11–13). When Rukeyser embraces presumption, I aim to follow her in order to discern meanings "that blaze up for our moment, meanings of struggle and wish and loneliness, meanings of war and structure and democracy that tie in with what we shall be doing tomorrow; meanings that must be reached" (13). These meanings may be inchoate remnants of another time or imaginative flashes of the fortunate inventor. "By suggestion," she announces, "by particles of intense life, the darkness of wish and love and abstract thought may be seen, and all the struggles in which they are caught" (325). This medium of suggestion is the presumptuous knowledge that binds poet and scientist as analogous discoverers devoted to life-expanding endeavors. Love binds their researches, Rukeyser explains, as desires that "bring a delicate and enormous human expansion to discovered images, so that they might grow and grow in the imagination." Its energy "enlarg[es] the capacity of those who see the images, indeed enlarging their desire, until new gifts arrive."

The scientist and the poet both give their energies to a creative process of combining, of tendering relations in the creation and description of systems. They share. Although their interests may seem far apart from each other, for Rukeyser their claims on systems are the same. Placing Gibbs's accomplishments next to those of his contemporaries, Herman Melville and Walt Whitman, Rukeyser finds that their writings "anticipate each other; welcome each other; indeed embrace" (11). Their knowledge is a pursuit not of types but rather of deviations, of new groupings, rhymes, and points where rules break down and history is made. A Yale scholar comes to listen to kidnapped Africans who had taken control of a slave ship. An aged ex-president who once ordered Andrew Jackson to attack the Seminoles steps up to defend those Africans. The trafficked Africans fade from the Gibbs's story, but they are not forgotten. Their traces appear in the public testimonies of African Americans a century later, traces that Rukeyser had already hinted at in her earlier work from the 1930s. They would haunt some of her most intimate relationships for the rest of her life.

Make Way for Eros, Sexuality, and Race

In 1903, a year after Gibbs published his highly influential textbook *Elementary Principles in Statistical Mechanics,* Alexandra Kollontai published *The State of the Working Class in Finland.* Gibbs died that year in New Haven, unmarried, at the age of sixty-four. Kollontai was thirty years younger, a mother who had hastily married an engineer in an act of rebellion and left him three years later. An ambitious intellectual, she had taken an interest in the Finnish fight for independence from Russia because her mother was Finnish. Kollontai would go on to become a leading supporter of women's struggles in the factories and at home. She wrote many books and pamphlets, among them *Sexual Relations and the Class Struggle* (1921) and *Red Love* (1923), both outlining the need for a revolutionary understanding of Eros. She held leading positions in the Communist Party, notably as head of the Women's Department and as a member of the Executive Committee, where she was the only leading Bolshevik to raise the question of the organization of women. By the 1920s, as Stalin rose to power, her ideas were stirring controversy. An oppositional voice within the party, she was eventually muzzled, her writings suppressed.[14] Because she was the only one raising fundamental questions regarding sexuality, her arguments were dismissed as extreme. She became more and more isolated and eventually retreated into self-imposed exile. She remains one of the most overlooked Marxist theorists. Her analyses open inquiry into the relation to capital of women's reproductive labor and sexuality and summon attention to the human capacity she called the "erotic." Only a handful of Western writers pursued that opening.[15] One of them was Muriel Rukeyser.

In raising the relation of the personal to class struggle and in confronting the intensified circulation of sexual discourses in the twentieth century, Kollontai was challenged to find an adequate vocabulary for what she called "the potential for loving," or Eros. She pointed to areas of social struggle that had been left to the utopian socialists and that expanded upon the work of Friedrich Engels and Isaac Babel. She aimed to articulate these features of human relationships as integral to the class struggle. Her 1923 essay "Make Way for Winged Eros: A Letter to Working Youth" targets what she calls "the relationships between the sexes" and addresses "a revolution in the outlook, emotions and inner world of the working people" that was taking place after the revolution.[16] One of the most interesting features of this essay is her attention to sexuality as historically produced and to Eros as energy "shaped by the aims of the historical moment" ("Make Way," 277). For Kollontai, Eros is a capacity that is organized historically and ideologically. She traces transitions in its historical forms as a feudal mode of life was displaced by a bourgeois social regime in which the family was no longer a productive unit but rather was being directed toward consumption and the accumulation and concentration of capital. She makes the case for understanding the historical appearances of this erotic capacity and its regulation in kinship, tribal, and state formations, in forms of friendship and loyalty, and in marriage and morality—all caught up in norms defining relations to the sinful, legal, or criminal. Eros was for her a complex capacity that had become privatized yet could be transformed and deprivatized into "love-comradeship" (285). For a social system to be built on solidarity and cooperation, she argues, it is essential that people educate the emotions into a sensitive understanding of others and a penetrating consciousness of the individual's relationship to the collective. "Working men and women, armed with the science of Marxism and using the experience of the past," she claims, "must seek to discover the place of love that corresponds to their class interests" (285). The task for developing such a consciousness was "not to drive Eros from social life but to re-arm him according to the new social formation . . . in the spirit of the great new psychological force of comradely solidarity" (291–92).

The terms she uses to name this erotic force can seem quaint and awkward today. Nonetheless, her attention to Eros opens the conceptual space to address affective intensity as historically shaped and as a powerful accompaniment to structural social change. In historicizing its cultural production across relations of property and reproduction, she is thinking of class and culture in dialectical terms and puzzling out how Eros features in a social transformation like the revolutionary one underway. Her theoretical insights both emerged from and spoke to a crisis of representation that was taking place in the early twentieth century as capital was transitioning into a new phase and as new social subjects and collectivities were appearing. That crisis was to constitute one of the limits of the Communist Party as its organizing efforts in the United States coalesced and transitioned into the popular front. Marxism and the party did not acknowledge Eros as a feature of political or social life, nor did they attend to its cultural formulations as sexuality or race. Eros's eclipse remains an undertheorized area of critical history and theory. Kollontai was one of the earliest Marxist theorists to confront that oversight. Her writings are both an analogue and a materialist precursor to the thinking of Muriel Rukeyser.

Kollontai's attention to Eros in the mid-1920s hovered as an undeveloped and eventually unrepresentable alternative to the abstraction of race and sexuality in the party's attention to the Negro question in the 1930s. Race and sexuality are both profoundly affective, erotic intensities. As hyper-ritualized, affectively saturated discourses, they are also part of the historical biopolitical process subsuming labor under capital, especially since

..e nineteenth century, when the commonsense understanding of race and sexuality began to translate what are essentially historical cultural products into discrete, biologically based identities. This strategy of body discipline differentiated the working-class subjects and bodies that became labor power.

Race and sexuality are cultural discourses—that is, historically produced representations. Although they may be presented as "natural," they are not, nor are their meanings fixed. They are better understood as sites of control and struggle over power relations in a way of life. To say that they are historical means that the affective intensities of their naturalized commonsense versions may be and have been thought otherwise, have been recast. A first step toward denaturalizing them is to comprehend race and sexuality as historical products and to see one's positioning by them as historical, too. In the wake of the 2020 murder of George Floyd, for example, many U.S. white people began to undertake this sort of work on race. The gay liberation movement of the late twentieth century and the materialist queer theory of the twenty-first provoked similar critical consideration of sexuality.

Kollontai's attention to the erotic was effectively suppressed just as the Communist Party's international political strategy focused on the so-called Negro problem in the United States and on support for the case of the Scottsboro Boys. Rukeyser was involved in that campaign. She attended the trial of Haywood Patterson in 1933, and she wrote about the case in terms that focused on working-class women's reproductive and affective labor. In these writings, Rukeyser explores the erotics of race and racism and implicitly advances Kollontai's forgotten legacy. Her own biography and personal papers offer a backdrop to this attention to the erotic life of race and racism, and I turn to them in chapter 7. Rukeyser's complicated relationship with a close friend from childhood, Nancy Naumburg, punctuated her 1933 trip to Patterson's second trial, and it conditioned her attention to the erotics of race in a poem about that legal lynching that she published a year later. Three years after the Scottsboro trip, Muriel drove with Nancy to West Virginia to document a mining disaster in which hundreds of men, most of them Black migrants, were dying of silicosis. The trip became the foundation for Rukeyser's extraordinary poem "The Book of the Dead." I consider one of the photographs Naumburg took on that trip as a hieroglyphic analogue to the poem, and I read it for the critical relation to race that it enacts. Finally, I turn to Rukeyser's complicated relationship with her student Alice Walker as it is represented in letters and in Rukeyser's last published poem. Here Nancy's shadow reappears, and we may glimpse a trace of Zora Neale Hurston as well, adhering to ineffable analogous intimacies in which the erotic life of race is instructively on display, entangled in the poem's intercepted music of lost loves and specular authority.

As I tracked Rukeyser's augmented concept of Eros, I found in her archived diaries and letters from the 1930s material that speaks to some of the energies that conditioned her imagination and her writing. Those energies remained an unruly undercurrent even to the end of her life. Throughout chapter 7, I consider this material for the evidence it offers of the tangled particles of intense life that shaped her attention to race in the 1930s and beyond. What emerges is an erotic infrastructure in which race and sexuality are encrypted. Most salient in her expansive conception of Eros is its attention to race and sexuality as covert companions and analogous agents. Their entanglement in her life and work offers instructive lessons on a cultural architecture whose scaffolding still conditions the presumptions of researchers and lovers, caregivers and students.

Seven
Shadowing the Erotics of Race Work in Muriel Rukeyser

"The Name Stands: Scottsboro"

The air was tense in the small town of Decatur, Alabama, during the last week of March 1933. The second trial of Haywood Patterson, one of the Scottsboro Nine, who had been convicted of rape and sentenced to death, was scheduled to begin. Muriel Rukeyser and two male friends, Hank Fuller and Ed Sagarin, had just arrived to report on it. They had driven from New York in a car she borrowed from her father. The presence of outsiders was already an irritant to officials and locals across the state, and the car's New York license plates made the group conspicuous. Muriel was reporting for the magazine of the National Student League (NSL), an organization of American Communist and Communist-sympathizing students at several New York colleges who were supporting the Scottsboro Boys' case.[1] Fuller was a reporter for the *Daily Worker*; Sagarin was the educational director for the Harlem section of the Young Communist League. On a previous trip, one of the men had been threatened with lynching, and in a few days, all three would be arrested for "contempt of court," the official euphemism for talking with Black organizers.[2]

In early 1931, a group of Black teenagers were riding the rails between Tennessee and Alabama. When a group of white hoboes got on the train, one of them stepped on Patterson's hand, and the incident sparked a fight. The Black youths succeeded in throwing the white boys off the train; the white boys then went to the nearest town and claimed they had been assaulted. A posse consequently intercepted the train and arrested the Black teens. Born in 1912, the son of a Georgia sharecropper, Patterson had left school in the third grade to work as a delivery boy. He soon became a veteran rider of the rails looking for work. That is what he was doing on the fateful day of March 25, 1931. Two years later, at the time of the trial, both Muriel and Heywood were twenty-one.[3]

In addition to the article she wrote for the NSL's *Student Review*, Rukeyser also wrote about the trial in an unpublished essay, "Women of Scottsboro," and in a poem entitled "The Lynchings of Jesus." She would include the poem in her award-winning volume *Theory of Flight,* published the year after the trip south. Both essay and poem offer the reader an unsettling orientation to the case by challenging common assumptions. The poem reinforces the effect with a structure of abrupt shifts. Disjointed formal structures were a signature modernist device appearing across written and visual culture after the Great War. They captured the deepening crisis taking place in the social relations of twentieth-century capitalism as an old order was cracking open and a new one was being patched together. Competition among imperial powers shifted global economic control after the war, and a decade of labor strikes and racial oppression simmered beneath the Roaring Twenties. New technologies were speeding up industrial production, changing the lived experience of time and space, and new consumer markets were invading and improving everyday life. Cultural norms that once seemed to hold the world together were fraying, too, and new forms of communication were emerging. Film was still a relatively new one, and Rukeyser was already working with it. Across genres, unexpected pairings and abrupt transitions conveyed the modern experience of fragmentation. High-modernist works from the 1920s registered this cultural crisis and responded; T. S. Eliot's "The Waste Land" (1922), James Joyce's *Ulysses* (1922), and Virginia Woolf's *Mrs. Dalloway* (1925) are three classic examples. If the center of an old order no longer held, they seemed to say, perhaps Art's myths and forms might offer a substitute, or at least some consolation.[4] Rukeyser used disjunction, however, to do something else. In these Scottsboro writings from the early 1930s, she explodes two central mythic figures of Western culture—woman and Jesus—to reveal the powerful erotic intensity marshaled by the public discourses of race and sexuality. In her essay and poem, these discourses appear as fragmented vectors of class struggle that ensure certain bodies will be devalued. Yet Rukeyser is quick to suggest what it might mean to recast both.

Her essay "Women of Scottsboro" does this by bringing into focus the women who are present in the courtroom. They include two of the mothers of the youths, the stenographer, a reporter from the *New Republic,* the sister of defense lawyer Joseph Brodsky, a white student, Black working women of Decatur (who made up one-third of the audience), and the white plaintiffs. Imagining "what the women must feel," she frames the courtroom scene in terms of the two most prominent pairs: the mothers, Ada Wright and Janie Patterson, and the accusers, Ruby Bates and Victoria Price.[5] She contends that "the fundamental issues of the Scottsboro case are more clearly tied up with the problem of the woman worker than has been pointed out," and she goes on to highlight two facts. First, "the boys were dependent on their mothers before they were sent out by freight to look for jobs"; and second, "prostitution has played so large a part" in their case. She reminds the reader that the state's star witnesses in the Sacco and Vanzetti case and in the case of socialist labor leader Tom Mooney were also prostitutes.[6] "All these," she asserts, "should bring the Scottsboro case home to the woman worker," adding, "the whole problem of employment for women must be examined, the facts of prostitution made clear."[7]

The essay demystifies white womanhood by making visible Black women's labor as mothers and white women's labor as sex workers. Rukeyser highlights the braided discourses of sexuality and race surrounding the case, and in doing so she confounds the commonsense separation of home and market, mother and whore. She discloses sexuality as a component of various forms of women's labor spanning the kitchen, the bedroom, and the streets where need and desire have been fragmented into the idealized asexual white mother and the Black maid, while the prostitute transgresses both respectability and whiteness.[8] She represents the Scottsboro mothers as doing the essential labor of care for their sons until the meager resources of a deprived Black household sent them both in search of other means for survival. At the trial, she sees these mothers as witnesses to their sons' sacrifice to a cause. Naming that cause "a deepening class struggle," Rukeyser challenges the Communist Party's neglect of domestic labor and echoes the organizing efforts of Black women in the streets and homes of Harlem. Thus, she astutely hints that the Scottsboro case brought race, gender, and sexuality into focus as integral to class conflict. It is a stunning assessment, one that would take over forty years to be fully elaborated by marxist feminists.

By April 8, Rukeyser was back in New York City, and on May 2, she was admitted to the hospital with typhoid fever. That month, Ruby Bates recanted her allegation of rape, but the Alabama jury delivered a guilty verdict nonetheless. On May 6, Louise Thompson led a caravan of buses to the march on Washington, a watershed event of women's solidarity that brought Ruby Bates, Janie Patterson, and Ada Wright so scandalously together, and she reported on the event in the June issue of *Working Woman*. Perhaps Rukeyser read Thompson's account of the march in the news or heard about the march from friends and allies in the NSL. I do not know when she wrote her essay on the women of Scottsboro or why she never published it. It remains buried in the archives, a shadow accompaniment to the writing and activism of Louise Thompson and the witness work of the Scottsboro mothers. Perhaps, as with Alexandra Kollontai's daring writing on Eros, Rukeyser's attention to sexuality and to women's labor as companionate features of this case was too at odds with the party's misrecognition of the entangled questions of woman and Negro. In any case, in these crossings historical opportunity cracks open. Then closes.

Throughout the early twentieth century, the U.S. Left, and the Communist Party in particular, were coming to terms with the imperial and biopolitical restructuring of class relations after World War I. As I mention in chapter 1, in 1928 the party embraced a policy that called for multiracial workers' solidarity and self-determination for the so-called U.S. Black Belt. It would materialize in their campaign of support for the Scottsboro Nine. Although the campaign kindled a wave of antiracist activity in the United States throughout the next decade, as a strategy it also had several drawbacks. The rhetoric of a "Black republic" did not speak to the immediate needs of poor Blacks and whites.[9] As Barbara Foley has argued, the premise that American Blacks in the South constituted a nation confused the concepts of nation and class. That is, it offered a Black alternative to nationalist ideology rather than exposing the concept of nation and the state itself as representing the interests of the ruling group. As such, the self-determination strategy ultimately contributed to the party's popular front direction in the mid-1930s, which represented the state as an arena open to control by all classes. This conception of the state, however, concealed its history as an apparatus that protects the interests of the owning class.[10] Furthermore, the nationalist framing of class in the party's Black Belt strategy foreclosed a more complex understanding of racist history and culture and its impact on the poor and working class of all races. Once party organizing focused on Alabama and the case of the Scottsboro Nine, violent repression hampered the recruitment of Black party members, and efforts to form interracial alliances were frequently suppressed by police raids and outright murder. The relation of both sexuality and race to a capitalist economy would remain opaque in the Left's political education and discourse until the 1960s.

Nonetheless, both were central to the Scottsboro case and were lethally distilled in the practice of lynching. Lynching thrived because of the fact of a Black majority, especially in the South, although lynching was not confined to that region. State and police impunity supported the practice, and intense emotional energies fueled it, channeled through the discourses of race and sexuality.[11] Anxieties about racial mixing adhered to the idealization of white womanhood by white men, who for generations feared the Black majority and the possibility that it would rise up to seize control of property and the social authority that control secured. In the antebellum South, access to the bodies of women both white and Black was reserved for white men, especially of the owning class, for whom it served as a sign of white patriarchal, economic, social, and legal power. The threat that newly emancipated Black men posed was symbolically represented through their imagined access to the bodies of white women. White anxieties about that threat translated into sexual fears attached to property and reproduction. Thus, the bodies of Black and white women and of Black men served as the symbolic and material ground on which white men staked their claim to authority.[12] Anxiety fueled that reality and propelled the call for the protection of white women. Retribution against fantastical miscegenation and emasculation was often the pretext for lynching. As a ploy for repressing the Black economic and political power achieved during Reconstruction and any hint of Black interference in white rule after that, the pretense of protecting white womanhood reinforced the state's mission. Alabama's Constitutional Convention had confirmed that mission two decades earlier when it affirmed that permanent white supremacy legitimized Jim Crow control over land and labor, wealth and women.[13]

Sexuality is in this sense the interdiscourse of a lethal form of racial violence. An "interdiscourse" is the sayable link that establishes a connection among material relations while keeping the purpose of those relations muted. As Ida B. Wells had contended decades earlier, lynching had nothing to do with actual rape. It was always about power. Reiterated in the smallest activities of daily life, it aimed to terrorize, silence, and dehumanize Black people. The fantastical image of white womanhood violated by a Black man was a powerful pretext for whites to ensure that Black people remained economically dispossessed, politically disempowered, and culturally subordinated and that the threat of organized Black power and resistance was kept in check. Reinforcing the divisions among the poor and working class, it also masked the history of Black and white consensual sexual intimacy and the lived realities of class dispossession in the South. Yet this potent ideological weapon eluded Communist organizing efforts in the South.[14]

The party's handling of the Scottsboro case was no help. Not only did it split the representation of sexuality and race, but it also used both in the most commonsense terms. In the Left's publicity and propaganda, the historical conditions driving the ideological distortion of the rape allegation remained opaque, as did the integral relation of sexuality and race to the division of labor. The white women accusers, twenty-one-year-old Victoria Price and seventeen-year-old Ruby Bates, were more or less the same age as the young men they accused. Both were poor young white women who lived, worked, and slept with Black and white people. Their contradictory testimony demonstrated they had fabricated the rape charge.[15] The defense attorney's tactic to discredit Price as a common prostitute unworthy of belief reignited the passionate defense of white womanhood in the courtroom and beyond. The

Left, meanwhile, had no theoretical weapons to confront the fury and panic marshaled by this discourse. Nor did the Left have any effective strategy to confront the anti-Semitism that surfaced in the case, linked to the claim that "Jew money" was coming in from New York. The claim circulated throughout the trial and flared up most dramatically during the summation for the prosecution at the second trial, when it was lodged against Communists as outside agitators and against defense attorney Sam Leibowitz, even though he did not work for the ILD. The bare facts of the case cannot convey the insidious and brutal power of these emotionally charged discourses. After their initial convictions, all nine of the young Black youths received death sentences, and appeals led to seven retrials and two landmark Supreme Court decisions. In the end, the defendants spent no less than six and as many as nineteen years in jail.

Rukeyser's first volume of poems, *Theory of Flight,* renders the Scottsboro case as a legal lynching. The poem "Gyroscope," which immediately precedes the poem on the case, serves as a preface of sorts because it introduces Eros as life-giving energy, a concept that will be central to her recasting of sexuality as an agent in lynching. As a meditation on "desire and its worth," "Gyroscope" posits material energy as elemental:

> Power electric-clean, gravitating outward at all points,
> moving in savage fire, fusing all durable stuff.

> (stanza 1, lines 2–3)

Importantly, this power is

> never itself being fused with any force
> homing in no hand nor breast nor sex.

> (stanza 1, lines 4–5)

Rather, it is associated with more diffuse forms of energy—modernization and desire. A gyroscope is a navigational instrument that guides aeronautic flight in relation to a fixed gravitational point. As such, it figures the poem's effort to understand the social orientation of dynamic energy.

"The Lynchings of Jesus" is a jarring sequel that brings together two modern technologies of power and energy: aeronautic flight and lynching. Here Rukeyser extends her attention to the cultural mediation of energetic intensities by confronting sexuality as a consolidation of energetic intensity into a charged public discourse. She confronts the Scottsboro trial's deployment of sexuality as rape and jams it into the figure of the Crucifixion, the Christian icon of salvation. In this rendering, quite pointedly, Scottsboro is not principally about race. Instead, the poem represents the trials as events in a long series of state-sponsored violent repressions of revolutionary struggle. In so doing, Rukeyser renarrates the sexual discourse used to justify lynching as historically and mythically produced erotic energy geared to confront a Black threat through brutal domination. At the same time, and importantly, the poem concludes that the energies swarming around the event of legal lynching might be marshaled for revolutionary aims.

A disjointed structure amplifies the poem's shock effect. Each stanza enacts a discursive jamming that unsettles and recodes the affects attached to the sexualization of lynching. In the opening stanza, the Crucifixion appears as a lynching and the false accusation of rape is translated into the lynched rebel's violation. Lynching is thus refigured as a spectacle of repression with the potential to incite rebellion. "This latest effort to revolution stabbed" appears in the arresting image of

> mild thighs split by the spearwound, opening
> in fierce gestation of immortality.

(1, stanza 1, lines 5–6)[16]

The image powerfully reorients the sexual discourse underpinning lynching and reroutes despair from a history of defeats to a celebration of

> eternal return, until
> the thoughtful rebel may triumph everywhere.

(1, stanza 2, lines 5–6)

The poem's second section, entitled "The Committee Room," features anonymous men who vote on the fates of several rebels: Sacco and Vanzetti, Tom Mooney, and "one Hilliard," a freeman and native of Texas lynched in 1897. The scope and reiterative force of lynching's affective power is implicit in the committee's consideration of sixteen large photographs of Hilliard's lynching. One member announces:

For place of exhibit watch the street bills.
Don't fail to see this.

(2, stanza 4, lines 12–13)

This attention to photography as a modern technology of spectacle and spectacular power is followed by a new voice inviting a listener to "Lie down dear, the day was long, the evening is smooth" (2, stanza 5, line 1). The disorienting effect of this intrusion, perhaps initiating a sexual encounter or merely the erotic pleasure of rest in a domestic space, is to jam the division between public and private, intimacy and abstracted violence. It also invites the reader to reconceive his or her own understanding of these distinctions as themselves violent abstractions.

The poem's third and final section, "The Trial," opens with an unnerving description of a verdant southern pastoral as the setting for state violence and impunity:

The South is green with coming spring ; revival
flourishes in the fields of Alabama. Spongy with rain.

(3, stanza 1, lines 1–2)

The gaps register a halting awareness of violation simmering beneath lush afternoons and spiritual redemption where

                              A red brick courthouse
is vicious with men inviting death.

(3, stanza 1, lines 6–7)

Mention of yards where hoboes are "gathering grains of sleep in forbidden corners" (3, stanza 2, line 5) draws attention to spaces of unmet need that conditioned the Scottsboro trial. A new form of transport interrupts the catalog of cities that the rails and migrants traverse (Atlanta, Chattanooga, Memphis, and New Orleans) as mail planes herald modern progress and communication. They

> burrow the sky,
> carrying postcards to laughing girls in Texas,
> passionate letters to the Charleston virgins.

> (3, stanza 3, lines 1–3)

In the early twentieth century, photographs of lynchings were promiscuous souvenirs that often appeared on postcards.[17] The irruption of that history and its sexual interdiscourse links pastoral and courthouse, laughing lovers and the Scottsboro Nine, making evident that the representation of the erotic, mediated by the cultural conventions that shape it, can be bound to ruthless state power. However, organized resistance also can marshal a very different Eros. The poem carries this insight into its promotion of a collective and passionate revolutionary subject: "all the people's anger finds its vortex here" (3, stanza 4, line 5), the speaker declares as she merges the Communist-led Scottsboro campaign with other revolts:

> Hammers and sickles are carried in a wave of strength, fire tipped,
> . . . .
> John Brown, Nat Turner, Toussaint stand in this courtroom,
> Dred Scott wrestles for freedom there in the dark corner,
> all our celebrated shambles are repeated here.

> (3, stanza 5, lines 1, 7–9)

This invitation to see the erotic in terms of a long American legacy of passionate revolt does not forget, however, the particularity of "Nine dark boys spreading their breasts against Alabama" (3, stanza 5, line 30). The ties that bind the spectacle of legal lynching to individuals whose lives are cut short in state prisons become clear as the poem paraphrases letters from a defendant to his mother:

> schooled in the cells, fathered by want.
> Mother : one writes : they treat us bad.   If they send us
> back to Kilby jail, I think I shall kill myself.
> I think I must hang myself by my overalls.

> (3, stanza 5, lines 31–34)

Colons and spaces convey the speaker's breathless anxiety in this desperate prison scene. The perspective then shifts abruptly to the

public square where the lynched Jesus has become a triumphant
risen rebel and

> a plane
> circles . . .
> . . . .
> The name stands :
> Scottsboro.

(3, stanza 7, lines 2, 3, 5, 6)

The poem that follows in the collection, entitled "The Tunnel,"
jams together the brutal loss of life and livelihood endured by coal
miners on strike in Harlan County with the nighttime rendezvous
of a pilot and his lover soon to be separated by his plane crash. It
ends by inviting the reader to find in loss across disjointed situations a "we" that is "beyond demand" and opens a scope to the
erotic that exceeds divisions between private and public, risk and
rebellion, summoning

> here is strength to be used
> delicately, most subtly on the controls and levers.

(3, stanza 17, lines 4–5)

Rukeyser's representation of Scottsboro thus draws out one of its
most virulent underpinnings, the affect-laden discourse of sexuality binding the twin alibis of Christian morality and white womanhood to racist ideology and a history of state-sponsored dispossession. Her essay's attention to the labor of Black mothers and sex
workers and her poem's focus on elemental energies that conceal
a violent history or inspire revolt is a stunning intervention. Here
she exponentially amplifies Kollontai's work, extends materialist
thought, and offers portable navigational maps of the uncharted
political power of Eros. She would continue to chart that terrain of
a national history in her next volume of poems, *U.S. 1*.

Looking for Nancy

When I first read the opening poem of *U.S. 1*, Rukeyser's "Book of
the Dead," I was struck by the figure of the photographer there, and
I went to the archives looking for her. What I found drew me into

a web of relationships inscribed in diaries, letters, and postcards, the richness of life making conveyed in particles of intensity. As anyone who has worked in archives knows, the experience is an intimate encounter. I often felt that I was getting to know and care deeply about those I met in the boxes of files, in the handwriting and typing of friends and family communicating their everyday news, joys, hurts, and recriminations. Rukeyser's clear penmanship in her diaries brought the anxieties and inspirations of her youth to life. Reading them, I felt like a spying sister. Letters from college friends with coded messages about forbidden love drew me in as a coconspirator. What I learned about her relationship with Nancy Naumburg gave me much to ponder as I set out to stitch that relationship into Muriel's involvement in the Scottsboro case as well as into other events in her life and what I was growing to understand as her broad conception of the erotic.

Before turning to their friendship, I begin with some details about Rukeyser. She was born in New York City in 1911, and grew up at 37 Riverside Drive with her sister, Frances, in an upwardly mobile Jewish family. Muriel's mother, Myra Lyons Rukeyser, was from Yonkers, an industrializing riverfront community in the Hudson Valley. Before her marriage to Lawrence Rukeyser, Myra worked as a bookkeeper. Lawrence was a construction engineer who came to New York from Wisconsin, where his grandfather had migrated in 1848.[18] By the 1920s, Lawrence was president of the Colonial Sand and Stone Company, and his business was thriving in the postwar building boom. Muriel later remembered him as "a businessman, a salesman really," who in her childhood and adolescence was building the "fierce skyscrapers" of New York.[19] As the Depression years unfolded and the building trades were no longer flourishing, Lawrence Rukeyser lost his business. Once he was able to find employment, however, the family weathered those years relatively comfortably. Bolstered by the resources of her upper-middle-class family, Muriel was able to attend college for two years.

Both her parents were secular Jews. Family legend held that Muriel's mother's family were descendants of the first-century Rabbi Akiba, the famous poet-scholar and martyr who resisted the Romans after the Bar Kokhba rebellion was defeated. She heard

Yiddish at home and "automatically" attended Hebrew school, where she became familiar with the Bible, but she characterized her family life as having no trace of the foods and songs that pass on tradition.[20] She recalled knowing that her governesses and maids were Christian but said she did not know what a Jew was until her mother quite suddenly turned to religion. For the next seven years, Muriel accompanied her to temple each week. Ever resourceful, during uninteresting sermons Muriel read the Bible and found it to be "closer to the city than anything that was going on or could possibly go on in the Temple."[21] Several years later, in her contribution to a symposium on the younger generation of American Jews, she wrote unapologetically about what it meant to her to be a Jew. It was an identity she neither denied nor embraced yet qualified, writing, "I grew up among a group of Jews who wished more than anything else, I think, to be invisible" ("Under Forty," 27). She renounced that impulse herself; reporting that in the search for ancestors, one can choose them "and go on with their wishes and their fight" (28). In that effort, she attempted to integrate four aspects of her life: as a poet, a woman, an American, and a Jew, yet she claimed not to know what part of that was Jewish (29).

Janet Kaufman's assessment that Rukeyser was essentially ambivalent about her Jewish roots thus seems right, as does her conclusion that Rukeyser's parents' resistance to Judaism was understandable given the anti-Semitism of the times and the assimilationist efforts of German Jews. Though not observant, Rukeyser nonetheless stayed in close contact with her rabbi for twenty years. She shared stories of Jewish history with her son but sent him to an Episcopal boys' prep school. Kaufman characterizes these choices as Rukeyser's management of the tensions "in a world where it was so important to 'pass.'"[22] The word "passing" captures some of the racial ambivalence of being Jewish in the twentieth century as Rukeyser returned to the subject multiple times, perhaps to learn its significance. She published a sonnet, "To Be a Jew" in the sequence "Letter to the Front" (1944), that opens with the lines

To be a Jew in the twentieth century
Is to be offered a gift.

(7, stanza 1, lines 1–2)

Much like the gift Du Bois mentions in *The Gift of Black Folk,* the gift is the wish for freedom that motivates "daring to live for the impossible" (line 14).[23] That gift would shape her relation to a heritage she mined for the political desires and energies that fueled "those who resist, fail, and resist" (line 7). It would also color her relation to race and racial justice.

As she dared to live for the impossible, Muriel refused to comply with convention and with her family's expectations that she would grow up to be a suburban matron. She married a man, and within two months the marriage was annulled. She decided to have a child (from a different man) and raised her son as a single mother. These refusals were not well received by her birth family, whose response was to disinherit her. She loved many women intimately, among them her literary agent and long-term partner for more than twenty years, Monica McCall. During the McCarthy era, the local chapter of the American Legion demanded that Sarah Lawrence College fire her, and the FBI hunted her.[24] She suffered a series of strokes beginning in 1965 but had the good fortune to live to see her poetry rediscovered by a new generation of women poets and her *Collected Poems* published. In 1978, she agreed to speak as part of a Modern Language Association panel on lesbians and literature, which would have been a public coming-out event for her, but her illness kept her from participating.

When the Great Depression hit, Muriel was just entering young adulthood and was still living with her family in New York City, where Communists were front-page news. Across the United States, as households crushed by the failed wage market were no longer able to provide for themselves, men and some women were taking to the road and the rails. In the next few years, over half a million transient men and women would wander across the country, either on foot or by train, searching for jobs. Some were desperate household supporters or young adults from the South, displaced from tenant farming and sharecropping or from cheap labor in southern mill towns, willing recruits to corporate projects like the one Muriel and Nancy would drive to visit in Gauley Bridge, West Virginia.

Nancy Naumburg (1911–1988) was Muriel's childhood friend. She also grew up on New York City's Upper West Side.[25] Like Muriel, she was the daughter of a Jewish family of means. Nancy's fam-

Nancy Naumburg, 1945. Courtesy of Margie Goldsmith and Lynne Miller.

ily had a more secure financial profile and ample social connections, due in large part to her extraordinary mother (about whom
I have more to say later). As girls, Nancy and Muriel both attended
the progressive Ethical Culture Fieldston School. Fieldston was
committed to racial equality, which made it a haven for secular
Jews who were restricted by quotas from attending other private
schools. Both attended Vassar College, Muriel enrolling the year

she turned sixteen.[26] Vassar was then a women's college with a reputation for producing progressive and politically minded students.[27] While there, both girls were part of Hallie Flanagan's Experimental Theater group. In May 1931, the group put on the play *Can You Hear Their Voices?* Written by Flanagan and her former student Margaret Ellen Clifford, it was based on a short story by Whittaker Chambers originally published in the *New Masses.* The play relates the effects of the first year of the Dust Bowl (and the second year of the Great Depression) on the farmers of a small town in rural Arkansas. Interjected into the story are scenes in Washington, D.C., that show a spectrum of reactions to the farmers' plight. This was agitprop theater and a precursor to the Living Newspaper theatrical form that Flanagan went on to champion as head of the WPA Federal Theatre Project from 1935 to 1939. The experience of working with Flanagan had a profound impact on the girls' future work and probably shaped their later collaboration.

By 1932, both young women were back in New York City from Vassar, Muriel having completed only two years of college as a result of her father's business's fall into bankruptcy. She took classes at Columbia and flying lessons at the Roosevelt Aviation School. She also maintained ties with two journals that she had helped found while at Vassar. Both she and Nancy became involved with Communist Party organizations that were supporting strikes and political prisoners and promoting the party's newly inaugurated attention to the southern Negro labor force. Muriel joined the NSL, which was providing relief, reporting on conditions in the Harlan County coal miners' strike, and supporting the case of the Scottsboro Boys. It was as a representative of the NSL that she took the trip south to Patterson's trial. She was also involved with the Film and Photo League, as was Nancy. This was an organization of film workers, many of whom were Marxists and Communist Party members dedicated to using film and photography for progressive social change. Muriel and Nancy both worked closely with a network of documentary filmmakers and writers and collaborated with them on numerous projects.[28]

Nancy began to establish herself as a filmmaker and photographer and became one of the scores of documentary photographers funded by the New Deal's WPA and Farm Security Administration, many of whom were inventing new narrative forms.[29] In 1934, in collaboration with the painter James Guy, and with the 16 mm camera that was a gift from her mother, Naumburg made a silent short film, *Sherriffed*, which documented the farm crisis. The following year, she photographed and coproduced another silent short, *Taxi*, detailing the taxi drivers' strike with footage of newspaper clippings and dramatized representations of union meetings. She also spent time in Hollywood, and in 1937 Norton published her edited anthology *We Make the Movies*, which documents the many hands required to produce a Hollywood motion picture.[30] Unfortunately, her short films, like many others from the 1930s, have been lost. The shifting cultural agenda of the following years in the United States conspired to eclipse her history as a pioneering filmmaker and eliminate the brief wave of federal support for independent filmmaking that she rode.

What more I know about Nancy and her relationship to Muriel is inscribed between the lines of Muriel's diaries and Nancy's letters to her from the Vassar years and after. They suggest that the young women had friends in common and that there was some tension between them. Writing to Muriel from Poughkeepsie, New York, in 1932, Nancy takes her to task for hurting people and for "actions that were predominantly experimental," a word that echoes the theater group's name but seems to refer to activities of another sort.[31] Muriel's diary indicates that she and Nancy spent a fair amount of time together in the city. By February 1933, the tension between them had increased. In one letter Nancy claims that Muriel "overdramatizes the romanticism": "It has been difficult, Muriel," she writes,

> for me to see you and not because I didn't want to. But I'm afraid in your demanding [my] presence that you demand more. I think you know how I feel about that. And whenever I tell you—there is that reiteration that lunging into a possibility which for me cannot exist. When you realize that it will be much easier for both of us. . . . But remember you are always very important to me.[32]

On March 19, 1933, Muriel wrote the following in her diary: "I love. I admire. I want. Hank Fuller at the *Daily*. NN." Fuller was one of the two friends from the NSL who would take the trip to the Scottsboro trial with Muriel. "NN" is the insignia she used for

Nancy—a hieroglyph of sorts written with the middle legs of the two Ns fused. The conflict in Muriel's feelings for Nancy continued through the next month as keeping up with the news of Scottsboro and organizing to attend the trial filled her time. By the end of March, as plans for the trip to Alabama solidified, the turmoil over Nancy did, too. The diary records Muriel's pain at Nancy's revelation that "there has never been any under layer or feeling." The next entry reads, "Wanted to phone NN didn't. Scottsboro trial slated for today. . . . Hank. The South. Vassar. Scottsboro. Negroes. Scottsboro possible." The next day the diary records a swirl of feelings: "Much talk. Scottsboro. Nancy, no, no Nancy, maybe Nancy. Hank for dinner. Scottsboro, Scottsboro, Scottsboro."[33] It is not clear if Scottsboro here is code for Nancy's potential presence on the trip, the trial itself, time with Hank, vengeance on Nancy, or all of these. By the morning of March 28, Muriel, Hank Fuller, and Ed Sagarin were on the road headed to Decatur and the trial.[34] Upon their return to New York, Muriel recorded in her diary: "Things different after Decatur experience. Two weeks without Nancy. Though time must have given me resolution and determination of a sort." Two days later, she sees Nancy and recorded, "Today I was given something without asking, without being forced. I think I'll sleep well," followed by the NN sign.[35]

At the end of April, Muriel wrote a note in her diary that is a reckoning with the environment of erotic intimacy she sees as elemental to the political aesthetic she was in the process of inventing:

> My hope for myself is in relationships as well as writing. . . . It is not sensationalism because it is all there always, in front of me, as long as I put my hand out for it. And if the hand, meeting flesh—Yes. I know. Little explosions in my thorax, like a face exploding, like a recurrent wave, like certain days. You see. And then there is the very personal love, which I have not spoken directly about in this book, of a line, a cadence of speech, a muscle's bending. This I keep. I want to write things down. I will too. And I will rest my love on whom I love. Selah.[36]

Ten days later, she was hospitalized with typhoid fever. After recovering, she attended the student conference at Columbia and wrote a report on the Scottsboro trip for the *New Masses*. Perhaps then she also drafted her eloquent essay "Women of Scottsboro." A year later, the tension between the friends had not abated. In August 1934 Nancy wrote from Cape Cod, "It would be a lot better seeing you without knowing your subtle insistence, your constant double strain of word and thought. There is nothing to be done about the situation, really."[37] The following summer, Muriel invited Nancy to join her in Provincetown, Massachusetts, but Nancy was on a filming expedition to Nova Scotia and could not get down. That year Muriel published her first volume of poems, *Theory of Flight*—which won the Yale Younger Poets award—with its extraordinary sequence on Scottsboro. In the spring of 1936, she and Nancy traveled together to West Virginia, and in 1937 Nancy's correspondence with Muriel from this period ended.[38]

Muriel's love for Nancy appears in the diary as a life-enhancing energy even as its refusal registers as loss and perhaps shame. As all of that, it leaves an unverifiable imprint on her work. Helen Lynd, who features later in this story, wrote of shame as "almost impossible to communicate," as it is concerned with uncodified details and a diffused feeling that lacks an expressive language.[39] One of the questions Nancy's appearance in the archive raises for me is how to read her irruption into Rukeyser's poetic documentation of racial injustice as a national problem. The relationship between what we might crudely call "sex and race" here is neither simple nor inconsequential.

Sharon Holland confronts some of this complexity by way of what she calls "the erotic life of racism": "The autonomy usually attached to erotic choices," she asserts "should be reevaluated to think through" the psychic life of racism embedded in these attachments.[40] She posits that the Black–white binary, still fundamental to race politics in the United States, is critical to such a project, and she wants us to "imagine what happens to the 'white' side of the equation" and "to our conceptualization of the 'us' when desire has been abstracted" (45). Holland recognizes that the life of the erotic is "cradled in the definition of what it means to be human in the first place, to be dependent on and enabled by sensations and affects" (46). If the psychic life of racism thrives in environments where intimacy is shadowed in abstracted desires, what would it mean, Holland asks, to return race to the landscape of the erotic and to address the erotic in terms of its value both for and against capital? Blackness, she contends, produces erotic value, and she wants to unearth the inescapable racial features of that value. Implicit in her argument is the fact that the historical formation of the erotic is premised on the abstracted devaluation of Blackness as object of the white gaze. It is encoded in cultural conventions of seeing, a visual culture that captures the other as object of the gaze, the white gaze. As such, Blackness is devalued culturally. This devaluation enables the provision of cheap labor that produces profits and legitimizes the state domination and policing that protects the profit margin. Thus, Blackness becomes valuable by virtue of its devaluation. That the erotic is nestled in that relation is Holland's insight into the dynamics of racial power, the energetic intensities that summon consent and drive the reproduction of racism. Lynching postcards are an extreme example. The technology of the camera and its photographic product made the postcard a ready tool in the reproduction of the white gaze and the erotic intensity attached to the devaluation of Blackness. As the critical history of photography has disclosed, however, there are gaps, apertures if you will, in the conventional dynamics of that technology when the photographer puts the erotic to work other-wise. What happens then to both sides of the race equation, to the conceptualization of an "us"?

Nancy and Muriel's collaboration offers some hints. They originally planned to combine photographic images and text from their trip to West Virginia in 1936 to document a mining disaster, but the collaborative project never materialized as initially planned. Rukeyser did write a film script about the disaster, however, and she documented it in her magisterial poem "The Book of the Dead."[41] Naumburg took hundreds of photographs during the trip; unfortunately, only three of them survive. In what follows, I consider one of them, *George Robinson's Kitchen in Vanetta*, in conjunction with the section of Rukeyser's poem entitled "George Robinson: Blues" as vestiges of that planned collaboration. I read them as analogous texts that invite the viewer to conduct "race work" on the erotic intensity and specular authority of whiteness, on the limits and possibility of an "us."

As I discuss in previous chapters, an ontological and propertied relation to space, often unconscious, conditions the authority of whiteness. This authority also informs the perspective of documentary witness. The powers of property ownership that propelled discovery, race difference, modernization, and scientific invention remained fundamental to the dialectical relation between progress and brutality under capitalism, and they preoccupied Rukeyser. The contradiction registers in her representations of the camera and the photographer's specular authority. As figures and agents of realist documentary, camera and photographer can mask the abstraction of white authority and desire in the specular history of race. What I am calling, after Holland, "the erotics of race work" is a critical relation to a text that works on that abstraction. Taking "race" as a social invention, race work tracks the erotic effects of race. To work on the erotics of race is to initiate an investigation of the energies consolidated in images (both graphic and photographic) and draw out their historical and social reasons for being. The "work" takes place as the reader maps the assemblage of images, attuned to the intensities that assembly conveys or elicits as well as the historical relations of property, power, and possibility the images reproduce, shelter, or interrupt. Rukeyser's "Book of the Dead" invites us to do this work.

"The Man on the Street and the Camera Eye"

"The Book of the Dead" is a daring renarration of American history as shaped by a heritage of vision, violence, discovery, and conquest. The poem is written in multiple voices (those of a social worker, miners, a mother, an engineer, official congressional testimony, even a chemical formula), and it includes excerpts from the Egyptian *Book of the Dead*. Its narrative voice places the accumulated documents into a sweeping national story. Its opening directs the reader:

> These are roads to take when you think of your country
> and interested bring down the maps again.

In the spring of 1936, Muriel and Nancy drove these roads to report on the Hawk's Nest Tunnel disaster. Five years earlier Union Carbide and Carbon Corporation had set out to dig a three-mile tunnel through the sandstone mountain promontory called Hawk's Nest outside the town of Gauley Bridge in Fayette County, West

Virginia. Race difference was central to the ensuing catastrophe, the Depression era's worst industrial poisoning. For the work of drilling, nipping, and mucking in the deepest part of the tunnel, the company hired migrant men, most of them Black recruits from southern coastal states. Only a small percentage of the workers were local white men.

Groundbreaking began on March 31, 1930. The tunnel was intended to divert a portion of the New River to a hydroelectric power station and dam. The project was supposed to provide hydroelectric power for the community, but in fact the power went to Union Carbide's nearby alloy plant. Once the company realized that the workers had encountered almost pure silica, a valuable compound used in processing steel, they expanded the tunnel project to become a mine. The cheaper, faster drilling process the company demanded exposed almost three thousand workers to silica dust. Lacking protection, within a few years hundreds of them died of the lung disease silicosis.[42] Estimates of the number of dead ranged from two hundred to one thousand, the majority of them Black men. Neither Union Carbide nor its contractor, the Rinehart and Dennis Company out of Charlottesville, Virginia, ever admitted wrongdoing.[43] In 1935, the *New Masses* broke the Hawk's Nest story nationally, and it became a cause célèbre of the New York Left. The Labor Subcommittee of the U.S. House of Representatives began a hearing on the incident the following January.[44] For a couple of weeks, the country absorbed the event's gruesome details through the mainstream media, but despite the subcommittee's urging, the federal government never took up a full investigation.

Like its Egyptian analogue, Rukeyser's poem is a hieroglyphic constellation. Images document deadly silica, spectacular technology, the camera lens, and a sweeping epic narrative of the ecology of a disaster.[45] Drawing from her work in film editing and production, Rukeyser likened the frame of a film to the image of a poem. The single image takes its place in a sequence that reinforces that image. Her term for the sequence was "cluster" or "constellation," a "gathering together of elements so that they move together according to a newly visible system."[46] In this sense, hers is a poetry of meeting places, and in that respect, it is much like the systemic thinking of Gibbs.[47] The camera lens joins a constellation of images of silica—the material for glass made into a technology of specular authority. Race, and its corollary racism, feature in the constellation as forces shaping what is seeable as a charged facet of a nation's long history. The Black bodies in "The Lynchings of Jesus" occupy space but do not speak history; in "The Book of the Dead," at least one of them does, George Robinson. Robinson came to West Virginia from Georgia. When silicosis took so many lives, he was the spokesperson for the Gauley Bridge Committee of workers and their families who advocated for the victims. In the poem, Robinson's testimony is rendered as blues, a musical genre that bears witness, at times ironically, to a long history of African American oppression. Robinson announces ironically in his section of the poem:

> Gauley Bridge is a good town for Negroes, they let us stand
>   around, they let us stand
> around on the sidewalks if we're black or brown.

> (lines 1–3)

Of course, in the Jim Crow South, Blacks were notoriously not allowed to stand around. Vagrancy laws kept them out of sight, subject to arrest or worse if they were standing around on the street. George Robinson goes on to map some of those street spaces, measured by the ailing lungs of affected workers:

> The hill makes breathing slow, slow breathing after you
>   row the river,
> and the graveyard's on the hill, cold in the springtime blow.

> ("George Robinson: Blues," stanza 2, lines 1–2)

It is hard to read these lines in 2020 and not think of George Floyd calling out, "I can't breathe." We learn later that in the cornfield of the undertaker's mother, hundreds of bodies were tossed into unmarked graves.[48] "The camps and their groves were covered with the dust," Robinson's breathy voice continues,

> Looked like somebody sprinkled flour all over the parks
> and groves.

> (stanza 8, line 2; stanza 9, line 1)

Silica appears in the poem as toxic dust and as the scientific formula for a component crucial to Union Carbide's profitable new alloy. The poison silica reduces the bodies of the workers to disposable objects and dissolves the distinction of whiteness in a tableau that perversely reinforces the value of Blackness. In the final stanza, George Robinson announces:

> As dark as I am, when I came out at morning after the
>   tunnel at night,
> with a white man, nobody could have told which man was
>   white.
>
> (stanza 10, lines 1–2)

The image captures color as the imaginary difference embedded in the calculus of labor's value. It both apprehends and interferes with the tyranny of the visual as the empirical anchor for race. In a flash, the spectator realizes that the toxic white dust indiscriminately abstracts the bodies of white and Black workers into a valuable disposable workforce. At the same time, Robinson's whitened image confronts the spectator with his or her own will to discriminate as it colludes with this abstraction. Displaying the marked/unmarked disposable body, the image simultaneously reiterates and suspends the long-standing value to capital of the concept of race, rooted as it is in a history of branded flesh and abstracted labor.

Nahum Chandler's book *X: The Problem of the Negro as a Problem for Thought* is a helpful guide for coming to terms with this image of Robinson's and its contribution to the critical race work of "The Book of the Dead." Chandler reads W. E. B. Du Bois's autobiography *Dusk of Dawn: An Essay toward an Autobiography of a Race Concept* (1940), another experiment in life writing, and finds in it a key to understanding race as a historical structure for identity, what Chandler calls "the question of difference or the question of the other."[49] Du Bois situates this structure within the long history of modernity in which the conception of the human rests upon a colonial, capitalist project that required the concept of race. He locates in the concept of racial difference an epistemic horizon, a problem for thought. For Du Bois, Chandler reminds us, "it was not the color that was crucial, but rather the way in which color was understood."[50] He recognizes the historical requirements and benefits—the value—of this understanding as it was lodged in the economic foundation of modernity. What he calls "the income bearing value of race prejudice as the cause and not the result of race inferiority" justified low or no wages for Negro or Asian laboring classes.[51]

⁂ Chandler follows Du Bois as he locates the hidden term in this marking, or that which is not abstracted as a nameable identity. Through this unnamed remainder, the inhabiting of identity takes place. For Du Bois, this hidden term is both "racial mixture" and, more fundamentally, the profitable use of labor and the effective political division of labor it challenges. In Robinson's image, we glimpse this hidden term when the silica dust erases racial difference. I want to read this figure as a dialectical image analogous to Naumburg's photograph *George Robinson's Kitchen in Vanetta*. By reading both poem and photograph as offering companionate dialectical images, we can apprehend in Nancy and Muriel's collaboration a practice of documentary witness provoking work on the erotic value of race. Robinson's testimonial, preserved in Rukeyser's poem, conveys imaginary racial difference as central to the value calculation of labor power in wage work. Naumburg's kitchen photograph draws us into a complementary value-making space. Similarly, Robinson's testimony, rendered as "George Robinson: Blues," captures race as a cultural invention in a temporal medium (music) while the photograph's title and image emphasize space. We know that at some point on their trip Naumburg visited Robinson's home in Vanetta, probably accompanied by Rukeyser. Vanetta was a segregated Black camp, more a cluster of shacks than a town, and by 1936 it was riddled with silicosis.[52] The photograph Naumburg took there is an interior still life, a form that appears in several of her other surviving photographs. In the photograph of Robinson's kitchen, objects function metonymically as parts that stand in for an absent whole—a household and the activities of subsistence. I am interested in this absence as negative space that thrusts unnamed actors into the present of the viewer.

Shawn Smith has claimed that at the heart of photography is an intense desire, and a failure, to see. She is interested in Walter Benjamin's thinking on photography, what he called "the optical unconscious," a photograph's ability to make visible what usually evades perception, to disclose how much we do not see, how much of ordinary seeing is blind. The optical unconscious of photography "draws us to the edge of sight." It offers "a deeply uncanny sensibility," the "revelation and recognition that we inhabit a world unseen." It reveals the "blind spots of the mind" as "the viewer is made aware of all one did not, and could not, see." As Smith comments, these things not seen invite leaps of imagination.[53]

Most immediately unseen in the photograph are the people who live there. Who are they, and how many of them were in the room when the photograph was taken? What relations shaped their life together and condition what we see? I imagine Nancy with her camera, Muriel there as well, taking notes as George talked. George's wife, Mary, must have been nearby, perhaps wondering why Nancy wanted to take a photograph of the wall. Imagining these invisible ones, I can feel the authority of the two white women with the tools of their profession in hand. Did their presence provoke an awkwardness, even apprehension, on the part of the family hosting them on this occasion of racial mixing? We do not know what navigations of space and time, desire and fear, might have taken place in this room. What we have is the photograph and the work it does on us and with us as what-has-been flashes into view. The spare objects set against a gray wall and the medium of the black-and-white photograph can easily conjure for some viewers the formalist conventions of modernist documentary. Inserting the photograph into a relation with the section of "The Book of the Dead" entitled "George Robinson: Blues," however, disrupts that formal aesthetic option. As in the poem's montage, here the concept of race seems barely operative, absorbed into a constellation of negative spaces. Hovering on the edge of the visible, this negative space is subsumed into an assemblage of unembellished life making and its invisible value. It confronts the viewer with a knot that characterizes the ubiquitous documentary form.[54] As Jeff Allred explains, the figure of a knot conveys that the image disrupts the viewer's comfortable position by "emphasizing the obscurity of the other . . . or, better, its constitution in a process that reveals subterranean connections linking self and other."[55] Let's linger with these negative spaces.

The photograph's title, *George Robinson's Kitchen in Vanetta,* incorporates into the propertied history of an English patronymic the anonymous ones who were most likely to have used these objects—Mary, surely, and perhaps others. We do not know if George and Mary had any children or other relatives living with

Nancy Naumburg, *George Robinson's Kitchen in Vanetta*. Metropolitan Museum of Art, Walker Evans Archive. Copyright Estate of Nancy Naumburg Goldsmith. Image copyright Metropolitan Museum of Art. Image source: Art Resource, N.Y.

them who might have cleaned and hung these pots and pans or chopped wood for the stove. It is likely that they did. We do not know what other labor Mary might have done—laundry, no doubt, for the family and perhaps others. She may have kept a garden, assisted births, nursed babies, or cared for elders. What we do know is that within four months of Nancy's and Muriel's visit, George Robinson had sickened and died "of heart trouble" at age fifty-one, leaving Mary to manage and carry on somehow.

In his autobiography, Du Bois traces his paternal line to a great-grandfather, James Du Bois, a landholder and slave owner who had as a common-law wife one of his slaves. In the Du Bois family tree, she has no name. "She appears, if she can be said to appear at all, as an absence, or under the sign of absence, an invisible X, perhaps."[56] *X* is the mark of the freed ones' signature of anonymity as well as the sign of the chromosomal X—both marks of difference. For

Chandler, this X is also the figure of the "structure of intermixture [that] remains operative and functioning, sedimenting its irreducible difference, its X, in the very space of supposed or projected purity."[57] This mark of the other, he explains, is the *residue* of violence across what-has-been, propelled into the reiteration of all racial and other categories. Echoing Hortense Spillers's mapping of the disavowal of slave mothers and their lineage within the paternal line of slavers, Chandler affirms the maternal X as the name of both an unnamed remainder and a possibility within the binary structure of white supremacy's racial violence, a crisis always to be managed.[58] The figure of this unnamed remainder also opens the abstracted lines of color (and gender or lineage) onto another possible line of thinking, an invitation "to look at ourselves in a radically *other* way."[59] Du Bois's realization that his grandfather could not be understood as categorically Black or white or neither is the paradox that underlies race or, as Chandler puts is, the nonpertinence of all social designation. An exorbitant idea indeed.

Like the *X*, the absent residents of the house and the visitors in the room are an unnamed remainder. This remainder is inseparable from Robinson's wasting body, from the useful objects that conjure the life-making labor of women that accompanies the life-wasting labor of wage work, and from the documentary collaboration unfolding through this particular encounter one day in March 1936. This remainder crystallizes the event of the photograph into a dialectical image. The dialectical image has a particular pertinence in visual culture, especially photography. "Dialectical image" is Walter Benjamin's term for the object of the reader's or viewer's gaze, an object that captures life at a standstill as the spectator takes up an image into her or his own time and in so doing throws a pointed light on what-has-been. In the process, the past is actualized and comes together with the present in a flash to form a constellation. For the dialectical image, the relation of what-has-been to the present is not temporal progression but "image, suddenly emergent" and bound to the possibility of a collective, revolutionary subject.[60] To read an image as dialectical is to enter into a coincident time and space and a collaborative effort.

Ariella Azoulay pursues this line of inquiry in her theory of photography. For Azoulay, "photography is much more than what is printed on photographic paper. It bears the seal of the photographic event."[61] Reconstructing this event requires what she calls "the civil contract of photography," a skill that is an extension of Benjamin's conception of the image. The skill of the hypothetical spectator enables the photographic image to do its work of forming a community around the image through the act of watching.[62] In the photo-event of *George Robinson's Kitchen in Vanetta,* a constellation of actors and relations is formed. Migrant laborers from the South come to carve a mountain tunnel in aid of hydropower. Young travelers from the North bring technologies to document a disaster that corporate profiteering created and the state ignored. Anonymous others sustain daily life with the tools for feeding, sheltering, and warming. We as viewers join them, collaborating in an event that is a distillation of losses and possibility.

That Nancy Naumburg and Muriel Rukeyser were Jews and were managing on this trip a love that dare not speak its name adds another dimension to their place in this event as artists bearing witness to a national emergency. Reading these fragments of their documentation as a collaboration with George and Mary Robinson and with anonymous others past and future allows us to discern the power of dialectical images. From an untimely encounter, a constellation of relations is produced in which the concept of race as the scaffolding of violence and loss materializes and fades. As in the dusk before dawn, distinctions blur and become seeable as something else. In a flash a different temporality appears, its erotic charge allowing us to grasp the concept of race in a radically new way and perhaps to also see a new relation to life making emerging from the darkness.

The most striking feature of Naumburg's photograph is its attention to objects in a room. What do we make of this strategy? I imagine Nancy and Muriel discussing whether still life might effectively interrupt documentary realism's pretense of transparent representation. Did they consider whether still life too closely mimics modernist celebrations of aesthetic form, or whether, rather, it amplifies documentary photography's conventions, which were well-known to them both? In this instance, does still life more effectively represent the unnamed wives and mothers as an absence perhaps all too soon to disappear from Vanetta like George Robinson himself? The conjuring powers of still life are, curiously, a tactic that Rukeyser also uses in her poem, where Nancy is both present and absent, appearing only in the form of an anonymous photographer and her camera: the documentary eye.

If the collaborative project that inspired the trip, like the intimacy Rukeyser desired with Nancy, was intercepted, then the poem plots a reparation of sorts in the emblematic figure of the photographer, an abstracted observer intimately bound to the I and the eye of the narrator and reader.[63] The photographer's perspective,

> surveying the deep country, follows discovery
> viewing on groundglass an inverted image,

("The Road," stanza 10, lines 2–3)

is fused with the technology of documentary, whose complicity with the relations it surveys is hinted at in the reference to the lens, whose glass is made from silica.[64] "Camera at the crossing sees the city" of Gauley Bridge, we are told, and it registers "the deserted Negro standing on the corner" as one item in a still life.[65] The poem intercepts this static tableau, however, as a little boy running with his dog "blurs the camera-glass fixed on the street."[66] The "deserted Negro" and the boy appear much like the men in one of Naumburg's other surviving photographs from the trip, an outdoor still life that also captures arrested motion: a railroad track curves past a handful of grey shacks into the misty distance where figures in white shirts and dark pants are barely visible, clustered under a white sign reading "Vanetta." Like George Robinson's testimony, this photograph makes still life a confounding experience for the viewer, who is drawn along the tracks toward the figures, the desire to discern racial difference in them thwarted as the figures blur and the space opens, pulling the viewer into the mist—or is it actually silica dust?

A somewhat different erotics of race work is elicited in the section of Rukeyser's poem entitled "Absalom." Here Emma Jones speaks as the grieving mother of three sons who died of silicosis and the wife of a husband who also contracted it from mining the tunnel. She was a member of the workers' defense committee, and the Jones case was the first of the lawsuits. The constellation formed by her account includes quotations from the Egyptian *Book of the Dead*, a collection of spells inscribed in hieroglyphs and found on papyrus scrolls and amulets in the pyramid burial sites of kings and queens. The spells were intended as protection for the deceased in the afterlife. Their purpose was to ensure safe passage through the tribunal before Osiris, god of the dead. The central ceremony in the tribunal was the weighing of the heart of the deceased, the heart being considered the source of thought, memory, and emotion. Inclusion of these spells in the tomb almost guaranteed the heart's proof of a life well lived and thus safe passage into the afterlife. The incantations resemble those found on Egyptian heart scarabs. Rukeyser may have known about heart scarabs, as U.S. archeologists had recently unearthed some from the tomb of Hatnefer, mother-in-law of Hatshepsut, only the second woman to become pharaoh. Spell 30B appears in Emma Jones's account as *"My heart my mother my heart my mother,"* aligning her with ancient African matriarchs and with a funerary ritual of protection and transformation.[67] In titling her testimony "Absalom," Rukeyser conjures the beloved son of King David, thus folding together Jewish and African histories.

Other excerpts from the Egyptian *Book of the Dead* punctuate Jones's testimony and conjure a constellation of relations:

> *I have gained mastery over my heart*
> *I have gained mastery over my two hands*
> *I have gained mastery over the waters*
> *I have gained mastery over the river.*

("Absalom," stanza 6, lines 1–4)

The incantation "gained mastery" recasts mastery's association with slavery and a history of dispossession as the voice claims control of the body and orients the deceased loved one into a quest for justice. The images of mastery span human and natural bodies and suggest the technological control over nature that the power plant represents, even as building the plant breeds the destructive power of chemical death. This unwinding and rewinding of mastery's connotations echoes Rukeyser's attention to the dialectical features of modernity even as it also solicits the reader to enact race work on the relations the poem enacts in bringing together Emma Jones, Absalom, Hatnefer, and Hatshepsut.

The poem sequence making up "The Book of the Dead" concludes with an expansive review in a section entitled "The Book of the Dead." The section catalogs what is revealed when

These roads will take you into your own country.

. . . .

into a landscape mirrored in these men.

(stanza 1, lines 1, 3)

In the sweeping final history, the speaker issues instructions to "widen the lens," to "photograph and to extend the voice," to bear witness "as epilogue, seeds of unending love."[68] Nancy's anonymous imprint morphs into the product of her work and the project of documentary witness, representing the labor of surveyors and planters, those who drill their deaths or farm and starve, strikers, soldiers, and pioneers. The affective residue of Nancy's relationship to Muriel is here distilled, as perhaps only literature or dreams can be, into an incommensurable essence between form and substance, expression and appearance—that is to say, a block of unprocessed material.

In his book on shame as a postcolonial event, Timothy Bewes reminds us that Marx writes of shame as an affective expression of unprocessed material: the simultaneous impossibility of identifying and disidentifying with one's own country. In a letter to his friend Arnold Ruge in 1843, Marx writes that shame is "a kind of anger turned in on itself. And if a whole nation were to feel ashamed it would be like a lion recoiling in order to spring."[69] It is an interesting diagnosis, to think of a country not as guilty but as ashamed. It would be a realization not that one's country *did* some things wrong but, rather, that in a fundamental way it *is* wrong. The difference turns from ethics measured by a moral code bent on reform to a politics that understands a nation as structurally and essentially based on incommensurable unprocessed material. "The Book of the Dead" elicits the fractured relations underpinning American history and registers them in awe and shame in the face of technological feats and avoidable death, a message conveyed by a photographer who views on ground glass an inverted image. That the speaker in the poem reads that inverted image is more than a trope for documentary realism's political task, however. It does the work of disclosing unspeakable losses symbolically compressed in the poem's fusion of history and art. They irrupt in the foreground of the poem and also in the companion photograph's still life. The erotics of race work that each solicits calls upon the reader/viewer to apprehend distinctions that we want to call "race" even as they blur into something else. Thus, we are provoked to see anew and to look at ourselves in a radically new way. The process touches only lightly on other unspeakable relations that condition the incomplete project of photographer and poet, an unnamed remainder belying mastery of the heart. I turn to that unprocessed material next.

"Deep in the Story of Us All"

The first testimony in "The Book of the Dead" and in the congressional hearings on the Hawk's Nest disaster was given by a social worker named Philippa Allen. Allen worked at the Jacob Riis Settlement House on Henry Street in New York City, and she traveled to West Virginia for several months over two summers in the early 1930s. Like Muriel and Nancy, Philippa Allen was a woman on a mission. She entered this community as a mediator, believing her investigation would "help in some manner."[70] She testified publicly to stories from the miners that otherwise might have gone unrepresented. As a contributor to a burgeoning documentary culture that aimed to give voice to the details of ordinary people's suffering, Allen shared her investigation in an article in the *New Masses* and in congressional testimony.[71] Describing her time hitchhiking alone back and forth along the mountain roads between the towns surrounding Gauley Bridge, however, Allen became suspect in the eyes of the state. Questions posed to her by the congressional committee insinuated that a good girl would not be out there on her own. Her answers dodged innuendos of a tarnished reputation, since a woman on the road alone was open to being seen as either a floozy or a lesbian.

Philippa Allen may have reminded Muriel of Nancy's mother, Elsa Herzfeld Naumburg, who is a pivotal figure in this story. Elsa Naumburg was a social worker and teacher. She graduated from Barnard College in 1903 with a degree in sociology, received her master's from Columbia University's School of Social Work two years later, and attended the New York School of Philanthropy. She conducted research while helping immigrants living in a New York City tenement, which became the basis of a book, *Family Monographs,* for which Elsie Clews Parsons, also a Barnard graduate (class of 1896), wrote the foreword. Parsons had a PhD in sociology from Columbia (1899), where she studied with Franz Boas, and she later took a position at the New School, where she was one of the cofounders of anthropology.[72] Elsa Naumburg pursued her interests in social welfare, education, and the emerging field of anthropology with a feminist perspective.[73] Supported by a network of women intellectuals, she conducted a variety of community activities. She sustained a relationship to the Alumnae Association of Barnard College and maintained an active professional life as a writer and researcher. The 1918 *Barnard Bulletin* cites a long list of her activities, among them volunteering in settlement and social work, lecturing for the National Child Labor Committee, and organizing for the Federation for Child Study. She also served on the boards of several organizations: the College Settlements Association, the New York section of the National Council of Jewish Women, the Women's Conference of the Ethical Society, and the Federation for Child Study. She authored *The Child's First Books* (1925), *Books for Young Readers* (1926), and a translation of a German children's book, and she conducted the research and collected the photographs for another children's book on the construction of the Empire State Building, paying particular attention to the men and the machines that built it. One of her collaborators was Lucy Sprague Mitchell, a leading figure in early childhood education and founder of the Bank Street School.[74] In 1963, Elsa Naumburg published an annotated bibliography of childhood mental illness.

As I imagine it, the Naumburg home must have been a lively place, nurtured by Elsa's associations and energy. Sometime during the mid-1930s, one of the visitors to this home was Zora Neale Hurston. We know this because of another intimate relationship three decades later. In 1965 when Rukeyser was teaching at Sarah Lawrence College, Alice Walker was her student. Like Hurston, Walker came to higher education in New York by way of a historically Black college—Spelman College for Walker, Howard University for Hurston. At Spelman, Walker met the historian Howard Zinn and the sociologist Staughton Lynd. Both encouraged her to pursue her studies and to apply to Sarah Lawrence; she did and was accepted. There she met Rukeyser as well as Lynd's mother, Helen Lynd, a sociologist and social philosopher, author of

Shame and the Search for Identity, and coauthor with her husband, Robert Staughton Lynd, of the best-selling *Middletown: A Study in Contemporary American Culture.* For a time in the early 1960s, Helen would be Muriel's lover.[75]

Letters from Alice to Muriel testify that their relationship in those years and beyond had elements of an intense affectionate mentorship punctuated by half-truths, fears, confessions, and push-back. In May 1975, nine years after Alice graduated, Muriel wrote Alice a letter in which she refers to a rift in their relationship and chastises Alice for a series of "grave omissions." She tells Alice that she has just seen her in a television interview discussing how she had "gone hunting" Zora Neale Hurston. The interview must have been discussing Walker's publication in *MS Magazine* of her now-famous essay "Looking for Zora," which documents her recovery of Hurston's gravesite and reputation. Walker's undertaking and the article were groundbreaking, effectively catapulting Hurston back into public recognition. "I have always regretted," Muriel writes Alice in the letter, "that I couldn't take up [Zora's] invitation to go south with her, to pass. It came at a time when I couldn't move. (I think I was recovering from the typhoid I picked up at Decatur during the second Scottsboro trial.)"[76]

What might the prospect of returning to the South with Hurston in 1933 have meant for Rukeyser, and what could she possibly have imagined "passing" to entail? Was the term merely a metaphor? A polite way of asking Zora to be her mediator? Or does this reference to passing conjure intimacies that conditioned that first trip south to the Scottsboro trial of Patterson, making "passing" a hieroglyph in which vectors of racial distinction and sexual intensity, past and present, are blurred and concentrated? It is also possible that the invitation from Zora never happened—or not as Rukeyser tells it. I can find no record that Hurston was in New York City in May 1933, when Muriel was hospitalized with typhoid, or any time that summer. Both Valerie Boyd's and Robert Hemenway's biographies of Hurston place her in Florida that year, where she was staging performances of her musical *The Great Day* at Rollins College near Eatonville and in other Florida cities and, by July, renting a small house in Sanford, Florida, and settling in to writing her first novel.[77] It is possible that the invitation came at a different time—perhaps the previous year. Or even in 1936, when Zora most certainly did return to New York for her brief affiliation with the PhD program at Columbia. In the fall of 1935, Hurston joined the WPA Federal Theatre Project, and she may have met Nancy Naumburg there. By mid-April of 1936, however, Hurston had left for Haiti, and at that point Rukeyser was departing for England. In any case, Rukeyser remembers the moment as a Scottsboro–typhoid time, a time when she was struggling with her feelings for Nancy.

In the letter to Walker, Rukeyser continues with her correction of Alice's grave omissions. She writes, "Zora was helped at Barnard, and to get into Barnard. In interest and seeing her value and with money. By white women. It's much more interesting, the truth. More true people, more the way it happens, and deep in the story of us all. You were helped at Sarah Lawrence in comparable ways." The letter goes on: "It was at the home of one of these friends that I met Zora. The white woman is still alive, in her nineties, and fantastic. She is Elsa Naumburg, and the mother of a close friend of mine, school and college."[78]

Carla Kaplan's groundbreaking study of the white women of the Harlem Renaissance details Hurston's complicated and painful relationships to her white benefactors, most significantly the philanthropist Charlotte Osgood Mason.[79] I have not found any evidence that Elsa Naumburg was another. Nonetheless, as this circle of relations closes around Alice, what is most striking is the direction of Rukeyser's affective energy. In chastising Alice for forgetting the white "help" both Alice and Zora received, she not only enacts an overinvestment in recognition but also draws out a buried agent in the environment of intimacies and help: Elsa Naumburg. Elsa and Zora were close in age—Elsa less than ten years Zora's senior. They shared alma maters and interests. I imagine Elsa's delight at meeting Zora Neale. It's probable that Hurston's reputation preceded her, perhaps conveyed to Elsa by Elsie Parsons, Ruth Benedict, or Franz Boas. Hurston studied with Boas, and Rukeyser later planned to write his biography.[80] I can almost picture Elsa introducing Muriel to Zora Neale as Nancy's good friend, as someone who shared an interest in anthropology and had also attended Columbia and taken classes with Boas and Benedict. That Muriel remembers Zora's invitation as occurring in 1933 just after her return from Alabama, when she was very much caught up in her unresolved relationship to Nancy, puts another spin on a history at whose heart is lodged an unmastered and unsettling erotic life. The charge of "grave omissions" that Muriel levels against Alice (despite so oddly echoing the unmarked grave that Walker confronts in her search for Zora) seems to be replete with psychic identifications and compensations. For one, the reprimand eclipses any recognition of Walker's enormously important rediscovery of Hurston. What made Rukeyser unable to see that? Competition with a former student now entering the limelight? Buried jealousy of Hurston? Shame? The letter goes on: "Elsa Naumburg helped me, too, by believing in me when my parents pulled me out of college because my father couldn't have a daughter in college while he went bankrupt."[81] Such an interesting way of putting it all. Even the most pedestrian version of shame does have a way of finding outlets after years.

Drawing upon the work of Silvan Tomkins, Elsbeth Probyn emphasizes that shame is a relational affect experienced when another's interest—in being accepted or educated or simply loved—is interrupted.[82] In Muriel's letter, it clings to the phrase "pulled me out," referring to the father whose financial failure interrupted Muriel's schooling. He is both blamed and replaced in the syntax that travels to Elsa, the woman of steady means who "believ[ed] in me," and who helped. Dependence on a wealthy white woman's help emerges as a potential basis for Muriel's identification with Zora and Alice, and for reclaiming her authority as the one who knows, the teacher.

What sort of help might Elsa Naumburg have offered her daughter's best friend? Telegrams from spring 1932 to Muriel, who was still at Vassar, let her know that Nancy and her mother were traveling to Poughkeepsie. There is no explanation, and the dates confused me when I found the card in the Nancy Naumburg correspondence file.[83] Did Elsa and Nancy bring Muriel back from Vassar when she was "pulled . . . out" in 1932? We know that Muriel took classes after she left Vassar, but if there was no money for college, given her father's financial straits during the Depression, did Elsa make those ventures possible? In any case, in the shadows of all of that helping stands Nancy.

Rukeyser's 1975 letter to Alice Walker ends with a shift back to the present, the rift between herself and Alice, and another set of helpers. Muriel refers to "a page from Hiram's book," which she enclosed in the letter. Hiram was Hiram Haydn, the editor at Harcourt, Brace who published Walker's first volume of poems in 1965 soon after she graduated from Sarah Lawrence. Haydn had recently published a memoir, from which the page was taken. "I know you would have seen it," Muriel writes, "because it is partly about you." This page, she adds,

> has part of the facts about Monica McCall who brought you to Langston Hughes and also to Hiram who fought for you and whom you left saying you could not talk to her—although you didn't even say that to her face and had never tried to talk to her and went down the hall to another agent in the same firm. That's a very painful scene to me and it's been what has been standing between us.[84]

Rukeyser describes the scene as if she were actually there in the hallway witnessing it. The painfulness turns on a perceived betrayal linked to a desire for racial passing whose roots ran deep—all the way to the Scottsboro years.

Monica McCall was Rukeyser's agent and her lover from the mid-1950s until Rukeyser's death. Their relationship remained an open secret for years and one that Alice Walker did not learn about until much later. Rukeyser goes on to describe the effect on her of this imagined scene: "To see it repeated about Zora is a kind of rhyming in life, and I hope you can go over both of them and do what you can to correct them. Although the harm is done. Tell me what you think. Love to Mel and Rebecca. Wishes to you. Muriel. Cc. Helen Lynd."[85] It is difficult to know what Rukeyser means by what Alice has "repeated about Zora," except that rhyming is repetition with a difference. Rhyme is a form of analogy akin to the logic of displacement in dreams or a poetics of juxtaposition, a form that can explore the unverifiable, what is buried in history and in the mysterious parts of the self, unknown even to oneself.

Muriel wants Alice to acknowledge the "white women" who helped her and instructs her to correct the harm by writing to Monica, who in some sense is a stand-in for the white women who helped Zora and Muriel; Muriel's racial identification thus becomes somewhat blurry. Moreover, this repeated omission of help is coded with erotic traces that are difficult to name. A letter from

Alice to Monica McCall dated February 20, 1976—nine months after Muriel's—does her part toward a correction and carries its own energetic charge. It begins "Dearest Monica, Muriel who loves you very, very, very much has not forgiven me for 'not being able to talk to you.'" The letter is a study in obsequious performance, with phrases like "I was such a small fish" and "Still (and though I cannot imagine it) I would not on my life wish to hurt you even in a minor way."[86] Alice's voice here echoes Zora's to her patrons. In her biography of Alice Walker, Evelyn White mentions another letter Alice sent to Muriel. In it she offers her version of the rift between them, recounting "how like a beggar" she felt all those times Rukeyser was "helping" her and the slight she felt when Rukeyser appeared to ignore her and her husband (Mel Leventhal) at Langston Hughes's funeral. She goes on to name the problem for herself, Zora, and others as being helped by white people, a group in which she clearly puts Rukeyser.[87] For Walker such help meant Black people could not support each other, and that is why she shrank from Rukeyser and turned to Langston Hughes.[88] The web of shame tightens and tangles. In the cast of white women helpers in Rukeyser's accusation of Walker, Muriel represents herself as both helper and helped, white and not white, an echo of the racial blurring in "George Robinson: Blues" and in the history of American Jews. Missing in the dream logic here is Nancy, who features so strongly in Muriel's private accounts of her first trip south, where we might be tempted to say she had performed a kind of racial and sexual passing. Surely, however, "passing" is not an adequate term for events whose truth calls for a fictional or poetic account.

Five years later, on February 12, 1980, Muriel Rukeyser died of a stroke. One year earlier McGraw Hill had published her massive volume *Collected Poems,* and the following fall *American Poetry Review* published a new poem titled "An Unborn Poet." It would later be added to the revised edition of the *Collected Poems* (2005). It stands today as the final poem in that volume and it is dedicated to Alice Walker. The speaker is a poet and a teacher who had put a poem aside in order to drive to work, where she encounters a student, recognizable as Alice. She is "a marvelous young woman," the speaker declares, "the daughter I never had." The poem shifts gears as another woman is introduced—Berenice Abbott, a photographer whom Rukeyser knew in New York. Abbott captures people and places in her photographs and desires a camera "that is a room, the child of the *camera* obscura." The speaker positions herself as this photographer's collaborator. As indeed she was. They met in 1939 when Rukeyser was just finishing her book on Josiah Gibbs, and the two were probably lovers before Rukeyser left New York for California.[89] In the figure of Abbott other collaborations hover. She is a kindred spirit, reminiscent of Willard Gibbs. A photographer as well as an open lesbian, Abbott spent part of her career documenting science.[90] In the late 1950s, MIT hired her to create photographs that could be used to teach physics, and she worked as part of MIT's Physical Science Study Committee documenting principles of physical science.[91] She and Rukeyser had collaborated on a photo-text project. Much like the planned collaboration with Nancy Naumburg, the project aimed to address far-flung relations and correspondences, and it, too, was never completed.

The poem returns to the student, who is a collaborator, too, her "one perfect eye" becoming the camera eye, and the subject "I" fused with the poet of the title who is being born. The question she asks, directed to an anonymous "friend" of the speaker, is "Can a Black person love a white person?" It is a question played out in the dynamics of patronage and pedagogy, politics, and the erotic in Walker's life. She married a white man, Mel Leventhal, but the query is surely more exorbitant and unruly. An answer is prefigured by an unnamed man in the poem's third stanza, a singer on the tarmac who encounters the speaker after the women's conference and amid "noises of the planes." He tells her:

"I'm not a woman. And I don't write poems.
And I just. Don't. Know."

(stanza 3, lines 4–5)

He stands as a figure for the web of desire, elusive identities, and intimacies that the poem goes on to trace, an environment of music and noise, of bodies and shuddering misconnections, the medium from which "we look through our lives at each other" (stanza 3, line 1). By way of an answer, the speaker leaps to the very scene Rukeyser describes in her letter to Alice: Zora's invitation to accompany her on a trip south. She introduces it as a story that reveals the complexity of whiteness as a nexus of desire, disavowal, identification, fear, and longing:

> Zora, you looked at me
> and asked me South on a journey I never went.
> "If I go with you," I questioned in my white blackness
> "Will I pass? How will I pass, Zora?"
> "Honey," she said, "you travellin' with me,
> don't you worry, you passin'."

(stanza 6, lines 4–9)

The speaker then addresses Alice directly, announcing their kinship with a declaration:

> Alice, we're handed down.
> Alice, there is a road of long descent.
> Cold and shivering and something of ascent.

(stanza 6, lines 10–12)

The penultimate stanza brings back the photographer:

> Early, before the huge explosions,
> Woman with her lens under the massive roadbed,
> in the stillness speaks to me, "You feel it,
> don't you? The entire city vibrating,
> causing me to tremble,
> causing my picture
> and the world to tremble."

(stanza 7, lines 1–7)

Conjuring Alice's perfect eye, Abbott's camera, and perhaps Nancy's, too, this photographer under the massive roadbed conveys an expansive yet intimate erotic environment, unrepresentable except as a vibration that registers in the body. Asking her interlocutor if she feels it, the speaker gives voice to an ample material ecology as stillness summons attention to an exchange of energy that is felt in the body and merges into the pulsating city and world. Here, as so often in Rukeyser's work, nothing is ever only one thing. The photographer merges with the poem's mention of other artists, the poets Grace (Paley) and Denise (Levertov) and Alice. The speaker concludes by instructing the young writer to "Bring me my next poem!" which arrives in the following lines:

> To do what we mean, in poetry and sex,
> to give each other what we really are.
>
> End of a time of intercepted music.

(stanza 8, lines 9, 11–12, 13)

How like Rukeyser to bring in "sex" slant rhymed to "intercepted music"—both media of affective energy, intimacy, and the imaginary. Encoded in the speaker's "white blackness" and longing for the absolution of "passin'" are referents that run all the way to Decatur, Alabama, conjuring the erotics of race work and intercepted love that Rukeyser wrestled with throughout her life and in her poetry of witness. If the "unborn poet" of the title is Rukeyser's last word, I want to think of the state of unbornness as an invitation to reckon with the time of "intercepted music," the untimely pause or interruption that reveals the fragility and fallacy of containing the erotic and the intimate environments it traverses across the fluid relations of history.

Nahum Chandler reads Du Bois's biography of the radical abolitionist John Brown as part of Du Bois's continued meditation on "the problem of the Negro as a problem for America."[92] Du Bois situates Brown as a figure of that very problem, a figure of exorbitance, who, like Du Bois himself, embodied the instability of racial difference, the fallacy of race. Brown was a "white" man who discovered "from the 'inside' out the enigmatic difficulty of living on the basis of a kind of death" by confronting the myth of race in one's relation to the self.[93] I want to think that Rukeyser's final poem enacts a similar confrontation with her own "white blackness" in the speaker's return to Alice by way of Zora, Elsa, and Nancy.

The problem of the twentieth century, as Du Bois articulated it, was the color line; the problem of the twenty-first is to uproot the persistent value of that line to life making under capitalism. As the terrified scramble to resecure white supremacy unfolds in the United States and as the pretense of a post-racial society is stripped away, the task for the Left is to peel back the operation of whiteness. More than that, the task is to consolidate a political bloc that challenges capital's persistent investment in the value of racial categories even as it flexes and pretends to suspend them. Like other writers of her generation, Muriel Rukeyser confronted racial injustice in collaboration with organized efforts. Her archive directs our attention to the architecture of whiteness as a spectacular, intimate, multilayered affective environment in which erotic losses circulate and are transferred. As Rukeyser knew, life writing in any genre opens onto much more than a singular biography. It can plot from the traces of a life's evidence a national grammar in which the predication of subjects reiterates the violence embedded in a democratic imaginary of the erotic energies, political desires, and movement of life making. We still have much to learn about the patterns of affective investment in race and, for many of us, about the losses whiteness shelters, the traps it sets, its melancholy, shame, uncertainty, unconscious longings and transferences. Rukeyser's life and work are a manual for that education. The gaps and detours in the maps to our country that she offers are the most instructive features of her legacy, resources waiting for us to take up in order to recoil and spring.

"We look for ancestors as if the world were completed. It is constantly being torn away," Rukeyser writes in her biography of Gibbs.[94] I set out to find Nancy, and I found instead a network of relations scattered across diary entries, letters, and poems in which a shadow adheres to ineffable intimacies and irrupts in the present. That shadow suffuses a national story of possession and dispossession in which race clings to flesh, to a social hieroglyphic, to a proprietary specular authority, and to the evidence of things unseen. "A line, a cadence of speech, a muscle's bending" leaves an imprint in auditory and specular analogues, a constellation of images whose meaning is opaque even to those who reiterate them, vibrations at times apparent only in the intercepted music of a shudder.

Love gets the last word here. Rukeyser knew all too well that it never saves the day, is unreliable, at times cruel, and in itself no sure guide to the future. Nonetheless, like so many others, ancient and now, she pursued it in multiple forms, and fiercely. If at times she fell in and out of its commonsense versions, she also relentlessly pursued it as Eros, life-giving energy. A thing unseen. I am convinced that this expansive energy led her and the other women from the 1930s she accompanies here to a political movement that set out to transform the modern world and to open the possibility of commonly held resources for the collective making and remaking of life. That possibility fueled their courage and imagination and their fearless amplification of American Communism's vision and practice. Perhaps it played a part as well in what led them to abandon the party, altogether or in part, frustrated by its blindness to women's value, to race as a lethal invention, to the gifts and incisive knowledge of the dispossessed. Their stories chart a legacy that reveals the life-giving energy tapped and exhausted in the labor of domestic care, renewed in friendships and in white women's unsettling turns. It spans a network of analogous energetic relations to labor and to the land. Hedged by the power of property, these relations nonetheless harbor a surplus that can limit capital's grip on matter's spin toward entropy. Even if it is a subtle and elusive agent in these histories, Eros remains. Embedded in the dependencies of collective survival, its particles of intense life are a material force to reckon with. In the company of these women, we can sense that force in their conviction and tenacity and in their affirmation of the relations that make and remake life. They infuse the past that comes alive through them and the ever-present possibility to claim and fashion a common future.

Acknowledgments

This book, like life, is the product of many hands and minds. In a fundamental way, writing it was a collaboration with both the dead and the living. These seven women who kept company with me taught me so much and, indeed, I came to love them. Any failures of imagination or fact about their lives and work are mine. I am deeply grateful to the living as well. For opportunities to present my work, I thank the Elaine Stavro Distinguished Visiting Scholar Series in Theory, Politics, and Gender at Trent University; the Dissenting Traditions Conference at Trent University; the Gensler Family Symposium of the Gender, Sexuality, and Feminist Studies Program at Middlebury College; and colleagues at many American Studies Association conferences and Marxist Literary Group gatherings. A sabbatical leave and release from teaching at Rice University gave me the precious time to read and write. Support from Rice's Creative Ventures Fund helped with manuscript preparation.

My contacts with family members of some of the women in this book have been deeply gratifying. I am especially grateful to Margie Goldsmith and Lynne Miller, who gave me permission to reproduce Nancy Naumburg's photographs and portrait. I am also thankful to William L. Rukeyser for permission to quote from Muriel Rukeyser's works and papers. David and Barb Tilsen welcomed me into their home and shared wonderful stories of David's grandmother, Meridel Le Sueur. I also deeply appreciate Nana Ayebia and the Ayebia Clarke, Ltd., Press for permission to reprint Claudia Jones's poem and Carole Boyce Davies for her support in that process.

I am indebted to the intellectual generosity of many colleagues whose thinking and guidance enriched the project: Paula Rabinowitz's suggestions on the manuscript made it stronger, as did the comments of the anonymous reader for the University of Minnesota Press. Joan Sangster's intellectual generosity and marxist feminist solidarity have been a long-standing support, as has Bryan Palmer's. Feminist scholars Carly Thomsen, Kelly Sharron, and Abraham Weil kept me uplifted in an American Studies / National Women's Studies Association team that goaded me to keep producing multiple chapters. Kelly Gawel and Cinzia Arruzza solicited the essay on Meridel Le Sueur that catalyzed chapter 5.

I extend special appreciation to Fay Yarbrough, who led the Rice Feminist Research Group seminar on a chapter of the book, and to colleagues who attended and offered helpful comments: Margarita Castromán, Krista Comer, Emily Houlik-Ritchey, Cymene Howe, Susan Lurie, Helena Michie, Brian Riedel, Virginia Thomas, and Lora Wildenthal. English Department research assistant Laura Bilheimer tracked down documents in the project's early phase.

I am fortunate to have had an exquisite editorial team at the University of Minnesota Press. Leah Pennywark, my editor, has been superbly supportive and available, envisioning the book beyond my wildest dreams. Editorial assistant Anne Carter was an invaluable resource with permissions. I am grateful to Kathy Delfosse for her detailed, generous, and discerning copyediting and to Doug Easton for expert indexing.

The loving attention of friends and family nourished me through months of writing. Krista Comer, my writing partner, brightened the dark time of Covid-19 with her thoughtful comments and persistent encouragement to put more of Rosemary on the page. Catherine Bridge, Helena Michie, and Ruth Pelham read chapters with keen interest and insight; the wisdom of Halie Maxwell encouraged me time and again to be dialectically attuned and mindful. Weekly Zooms with family uplifted me with laughter and lively debates. I extend a heartfelt thank-you for that to Molly Hennessy-Fiske and Jeffrey Moran, Kate Hennessy-Fiske and Tom Bostelmann, Frida and Lucy H. F. Bostelmann, Margaret and Al Bostelmann, Fred and Chris Fiske, and my ever-faithful sisters: Christine, Claire, Patty, Anne, and Barbara Hennessy. To Martha Ojeda I owe more than I can ever say for endless hours of listening and for sharing our long road together.

My mother, Mary-Jane Carson Hennessy, was a child of the 1930s. Her love of literature and history were with me on every page. I dedicate this book to her.

Notes

Introduction

1. Milton, *U.S. Labor*, 7.
2. Sowinska, "American Women Writers"; Ware, *Holding Their Own*, 5.
3. Throughout I have capitalized the word "Left" when referring to a collective progressive political stance. It appears in lower case when used as an adjective (left-leaning, leftists, left politics).
4. My use of the concept "life making" amplifies and is indebted to Bhattacharya, "What Is Social Reproduction Theory?"; and Ferguson, *Women and Work*.
5. Federici, *Re-enchanting*, 15; and Federici, *Beyond the Periphery*, 77–78.
6. Federici, *Re-enchanting*, 18.
7. Federici, *Re-enchanting*, 29.
8. On similarities between the Great Depression and the economic recession of the twenty-first century, see Rabinowitz, "'Between the Outhouse and the Garbage Dump.'"
9. Horne, "Red and Black," 207.
10. Wiegand, *Red Feminism*, 20.
11. Roediger, *Working toward Whiteness*, 57–132, characterizes this position as an "in betweenness" shared by multiple immigrant groups. Jacobson, *Whiteness of a Different Color*, 170–199, calls it "probationary whiteness." On the complicated history of "the Jewish race," see also Brodkin, *How Jews Became White Folks*; Goldstein, *Price of Whiteness*.
12. Goldstein, *Price of Whiteness*, 1. Further citations appear as page numbers in the text.
13. Friedman, *What Went Wrong?*, 44.
14. Brodkin, *How Jews Became White Folks*, 103–4; see also Löwy, "Jewish Radical Intellectuals."
15. Wald, *New York Intellectuals*, 45.
16. Schere, "Irene Paull," 27. See also Wald, *New York Intellectuals*, 27–45, on non-Jewish Jews among radical intellectuals.
17. In addition to these seven, many women writers in the 1930s worked closely with American Communist-supported organizations. See Balthasar, *Anti-Imperialist Modernism*; Coiner, *Better Red*; Ehlers, *Left of Poetry*; Nekola and Rabinowitz, *Writing Red*; Rabinowitz, *Labor and Desire*; and Wald, *Exiles*.
18. On the Communist approach to race and the woman question as distinct from the U.S. feminist mainstream, see Wiegand, *Red Feminism*, 98.
19. Wald, "Culture and Commitment," 286.

20. Palmer and Sangster's "Legacies of 1917" traces that history and the fate of revolution through colonial uprisings, the feminist movement, the rise of the New Left, and the new millennium's Occupy movement.

21. Wiegand, *Red Feminism*, 15.

22. Palmer, "Rethinking the Historiography," 145.

23. Horne, "Red and Black," 227.

24. Katz, "Vagabond Capitalism," 711.

25. Palmer, "Rethinking the Historiography," 146.

26. Palmer, "Rethinking the Historiography," 143.

27. For background on the International Left Opposition in America, see Palmer, *Revolutionary Teamsters*.

28. On the impact of the popular front on American culture, see Denning, *Cultural Front*.

29. Palmer, "Rethinking the Historiography."

30. Sowinska, "American Women Writers," 8.

31. Hapke, *Daughters*, xiii. See also Ware, *Holding Their Own*.

32. See Gosse, "'To Organize in Every Neighborhood,'" on the shift in the party's direction in the early 1930s from factory to neighborhood, consumer needs, and homelife.

33. Wiegand, *Red Feminism*, 24.

34. I refer to marxist feminism with a lower case *m* in order to signal the distinct standpoint that feminism advances through its critical encounter with historical materialism or Marxism.

35. Cited in Federici, *Beyond the Periphery*. See also Le Sueur, *Women on the Breadlines*.

36. Reilly, "Involuntary Sterilization." See also Lira and Stern, "Mexican Americans and Eugenic Sterilization"; and Tajima-Peña's documentary *No más bebés* on the sterilization of Latina immigrant women as late as the 1970s.

37. On the relevance of Le Sueur's writing to the exhausted care workers of Covid times, see Balthasar, "'Don't Work.'"

38. Early feminist theorists of social reproduction were Margaret Benston, Selma James, Mariarosa Dalla Costa, and Lise Vogel. For recent work, see Arruzza and Gawel, "Politics of Social Reproduction"; Battacharya, *Social Reproduction Theory*; Ferguson, *Women and Work*; and Giménez, *Marx, Women*.

39. Rukeyser, *Willard Gibbs*, 12.

40. Rukeyser, *Willard Gibbs*, 13.

41. Rukeyser, *Willard Gibbs*, 390, 325.

42. Trethewey, Introduction to *Essential Muriel Rukeyser*, x.

43. Rukeyser, *Collected Poems*, "The Book of the Dead," lines 1–2.

1. Black and Red

1. Cooke, "I Was Part of the Bronx Slave Market," reports that there were rumored to be twenty or thirty of these market corners in the 1930s in the Bronx alone.

2. Baker and Cooke, "Bronx Slave Market," 330–32.

3. Cooke, interview by Kathleen Currie.

4. Vivian Morris interviewed Black women across New York City who worked as domestics, laundresses, and needle workers, and she seems to have disappeared after 1941. On these Works Progress Administration (WPA) interviews, see Morris, "Domestic Workers Union." See also Bascom, *Renaissance in Harlem*; Russell, "Who Was Vivian Morris?" Hapke, "Who Are You Calling Un-American," speculates that "Morris" was probably a pen name.

5. See Washington, *Other Blacklist*. On these writers as contributors to the Left and to feminism, see Gore, *Radicalism at the Crossroads*; L. Harris, "Running"; Lindsey, "Black Lives Matter"; McDuffie, *Sojourning*; and May, "Airing Dirty Laundry."

6. L. Harris, "Running," 24.

7. L. Harris, "Running," 22.

8. L. Harris, "Running," 40. See also McDuffie, *Sojourning*.

9. Hartman, *Wayward Lives*.

10. McDuffie, *Sojourning*, 3.

11. According to Wiegand, *Red Feminism*, 99, among all majority-white organizations in the 1940s, Communist associations were the chief defenders of Black women's rights; moreover, Communist publications regularly used the terms "triple burden" and "triple oppression" to describe the status of Black women exploited because of their race, gender, and class.

12. Fields and Fields, *Racecraft*, 25.

13. Hartman, *Wayward Lives*, 268, teases out the connotations of "wayward" as "unregulated movement," "sojourn without fixed destination," an "attempt to elude capture by never settling," or "to claim the right to opacity, to strike, refuse, riot."

14. On the call for "Negro self-determination" in the Black Belt, see Solomon, *Cry Was Unity*; Naison, *Communists in Harlem*; Foley, *Radical Representations*, 170–212; Higashida, *Black Internationalist Feminism*, 33–56; and Smethurst, *New Red Negro*, 21–32.

2. Centering Domestic Workers

1. For an account of this building as a space for radical Black left collaboration in the 1930s and 1940s, see Burden-Stelly, "Radical Blackness."

2. Cooke, interview by Mary Licht.

3. Cooke, interview by Kathleen Currie. The reservation was possibly the Lower Brule Indian Reservation and the Native people were probably Lakota.

4. Cooke, interview by Licht.

5. Cooke, interview by Currie, 6; L. Harris, "Marvel Cooke," 110.

6. Cooke, interview by Currie.

7. Delegard, "Hemmed In." See also D. Taylor, *African Americans*; *Minneapolis Tribune*, "Negro Building House"; and *Minneapolis Tribune*, "Race War."

8. Cooke, interview by Currie, 5.

9. L. Harris, "Marvel Cooke," 111. Du Bois joined the Communist Party at the age of ninety-three, when he was living in Ghana. Throughout the 1920s and 1930s, he questioned the party's failure to address fully the Negro question.

10. McDuffie, *Sojourning,* 3. According to Naison, *Communists in Harlem,* xvii, no socialist organization before or since has touched the life of an African American community so profoundly. At its high point in 1938, the Communist Party in Harlem had close to one thousand members. Further citations from Naison, *Communists in Harlem,* appear as page numbers in the text.

11. McDuffie, *Sojourning,* 2. On the housewives' strike, see Orlick, "'We Are That Mythical Thing.'"

12. *New York Amsterdam News,* September 1, 8, 1934. See also *New York Age,* September 29, 1934; and *Negro Liberator,* September 1, 1934.

13. *New York Amsterdam News,* Aug. 11, 18, September 1, 1934; *Negro Liberator,* August 18, 1934. On the atmosphere of protest in Harlem during the spring and summer of 1934, see Naison, *Communists in Harlem,* 115–24; and Naison, "From Eviction Resistance."

14. McDuffie, *Sojourning,* 45.

15. McDuffie, *Sojourning,* 45.

16. McDuffie, *Sojourning,* 79.

17. Baker and Cooke, "Bronx Slave Market," 327.

18. Cooke, interview by Currie, 33.

19. Cooper, "Negro Woman Domestic Worker," 13. The groundbreaking study by Esther Cooper (Jackson) remains the most thorough empirical examination of Black women's domestic labor.

20. See Rabinowitz, "Domestic Labor," for a detailed history of Black women's domestic labor and its representation in mid-twentieth-century popular culture.

21. Baker and Cooke, "Bronx Slave Market," 340. Further citations appear as page numbers in the text.

22. J. Jones, *Labor of Love,* 206.

23. I understand sexuality to be a historical discourse that gives meaning to bodily sensation and pleasure. It is also a vocabulary for naming the body's role in biological reproduction. In both these senses, it is both a cultural discourse and a domain of social reproduction.

24. As Federici, *Beyond the Periphery,* 89–105, argues, the early capitalist division of labor provided avenues for working-class men to enjoy "the only pleasure of the poor," often outside marriage in taverns where sex workers gathered. Because women factory workers in the nineteenth century who left home for the street or bar threatened the production of a stable workforce, state policy eventually enticed married women to provide the physical and emotional services required of a more disciplined male workforce.

25. The five-part series included "I Was Part of the Bronx Slave Market" and "Where Men Prowl."

26. Cooke, "I Was Part of the Bronx Slave Market," 1. Further citations appear as page numbers in the text.

27. Cooke, "'Mrs. Legree,'" 1.

28. Higashida, *Black Internationalist Feminism*, 37.

29. On the impact of her stories, see Streitmatter, "Marvel Cooke."

30. Cooke, "Some Ways."

31. Cooke, interview by Currie.

32. L. Harris, "Marvel Cooke," 94; Hine, "Rape and the Inner Lives of Black Women"; Ransby, *Ella Baker,* also refers to the practice.

33. Mason's husband practiced parapsychology and hypnotherapy and had patients who believed he helped them through psychic healing. She traveled in the Southwest, lived with Native Americans, and helped Natalie Curtis publish *The Indians' Book*. Cornelia and Katherine Chapin lived with her for thirty years. Katherine's husband, Francis Biddle, would become U.S. attorney general. The Chapins and Biddles were old Philadelphia families. For more on Mason's background, see Kaplan, *Miss Anne*; Hemenway, *Zora Neale Hurston*; and Y. Taylor, *Zora and Langston*, 86–87.

34. Kaplan, *Miss Anne*, 237.

35. Gilyard, *Louise Thompson Patterson*, 73; Hemenway, *Zora Neale Hurston*, 36–47; Kaplan, *Miss Anne*, 237.

36. Gilyard, *Louise Thompson Patterson*, 70–73. For more on the life of Thompson, see Crawford and Patterson, *Letters from Langston*; Maxwell, *New Negro*, 143–51.

37. Gilyard, *Louise Thompson Patterson*, 7.

38. Gilyard, *Louise Thompson Patterson*, 1–7; Crawford and Patterson, *Letters from Langston*, 10–11. While at Berkeley, Louise met Du Bois, who inspired her when he came to give a lecture. In New York, he remained a close supporter, although he disapproved of her joining the Communist Party.

39. Gilyard, *Louise Thompson Patterson*, 47–49.

40. Scholarly attention to Red Harlem blossomed belatedly in the late twentieth century. See Naison, *Communists in Harlem*; Solomon, *Cry Was Unity*; and literary histories by Crawford and Patterson, *Letters from Langston*, 25; Higashida, *Black Internationalist Feminism*; Maxwell, *New Negro*; and Smethurst, *New Red Negro*.

41. McDuffie, *Sojourning*, 77.

42. Thompson, "And So We Marched," 6.

43. Crawford and Patterson, *Letters from Langston*, 29; Gilyard, *Louise Thompson Patterson*, 73.

44. Thompson, quoted in Gilyard, *Louise Thompson Patterson*, 103, from an interview by Ruth and Bud Schultz.

45. On Metropolitan Life's notorious discrimination against Black policyholders, see McGlamery, "Race Based Underwriting."

46. McDuffie, *Sojourning*, 77. Further citations appear as page numbers in the text.

47. On Thompson's and other left women's travel to Russia, see Mickenberg, *American Girls*. See also Maxwell, *New Negro*, 113.

48. Gilyard, *Louise Thompson Patterson*, 92–96.

49. Gilyard, *Louise Thompson Patterson*, 96; McDuffie, *Sojourning*, 77.

50. The standard histories of the Scottsboro case are Carter, *Scottsboro*; and Goodman, *Stories of Scottsboro*. See also Maxwell, *New Negro*. On the international support the case provoked, see Miller, Pennybacker, and Rosenhaft, "Mother Ada Wright."

51. Gilyard, *Louise Thompson Patterson*, 101.

52. Thompson, "And So We Marched," 6.

53. Gilyard, *Louise Thompson Patterson*, 100.

54. Daniel, "Challenges Story by Victoria Price," 3.

55. Thompson, "And So We Marched," 6.

56. Thompson, "Southern Terror," 328.

57. Thompson, "Southern Terror," 328. See also Maxwell, *New Negro*, 144–48.

58. Gilyard, *Louise Thompson Patterson*, 110.

59. On this assignment of Thompson's, see Gilyard, *Louise Thompson Patterson*, 110–11. For more on the Scottsboro mothers, see Damon, "Scottsboro Mothers"; R. Moore, "Think of Them"; Van Deen, "Save the Scottsboro Boys."

60. Thompson, "Toward a Brighter Dawn," 14. Further citations appear as page numbers in the text.

61. See also Gilyard, *Louise Thompson Patterson*, 118–19.

62. Gilyard, *Louise Thompson Patterson*, 68. For more on Mary Louise's memories of her mother, see Crawford and Patterson, *Letters from Langston*.

63. Gilyard, *Louise Thompson Patterson*, 60.

64. The Alien Registration Act, widely known as the Smith Act, was approved by Congress in 1940 and set criminal penalties for advocating the overthrow of the U.S. government.

65. Other committee members included Bettina Aptheker (then an official of the CPUSA) and Sallye Bell Davis. Among the group's sponsors were Maya Angelou, Ella Baker, Alice Childress, Ruby Dee and Ossie Davis, Beah Richards, Pete Seeger, and Herbert Aptheker.

66. Cited in Gilyard, *Louise Thompson Patterson*, 223.

67. Claudia Jones, "The Elms at Morn" (1950), quoted in Davies, *Claudia Jones*, 186.

68. Carole Boyce Davies's groundbreaking research on Jones's poetry, in *Claudia Jones: Beyond Containment*, and her political biography of Jones, *Left of Karl Marx*, are the basis for much of what I learned about Jones. The original of the poem can be found in the Claudia Jones Memorial Collection, Sc MG 692, Schomburg Center for Research in Black Culture, Manu-

scripts, Archives and Rare Books Division, New York Public Library, box 1, folder 5. On Jones's prison poetry, see also Bernard and Hunter, "Roses Full of Flame."

69. Davies, *Left of Marx*, 104.

70. Davies, *Left of Marx*, 1.

71. Davies, *Left of Marx*, 141. For more on Jones's involvement in anticolonial struggles, see Higashida, *Black Internationalist Feminism*, 40–48.

72. Davies, *Left of Marx*, 138. Davies argues that the convergence of the Smith Act (1940), the McCarran Internal Security Act (1950), and the Immigration and Nationality Act (also known as the McCarran–Walter Act; 1952) targeted diaspora dissenters as punishable with deportation.

73. Sherwood, *Claudia Jones*, 22.

74. Betty Gannett, an immigrant from Poland, joined the Young Communist League in 1923. In the 1930s, she was an editor of numerous Communist Party publications, and by the 1950s, she was the party's national education director. Elizabeth Gurley Flynn joined the Communist Party in 1936 and later became its chair. Older than both Gannett and Jones, she spent her youth as an organizer for the Industrial Workers of the World (IWW), supporting workers in strikes across the country, and was a strong supporter of women's rights and reproductive freedom. Flynn writes about her friendship with Jones and their time in prison in *The Alderson Story*.

75. Sherwood, *Claudia Jones*.

76. Davies, *Claudia Jones*, 6.

77. Davies, *Claudia Jones*, 2.

78. Davies, *Claudia Jones*, 7.

79. Sherwood, *Claudia Jones*, 43.

80. Davies, *Left of Marx*, 209, points out that the strategy actually kept the FBI from making the connection between Claudia Cumberbatch and Claudia Jones for a number of years.

81. C. Jones, "Autobiographical History," 11.

82. C. Jones, "Autobiographical History," 199.

83. Davies, *Claudia Jones*, 12.

84. Sherwood, *Claudia Jones*, 20; Davies, *Left of Marx*, 35.

85. Davies, *Left of Marx*, 6.

86. Davies, *Left of Marx*, 14.

87. See C. Jones, "Sojourners for Peace and Justice."

88. Sherwood, *Claudia Jones*.

89. Sherwood, *Claudia Jones*.

90. Davies, *Claudia Jones*, 31.

91. Davies, *Claudia Jones*, 59.

92. Wiegand, *Red Feminism*, 107–9, claims that Jones overstated her case and that in fact the party worked to make her arguments accessible to a broader audience and to support the Sojourners.

93. C. Jones, "End to the Neglect," 58. Further citations appear as page numbers in the text.

94. Wiegand, *Red Feminism*, 101–2, argues that Jones brought Black women's experiences to the center of Communist writings and helped promote recognition that even though women share gender oppression, it takes different forms.

95. Some accounts indicate she was born in 1916; others, 1920. It may be that, like other women, she changed the date to appear younger, or that procuring a birth certificate took place belatedly and creatively.

96. C. Jones, "Autobiographical History," 14.

97. According to Washington, *Other Blacklist*, 132, Alice lived with her grandmother at 118th Street in Harlem, between Lennox and Fifth.

98. Washington, *Other Blacklist*, 131. For more on Childress's life and her influential contributions to building a people's theater and an international Black Arts movement, see Higashida, *Black Internationalist Feminism*, 82–111.

99. Higashida, *Black Internationalist Feminism*, 126.

100. Childress, Marshall, and Wright, "Negro Woman."

101. Mary Helen Washington, in *Other Blacklist*, 137, reports that Herbert Aptheker told her in an interview that Childress let him use her apartment for meetings with underground Communists.

102. Washington, *Other Blacklist*, 143.

103. See Washington, *Other Blacklist*, 140–45, on Childress's undercover relationship to the party and her probable knowledge of Jones.

104. Washington, "Alice Childress," 195; T. Harris, introduction to *Like One of the Family*, xiii.

105. T. Harris, introduction to *Like One of the Family*, xiii.

106. Washington, *Other Blacklist*, 141.

107. Washington, *Other Blacklist*, 142.

108. See T. Harris, *From Mammies to Militants*, 111.

109. T. Harris, introduction to *Like One of the Family*, xiv. T. Harris, *From Mammies to Militants*, 33, refers to Mildred as exemplifying a "militant" posture. Harris's book documents many instances of fictional representations of maids, among them Alice Walker's *Meridian*.

110. Childress, *Like One of the Family*, 66, 33. Further citations appear as page numbers in the text.

3. The Ground We Tread

1. Paula Rabinowitz's *Labor and Desire* and Nekola and Rabinowitz's *Writing Red* have been major contributions to American literature and have been influential to my own thinking.

2. I want to thank Virginia Thomas for bringing Dillon's *New World Drama* to my attention.

3. Dillon, *New World Drama*.

4. Dillon is most interested in the theater as a public space where the question of who comprised the sovereign notion of "the people" was being worked out on both sides of the Atlantic through representations of regicide, New World Natives, and former African slaves.

5. The explanation of nature that follows is based on works that address Karl Marx's thinking on ecology: Saito, *Karl Marx's Ecosocialism*; Foster, *Marx's Ecology*; Löwy, "Marx, Engels and Ecology"; Foster and Burkett, *Marx and the Earth*; Merchant, *Death of Nature*; Merchant, *Radical Ecology*; L. Marx, "Idea of Nature"; J. Moore, *Capitalism in Web*; and N. Smith, *Uneven Development*.

6. Federici, *Caliban,* 97.

7. Federici, *Caliban,* 49.

8. Dillon, *New World Drama,* 98.

9. Federici, *Caliban,* 16.

10. Preservation Alliance for Greater Philadelphia, Roxborough, "Neighborhood History," https://www.preservationalliance.com/explore-philadelphia/philadelphia-neighborhoods/roxborough/#:~:text=Roxborough.

11. Valley Green Inn was built on a tract of land purchased from Penn by absentee property owners in England and Ireland. In the mid-nineteenth century Thomas Livezey, who owned a grist mill farther down the creek, purchased some of it and rented it to Edward Rinker, who in 1850 built the inn. It still stands on what had been the Wissahickon Turnpike, now a bridle path restricted to pedestrian use and officially named Forbidden Drive.

12. Middleton, "Some Memoirs."

13. Some remained in Pennsylvania, living in secret. See *Fulfilling a Prophecy: The Past and Present of the Lenape in Pennsylvania,* exhibition organized by the Penn Museum and the Lenape Nation of Pennsylvania, Penn Museum, September 13, 2008–July 2010, Philadelphia, https://www.penn.museum/sites/fap/index.shtml.

14. *Fulfilling a Prophecy.*

15. The research on whiteness is now considerable. Especially pertinent is the Native perspective of Aileen Moreton-Robinson, in "Whiteness, Epistemology, and Indigenous Representation." She elaborates Indigenous knowledge of whiteness and the distinctions whereby "race" is made synonymous with blackness, placing it outside colonial history, while Indigenous people are collapsed into the land whites control and are considered aside from their claims to sovereignty. On this point, see Moreton-Robinson, *White Possessive,* 54–57.

16. Alcoff, *Future of Whiteness,* 22–23. Further citations appear as page numbers in the text.

17. Sullivan, *Revealing Whiteness.*

18. Wynter, "Rethinking 'Aesthetics,'" 259.

4. Unsettling the Grass Roots

1. Langer, *Josephine Herbst,* 7–11.

2. *New York Times,* "Josephine Herbst Dead," 38.

3. For criticism of Herbst's writing, including her novel trilogy and journalism, see Ehrhardt, *Writers of Conviction*; Kosiba, "Feet in the

Grassroots"; N. Roberts, *Three Radical Women Writers*; Rabinowitz, *Labor and Desire*; Wiedmann, *Herbst's Short Fiction*; Foley, *Radical Representations*; Wald, *Exiles*; and Wald, *American Night*.

4. Kosiba, "Feet in the Grassroots," 47–64.

5. Herbst, "Feet in the Grass Roots," 46–51.

6. Rabinowitz, *Labor and Desire*, 139, 157–70, reads Herbst for her representation of the female intellectual marked as spectator to history, a reading that complements mine although it is not focused on that spectator's relation to the land.

7. Schwieder, "History of Iowa."

8. Langer, *Josephine Herbst*, 17.

9. Langer, *Josephine Herbst*, 9.

10. Langer, *Josephine Herbst*, 19.

11. Herbst "Feet in the Grass Roots," 46.

12. Herbst "Feet in the Grass Roots," 46.

13. Herbst, *Starched Blue Sky*, 25. Further citations appear as page numbers in the text.

14. Johnson, introduction to *The Starched Blue Sky of Spain and Other Memoirs*, x.

15. Langer, *Josephine Herbst*, 18; Herbst, *Starched Blue Sky*, 40.

16. Langer, *Josephine Herbst*, 35. Further citations appear as page numbers in the text.

17. See *Sioux City Journal* archives for 1900–1915 on "Indians" and "lynching." According to census figures for 1910, of the state population of two million, fewer than five hundred were Native American and only fourteen thousand were Negro. "Thirteenth Census of the United States: 1910-V~4: Population 1910," 617–18, https://www2.census.gov/prod2/decennial/documents/36894832v2ch05.pdf.

18. Kelley, *Hammer and Hoe*, documents working-class and rural radicalism in the South during the 1930s when the Communist Party gradually came to support Black farmers who were already the center of rural labor movements.

19. See Harrow, "Factory Farm"; Richman, "Mass Migration"; Lenin, "Capitalism and Agriculture"; and Shover, *Cornbelt Rebellion*.

20. Shover, *Cornbelt Rebellion*, 35–37. From the early twentieth century, the IWW had been organizing unskilled workers and farmers across the Midwest. In the 1930s, there were multiple Communist Party efforts to form a united front of progressive agrarian groups. In 1932, the first unit of the Farmers' Holiday Association was formed, with Milo Reno as president. Because it aimed for government reforms rather than a proletarian revolution, Communists opposed it.

21. Shover, *Cornbelt Rebellion*, 36.

22. Shover, *Cornbelt Rebellion*, 22–26.

23. In 1922 Ware went to Russia, where he held managerial posts on several Soviet collective farms. Mother Bloor lived in Herbst's Erwinna home in 1936 when Herbst traveled to Spain. Langer, *Josephine Herbst*, 207.

24. Brown, "Savagely Fathered and Unmothered World," 527.

25. Ware later became widely known because Whittaker Chambers charged him with heading a Communist cell in the Department of Agriculture.

26. Shover, *Cornbelt Rebellion*, 42.

27. Herbst's article appeared in the same number as Le Sueur's story "The Trap."

28. Herbst, "Feet in the Grass Roots," 46. Further citations appear as page numbers in the text.

29. Langer reads the Mexico arrangement as one of several love triangles Josie was drawn to, exemplified in her relationship with Maxwell Anderson and her friendship with his wife, Margaret; her initial attraction to Marion, who was in a relationship with Philip Stevenson; and then in the triangle with John and Marion.

30. Communism had wide appeal, and many government officials expressed an interest in it. During her visits to John in D.C., Herbst met a man she knew only as "Karl" who at one point expressed an interest in meeting Alger Hiss, a young lawyer with the Agricultural Adjustment Administration. Many years later, seeing a photograph of Whittaker Chambers, she recognized him as Karl.

31. Herbst, "Farmer Looks Ahead."

32. Herbst, "Farmer Looks Ahead," 212.

33. Herbst, "Soviet in Cuba."

34. Herbst, "Soviet in Cuba," 11.

35. Swanger, *Rebel Lands*, xi–xiv, points out that slavery was abolished in Cuba in 1886 but the coupling of race and class continued. Skin color was the first thing parents had to state when registering a newborn child. Public spaces were segregated, and a narrow range of movement was designated for Blacks.

36. Swanger, *Rebel Lands*, xi–xiv. From 1933 on, the Communist Party championed full civil and social equality for Blacks and pushed for self-determination in Oriente after the call for that approach to the Negro question.

37. Swanger, *Rebel Lands*, 100.

38. Herbst, "Soviet in Cuba," 9; Herbst, "Passport from Realengo," 10.

39. Herbst, "Soviet in Cuba," 9.

40. In 1902, three years after Cuban independence and during the U.S. occupation, the U.S. Congress passed an ordinance requiring those holding title to collective lands to procure a physical document. Many property owners never knew they had to do this, and the result was a wave of dispossessions and evictions. Many U.S. companies took advantage of the order, and by the following year, there were thirty-seven U.S.-owned agricultural establishments in Cuba; three years later, there were seven thousand. Swanger, *Rebel Lands*, 86.

41. Herbst, "Soviet in Cuba," 9.

42. Swanger, *Rebel Lands*, 90.

43. Herbst, "Soviet in Cuba," 10.

44. Herbst, "Cuba Sick for Freedom," 17.

45. The Platt Amendment of 1901 declared that the United States had the right to protect its commercial interests by overseeing Cuban affairs and maintaining a military base at Guantánamo.

46. Herbst, "Cuba Sick for Freedom," 17.

47. Herbst, "Passport from Realengo." Further citations appear as page numbers in the text.

48. Herbst, *Rope of Gold*, 362. Further citations appear as page numbers in the text.

49. See also Herbst, "Passport from Realengo."

50. Balthasar, *Anti-Imperialist Modernism*, 69–72, remarks on the novel's suggestion that U.S. imperialism was in essence an extension of the U.S. frontier and a continuation of its Indian Wars.

51. Dillon, *New World Drama*, 3.

52. Herbst, *New Green World*, 133. Further citations appear as page numbers in the text.

53. Jameson, *Allegory and Ideology*, 10.

54. "The Loganian Library was created [by James Logan] in 1754 as a trust for the public with Logan's two sons and Benjamin Franklin among the trustees." Library Company of Philadelphia, https://www.librarycompany.org/treasures/ad6.htm.

55. Herbst spells his name "Petrie."

56. Herbst refers to them as the Five Nations. The nations of the Haudenosaunee, or "People of the Longhouse," are the Mohawk, the Onondaga, the Oneida, the Cayuga, and the Seneca, joined after 1722 by the Tuscarora. They were known to the French as the Iroquois Confederacy.

57. Schafer, *William Bartram and the Ghost Plantations*. See Braund, "Real Worlds of Bartram's Travels."

58. Wynter, "Rethinking 'Aesthetics,'" 247–48.

59. For extensive research on Black society in Florida, see Landers, "Africans and Native Americans"; and Landers, *Black Society in Spanish Florida*. On the relations between the Cherokee and enslaved Blacks in the Carolina region during the eighteenth century, see Miles, *Ties That Bind*; and King, *Black Shoals*.

60. Wood, *Black Majority*, xvi.

61. Schafer, *William Bartram and the Ghost Plantations*, 32.

62. Schafer, *William Bartram and the Ghost Plantations*, 32. It is also possible that the term "cromantee" refers to the Akan ethnic group taken from the Gold Coast region or to enslaved members of that group who became known in the Caribbean for organizing dozens of rebellions.

63. Schafer, *William Bartram and the Ghost Plantations*, 36–37.

64. Bartram, *Travels*, 31.

65. Schafer, *William Bartram and the Ghost Plantations*, 46. See also Landers, "Africans and Native Americans."

66. On later controversy over Black Indians' membership in the Seminole Nation, see S. Miller, "Seminoles and Africans."

67. Dunbar-Ortiz, *Indigenous Peoples' History*, 71. See also Grenier, *First Way of War*; and S. Miller and Riding In, *Native Historians*.

68. Dunbar-Ortiz, *Indigenous Peoples' History*, 70–71; Wolfe, "Settler Colonialism and the Elimination of the Native"; and Wolfe, *Settler Colonialism and the Transformation of Anthropology*.

69. Dunbar-Ortiz, *Indigenous Peoples' History*, 70.

70. Dunbar-Ortiz, *Indigenous Peoples' History*, 75–76.

71. Dunbar-Ortiz, *Indigenous Peoples' History*, 82.

72. Wolfe, "Settler Colonialism and the Elimination of the Native," 387.

73. Wolfe, "Settler Colonialism and the Elimination of the Native," 392.

74. Gilio-Whitaker, *As Long As the Grass Grows*, 38; Dunbar-Ortiz, *Indigenous Peoples' History*, 110.

75. Gilio-Whitaker, *As Long As the Grass Grows*, 27, 36. See also Deloria, *God Is Red*, 61–75.

76. The Termination Act was to be implemented by the commissioner of Indian Affairs, Dillon S. Meyer, who had headed the War Relocation Authority, which administered the Japanese concentration camps. See Dunbar-Ortiz, *Indigenous Peoples' History*, 174.

5. The Radical Ecology of Meridel Le Sueur

1. Meridel Le Sueur, "The Origins of Corn," 261.

2. My thinking on Le Sueur is indebted to Schleuning, *America,* who characterized Le Sueur's political philosophy as "dialectical relativity," an acknowledgment of the interdependence of life forms. J. Allen, "'We Must Have Writers,'" argues that Le Sueur's dialectical thought drew on her reading of Friedrich Engels's *Dialectics of Nature* and the writings of Vladimir Lenin.

3. In this respect, her work prefigures feminist political ecology. See Alaimo, *Bodily Natures*; Bennholdt-Thomsen and Mies, *Subsistence Perspective*; Federici, *Caliban*; Federici, *Re-enchanting*; Federici, *Beyond the Periphery*; Mies and Shiva, *Ecofeminism*; Salleh, *Eco-sufficiency*. See also Hennessy, "Toward an Ecology of Life-Making."

4. John Crawford, editor of West End Press, and several others, among them Elaine Hedges at the Feminist Press, helped Le Sueur republish her work, and in some cases, publish it for the first time.

5. For a discussion of biological determinism in Le Sueur, see Coiner, *Better Red*; and Rabinowitz, *Labor and Desire*.

6. Extensive critical writing on Le Sueur accompanied feminist recovery of her work. In addition to the works mentioned above, the editions of Le Sueur's writing edited by Elaine Hedges and by Linda Ray Pratt have important critical commentary. See also Schleuning, "Le Sueur: Toward a New Realism." Le Sueur's family circle has compiled an archival project housed at Meridel LeSueur: The Official Website, https://meridellesueur.org/.

7. Alaimo, *Bodily Natures*, 33.

8. Several scholars have analyzed Le Sueur's contributions to a radical midwestern regionalism aligned with the popular front and American Communism but not taking orders from the party. See, for example, Griffin, "Geographies of (In)Justice"; Mickenberg, "Writing the Midwest"; Wixson, *Worker-Writer in America*.

9. Le Sueur, "Dark of the Time."

10. Le Sueur, "Dark of the Time," 231.

11. Biographical details can be found in Le Sueur, *Crusaders*; Coiner, *Better Red*, 102–7; Hedges, Introduction to *Ripening*; Pratt, "Woman Writer"; Schleuning, *America*; and Schleuning, "Toward a New Regionalism."

12. Le Sueur, *Crusaders*, 45; Le Sueur, "Meridel Le Sueur"; Coiner, *Better Red*, 74. See also J. Allen, "'Dear Comrade,'" 121; and Greer, "No Smiling Madonna," 248–71.

13. Le Sueur, "Meridel Le Sueur," 194.

14. J. Allen, "'Dear Comrade,'" 121; Coiner, *Better Red*, 74–75; Greer, "No Smiling Madonna," 256; Le Sueur, *Crusaders*, 14. See also Debs, "School for the Masses."

15. Hedges, Introduction to *Ripening*, 2–4.

16. Pratt, "Woman Writer," 250.

17. Pratt, afterword to *I Hear Men Talking*, 227.

18. Le Sueur, "Meridel Le Sueur," 193, 194.

19. Le Sueur, "Meridel Le Sueur," 194.

20. Schleuning, *America*, 20.

21. Quoted in Pratt, afterword to *I Hear Men Talking*, 226.

22. Pratt, "Woman Writer," 249, suggests that Le Sueur may not have officially joined the Communist Party until the 1930s, although Le Sueur often dated her affiliation to 1924. Pratt suggests that date may mark her separation from her parents' progressive socialism because 1924 was a year of bitter conflict between the Communist Party and the Farmer–Labor Party over Progressive Party presidential nominee Robert La Folette, whom her parents supported.

23. Coiner, *Better Red*, 77.

24. Hedges, introduction to *Ripening*, 9.

25. "Call for an American Writers' Congress"; J. Allen, "'We Must Have Writers,'" 4.

26. "Call for an American Writers' Congress."

27. Steiner, *Regionalists*.

28. Steiner, *Regionalists*, 32.

29. J. Allen, "'We Must Have Writers,'" 4.

30. Pratt, "Woman Writer," 247.

31. Hedges, Introduction to *Ripening*, 4.

32. Hedges, Introduction to *Ripening*, 19.

33. Hedges, Introduction to *Ripening*, 15.

34. David and Barbara Tilsen, interview by the author, June 21, 2021.

35. Hedges, Introduction to *Ripening*, 19.
36. Le Sueur, "American Bus," 134.
37. Le Sueur, "Dark of the Time," 232.
38. Le Sueur, "Dark of the Time," 141.
39. Le Sueur, "Dark of the Time," 141.
40. Le Sueur, "Women on the Breadlines," 137–43.
41. Le Sueur, "Women on the Breadlines," 143; Le Sueur, "Women Are Hungry," 144–57.
42. Le Sueur, "Women on the Breadlines," 137.
43. Le Sueur, "Women on the Breadlines," 137.
44. Le Sueur, "Women on the Breadlines," 137.
45. Le Sueur, "Women Are Hungry," 149.
46. Le Sueur, "Women on the Breadlines," 140.
47. Le Sueur, "Women Are Hungry," 151.
48. Le Sueur, "Annunciation," 124–32. Further citations appear as page numbers in the text.
49. Le Sueur, *The Girl*, 1. Further citations appear as page numbers in the text.
50. Le Sueur, *Crusaders*, 13–14. Further citations appear as page numbers in the text.
51. The earliest Natives in what came to be Oklahoma were the Spiro mound builders (500–1300 CE), followed by the Caddos, Suens, and Athabascans; joined by tribes removed from the southeast—Cherokee, Creek, Seminole, Chickasaw, and Choctaw—and, by the mid-nineteenth century, by tribes from the northeast, among them the Delaware. See Debo, *And Still the Waters Run*.
52. Le Sueur, *North Star Country*. Further citations appear as page numbers in the text.
53. The Grange was a farmers' association and grassroots collective movement founded in the mid-nineteenth century by Minnesotan Oliver Hudson Kelly to fight the land grabs and monopolies of the business titans. Bourne, "Midwest Farmers' Movement."
54. Le Sueur, "Iron Country," 53; further citations from "Iron Country" appear as page numbers in the text. See also Le Sueur "Eroded Woman," 121.
55. Le Sueur, "Eroded Woman," 225. Further citations appear as page numbers in the text.
56. In 1870, the discovery of zinc in southeastern Kansas marked the beginning of a century of lead and zinc mining in the tristate mining district extending into Missouri, Oklahoma, and Kansas. Kansas Geological Survey, "Lead and Zinc Mining."
57. The town of Picher, Oklahoma, fifteen miles from Galena, sounds a lot like the town she visited. The lead and zinc mining region is now a ghost town. Sawyer, "Story behind America's Most Toxic Ghost Town."
58. Pratt, "Woman Writer," 256.

59. For these biographical details, see Coiner, *Better Red*, 82–84; Hedges, Introduction to *Ripening*, 16–17; and Schleuning, *America*, 19–25.

60. Irene Paull, letter to Neala Schleuning, 1989, MSS 0488, Neala Schleuning–Meridel Le Sueur collection, Special Collections, University of Delaware Library, Newark, Delaware.

61. Schleuning, *America*, 24, cites a profile of Le Sueur, incongruously appearing in the society pages of the *St. Paul Pioneer Press* in 1944, telling of a time when, late for a play and looking for something to wear at the last minute, she spied her colorful tablecloth and wore it as a wrap.

62. Sullivan, *Revealing Whiteness*.

63. Sullivan, *Revealing Whiteness*, 146.

64. Le Sueur, *Mound Builders*; and Le Sueur, "Zapata!"

65. Coiner ascribes Le Sueur's unconventional relation to time to her extended visits with Native groups, among them the Oglala Lakota in South Dakota and Hopi in Arizona. See Coiner, *Better Red*, 86.

66. Le Sueur, "Dark of the Time," 36.

67. Le Sueur, "American Bus," 136. Further citations appear as page numbers in the text.

68. For a fuller discussion of the unconscious pleasure of white good intentions, see Sullivan, *Revealing Whiteness*, 180–85.

69. Le Sueur's extended family has remained active in Native American struggles. David and Barbara Tilsen's grandchildren, Nick Tilsen, Mark Kenneth Tilsen, and Kimberly Tilsen Brave Heart, are enrolled members of the Oglala Lakota Sioux tribe. They and other family members maintain strong ties and commitments to the Lakota and Dakota people.

70. Barbara and David Tilsen, interview by author, June 21, 2021.

71. Le Sueur's family members are pursuing its publication.

72. Le Sueur, "Dakotas Look Back," 4.

73. Le Sueur, "First Farmers' Revolt," 21. Further citations appear as page numbers in the text.

74. Le Sueur, "The Ancient People and the Newly Come," 40. Further citations appear as page numbers in the text.

75. J. Crawford, "Note on the History of Ludlow," 55.

76. J. Crawford, "Note on the History of Ludlow," 55.

77. J. Crawford, "Note on the History of Ludlow," 56.

78. Thousands of workers in the United States are still contracting and dying of silicosis because their workplaces lack appropriate protection under safety standards from the companies and from federal regulations. One culprit is the cutting process for quartz kitchen counters. On lax regulation by the Occupational Safety and Health Administration (OSHA) under the administration of Donald Trump, see Michaels, "Silicosis Outbreak."

79. Le Sueur, *Dread Road*, 14. Further citations appear as page numbers in the text.

80. Le Sueur, author's note to *Dread Road*, 61–62.

81. Sullivan, *Revealing Whiteness*, 122.

82. I am reminded of the requirement to get rid of her "Semitic" nose that Le Sueur confronted in the Hollywood dream machine, an indicator of the evolving definition and commodification of the white female body and of the film industry's role in crafting and reproducing embodied racial values.

83. Byrd, *Transit of Empire*, xvii.

84. Kuokkanen, *Reshaping the University*, ch. 1; Kimmerer, *Braiding Sweetgrass*, 382–83.

85. Kuokkanen, *Reshaping the University*, 32, 33.

86. Zadik, "Iberian Pig," 52–59. See also Vann, "History of Pigs."

87. Le Sueur, "Meridel Le Sueur."

88. Le Sueur and Twin Cities Women's Film Collective, *My People Are My Home*, 3:34–3:57.

6. Particles of Intense Life

1. The scholarship on Rukeyser is extensive, much of it in articles and chapters. For major studies, see Kertesz, *Poetic Vision*; and Kennedy-Epstein, *Unfinished Spirit*. Ongoing research is featured on the website Muriel Rukeyser: A Living Archive, http://murielrukeyser.emuenglish.org/scholarship/.

2. Kennedy-Epstein, *Unfinished Spirit*, 144.

3. Rich, Introduction to *Muriel Rukeyser Reader*, xv. See also Rich, "Muriel Rukeyser."

4. Keenaghan, "Biocracy," 258.

5. Lorde, "Uses of the Erotic," 41.

6. Rukeyser, *Life of Poetry*, 55.

7. Keenaghan, "Biocracy," 268.

8. Däumer, "Introduction: Muriel Rukeyser's Presumptions," 254–55.

9. Rukeyser wrote a poem about Gibbs that appeared in *U.S. 1*. She also published a commentary on him in *Physics Today* and referred to him in her book on poetics, *The Life of Poetry*. For the influence of Gibbs on her work, see Morehead, "Negative Entropy."

10. Däumer, "Introduction: Muriel Rukeyser's Presumptions," 249; and *Journal of Narrative Theory*, special issue on Muriel Rukeyser, 43, no. 3 (2013).

11. Murphy, "Chemical Regimes of Living." The phrase refers to the transformations at the molecular level produced in over a century of petroleum capitalism as synthetic chemicals have traveled across the globe, penetrating air, water, soil, and the flesh of human and nonhuman animals.

12. Rukeyser, *Willard Gibbs*, 404. Further citations appear as page numbers in the text.

13. Däumer, "Introduction: Muriel Rukeyser's Presumptions," 250.

14. Holt, *Alexandra Kollontai*, 202.

15. See, for example, Inman, *In Woman's Defense*; and discussion of

Inman in Wiegand, *Red Feminism*. On sexual dissidents on the Left, see Brown and Faue, "Revolutionary Desires"; and Lecklider, *Love's Next Meeting*. For treatments of Kollontai's attention to Eros, see Barraclough, Bowen-Struyk, and Rabinowitz, "Introduction: Sex, Texts, Comrades." In that collection see Zavialova, "Red Venus," 221–31; and Rabinowitz, "Class Ventriloquism," on Rukeyser's "Absalom" as an instance of speaking through another as a practice of Red love.

16. Kollontai, "Make Way," 276. Further citations appear as page numbers in the text.

7. Shadowing the Erotics of Race Work in Muriel Rukeyser

1. That year the NSL organized a conference at Columbia University on Negro students' problems. In 1932, they organized support for the miners' strike in Harlan County, Kentucky.

2. Rukeyser mentions in the story for the NSL *Student Review* that one of the men had been threatened with lynching three weeks before "on a trip to do newspaper work." It was probably Fuller, who was often reporting on the case for the *Daily Worker*. Muriel Rukeyser Papers, part 2, box 5, Manuscript Division, Library of Congress, Washington, D.C.

3. On November 22, 2013, a three-judge panel of the Alabama Board of Pardons and Paroles posthumously pardoned Haywood Patterson, Charlie Weems, and Andy Wright. Bellamy, "The Scottsboro Boys: Injustice in Alabama."

4. Larsen, *Modernism and Hegemony*, xxi, argues for seeing modernism as an ideological formation stretching across many cultural activities that managed capital's transition from a liberal free market to a more abstract monopolistic form and the crisis of representation (of subjects and relations) that transition entailed.

5. Rukeyser, "Women of Scottsboro."

6. Tom Mooney (1882–1942) was one of the most famous political prisoners in America, an industrial worker and labor leader who many believed was wrongly imprisoned for planting explosives. His life sentence sparked a worldwide campaign to free him. Mooney worked for the Socialist Party of America and in Eugene Debs's campaign for president. His father was a militant miner who died of silicosis.

7. Rukeyser, "Women of Scottsboro."

8. Rukeyser's representation of the women is at odds with the narratives the Communist Party prepared for the boys' mothers to deliver in speeches they made during national and international tours.

9. Carter, *Scottsboro*, 150, 169.

10. Foley, *Spectres*, 78.

11. On the specular cultural logic of lynching, see Goldsby, *Spectacular Secret*.

12. S. Smith, *At the Edge of Sight*, 203.

13. This last point drove the initial political struggles over jury selection in the Scottsboro trials. Carter, *Scottsboro*, 196.

14. See Wells, *Southern Horrors*; Feimster, *Southern Horrors*.

15. Judge James E. Horton, who presided over Patterson's second trial, overturned the jury's guilty verdict, based on his analysis of evidence offered by the doctor who examined Victoria Price immediately after the incident. A Dr. John Lynch (Carter adds, "no pun here") also examined Price and did not believe the "girls" had been raped but was unwilling to testify to this, fearing his professional future in the town. See Carter, *Scottsboro*, 215.

16. Some poems have numbered parts or sections. I've given the part or section number where the stanza count is within a part or section, as here.

17. On photographs of lynching, see Smith, *At the Edge of Sight*, 279; Apel and Smith, *Lynching Photographs*.

18. Rukeyser, "Under Forty," 27.

19. Rukeyser, "Under Forty," 27.

20. Kaufman, "'But Not the Study,'" 49.

21. Rukeyser, "Under Forty," 27. Further citations appear as page numbers in the text.

22. Kaufman, "'But Not the Study,'" 50.

23. Wolosky, "What Do Jews Stand For?," 201; see also Engelhardt, "Muriel's Gift"; Kaufman, "'But Not the Study.'"

24. In 1952, her editor at Little, Brown, Angus Cameron, was accused of Communist sympathies and named before the Senate Internal Security Subcommittee, also known as the McCarran Committee. He was fired and went into hiding. Consequently, Rukeyser's advance contract and copyrights were frozen at the press.

25. For biographical information and details of Naumburg's film work, see Koszarski, "Nancy Naumburg."

26. Founded as the Workingman's School on principles developed by Felix Adler, the Fieldston School emphasized moral education, psychological development, and the integration of the creative and manual arts with academics.

27. Vassar already had famous alumnae to its credit, among them Edna St. Vincent Millay. Elizabeth Bishop, Eleanor Clark, and Mary McCarthy were classmates of Nancy and Muriel.

28. Davidson, *Ghostlier Demarcations*, 141.

29. Among them were Berenice Abbott, *Changing New York* (1939); Margaret Bourke-White and Erskine Caldwell, *You Have Seen Their Faces* (1937); Richard Wright and Edwin Rosskam, *12 Million Black Voices* (1941); Dorothea Lange and Paul Taylor, *An American Exodus* (1939); and James Agee and Walker Evans, *Let Us Now Praise Famous Men* (1941).

30. Each chapter in *We Make the Movies* is a contribution by a different leading artist or technician. The collection demystifies the glamour and lays bare the realism of the movies by showing how they are made, for example, by directors and technicians working in close proximity with the actors in a scene. Blaming well-funded big studios for the mythic versions of American life produced in Hollywood—the very studios represented in

the collection—she advocates for the revival of the "short subject" film, the format promoted by the Film and Photo League, because it offered "one of the most flexible means of experimentation in motion pictures." Naumburg, *We Make the Movies*, xxv.

31. Nancy Naumburg to Muriel Rukeyser, 1932, Muriel Rukeyser Papers, Berg Collection of English and American Literature, New York Public Library.

32. Nancy Naumburg to Muriel Rukeyser, February 1933, Muriel Rukeyser Papers, Berg Collection.

33. Diary entries, March 19, March 19, and March 20, 1933, Muriel Rukeyser Papers, part 1, box 2, Manuscript Division, Library of Congress, Washington, D.C.

34. Sagarin, who was two years older than Rukeyser, went on to become a well-known sociologist and a prolific writer. Cited as one of the most influential gay theorists of the 1950s, he authored *The Homosexual in America* (1951) under the pseudonym Donald Webster Cory. See Duberman, *Martin Duberman Reader*, 173–205.

35. Diary entry, April 9, 1933, Muriel Rukeyser Papers, part 1, box 2, Library of Congress.

36. Diary entry, April 22, 1933, Muriel Rukeyser Papers, part 1, box 2, Library of Congress. "Selah" is a Hebrew word that appears throughout the Psalms. It has no specific literal translation; rather, it marks a musical pause, both an interception and an affirmation.

37. Nancy Naumburg to Muriel Rukeyser, August 1934, Muriel Rukeyser Papers, Berg Collection.

38. Their correspondence resumed with a flurry of letters around the time of Muriel's brief marriage to the painter Glyn Collins in June 1945. It appears that Nancy attended the wedding reception because she wrote to Muriel that she corresponded with Muriel's parents about it. Nancy was living then in Redwood City, California, and was pregnant with her first child. The correspondence resumed in 1947 when Muriel was about to give birth to her son and Nancy was in the process of getting a divorce. At this time, Nancy seems adrift in her life and somewhat lost. Later she would marry Eugene Goldsmith, settle into domestic life in New York City, and raise three daughters, Katherine Ann Smith [d. 1999], Margie Goldsmith, and Lynne Goldsmith Miller. Muriel Rukeyser Papers, part 2, box 2, Library of Congress.

39. Lynd, *On Shame*, 65–66.

40. Holland, *Erotic Life of Racism*, 7. Further citations appear as page numbers in the text.

41. Publication of Rukeyser's film script "Gauley Bridge," in the magazine *Films*, featured an ad for books on film, among them Nancy Naumburg's edited book *We Make the Movies*.

42. For more on this project, see Cherniak, *Hawk's Nest Incident*; Dayton, *Muriel Rukeyser's "Book"*; Kadlec, "X-ray Testimonials"; Kalaidjian,

American Culture; C. Moore, "The Book of the Dead"; Morehead, "Negative Entropy"; Alaimo, *Bodily Natures*.

43. C. Moore's Introduction to Rukeyser's *Book of the Dead* recounts her interviews with several family members of survivors and includes three of Naumburg's photographs from the trip. She reads them, as well as Rukeyser's hand-drawn map of the area and the Rinehart and Dennis Company's list of employees who died from 1930 to 1935, a small sample of the probable total.

44. U.S. House of Representatives, H.R. Res. 449, 1936.

45. In 1939, Rukeyser published a photo-text portfolio in *Coronet* magazine entitled "Worlds Alongside," for which she wrote the narrative. See Gander, "Facing the Fact."

46. Rukeyser, *Life of Poetry*, 143, 19; see also Gander, "Facing the Fact," 317.

47. Gander, "Facing the Fact," 320.

48. C. Moore, "The Book of the Dead," 106.

49. Chandler, *X*, 69.

50. Chandler, *X*, 90.

51. Du Bois, *Dusk of Dawn*, 65.

52. In an interview with Catherine Moore, Bernard Jones said that merchants in Gauley Bridge, disturbed that their town was receiving so much bad publicity, blamed "the undesirables, mainly Negros." When someone burned a cross on the hill above Vanetta, the residents all headed to the bus station, "going back home to the South." C. Moore, introduction to Rukeyser's *Book of the Dead*, 32–33.

53. S. Smith, *At the Edge of Sight*, 2, 4, 7, 17.

54. On the "knottiness" of 1930s documentary photography, see Allred, *American Modernism*, 6. On Rukeyser's use of documentary, see especially Ehlers, *Left of Poetry*, 65–102; Gander, *Rukeyser and Documentary*; Thurston, *Making Something Happen*, 169–210.

55. Allred, *American Modernism*, 6.

56. Chandler, *X*, 101.

57. Chandler, *X*, 105.

58. Spillers, "Mama's Baby, Papa's Maybe."

59. Chandler, *X*, 111.

60. Eiland and McLaughlin, translators' introduction to Benjamin's *Arcades Project*, 462.

61. Azoulay, *Civil Contract*, 14.

62. Azoulay, *Civil Contract*, 22–23.

63. Like Rukeyser's film script "Gauley Bridge," "The Book of the Dead" recognizes that witnessing depends not merely upon the evidence of outside observers but also upon relations among narrator, camera, witnesses, committees, and spectators/readers, relations that are part of the material environment.

64. Rukeyser, "Book of the Dead," "The Road," stanza 10, lines 2–3.

65. Rukeyser, "Book of the Dead," "Gauley Bridge," stanza 1, lines 1, 4.

66. Rukeyser, "Book of the Dead," "Gauley Bridge," stanza 2, line 4.

67. Rukeyser, "Book of the Dead," "Absalom," stanza 2, quoting Spell 30B, *The Book of the Dead*. See A. Roberts, *My Heart My Mother*, 2000. On funerary heart scarabs, see Arico and Foley, "Ancient Egyptian Amulets: Heart Scarab." The heart scarab of Hatnefer was exhibited in the Metropolitan Museum in 1937. Rukeyser may well have seen it there or in the British Museum in London when she traveled to the UK in 1936. For more on the exhibit, see Kadlec, "X-ray Testimonials."

68. Rukeyser, "Book of the Dead," "The Book of the Dead," stanza 37, line 1; stanza 41, line 2; stanza 45, line 3.

69. Marx, quoted in Bewes, *Event of Postcolonial Shame*, 13.

70. Rukeyser, "Book of the Dead," "Statement: Philippa Allen," line 63.

71. P. Allen, "Two Thousand Dying." See Rabinowitz, *Labor and Desire*, 146–49, on the reputation of social workers and on their representation in the pulp fiction they populated during this time.

72. One of Parsons's students at the New School was 1909 Vassar graduate Ruth Benedict, who pursued her studies with Boas at Columbia, where she earned her PhD and joined the faculty in 1923.

73. Naumburg's 1913 review of *The Old Fashioned Woman* by Parsons appeared in the *Survey*, a prominent social work journal whose editors included Jane Addams. Her 1914 article in the *New York Times Magazine* makes a strong feminist argument and demonstrates familiarity with writings across a range of fields.

74. Sprague Mitchell was a Radcliffe graduate (1896) and the first Dean of Women at the University of California, Berkeley. She became a pioneer in early childhood education and a champion of experiential learning. In 1916, she established the Bureau of Educational Experiments, which later became the Bank Street School. She was the author of multiple children's books, among them the highly successful *Here and Now Storybook* (1921), which focused on the everyday lives of children.

75. The loosely Marxian model of shame that Helen Lynd advocated insisted on the importance of historical context and transcultural analysis.

76. Muriel Rukeyser to Alice Walker, May 1975, Muriel Rukeyser Papers, General Correspondence, part 2, box 3, Library of Congress.

77. Boyd, *Wrapped in Rainbows*, 247; Hemenway, *Zora Neale Hurston*, 189.

78. Muriel Rukeyser to Alice Walker, May 1975, Muriel Rukeyser Papers, General Correspondence, part 2, box 3, Library of Congress.

79. See Kaplan, *Miss Anne*; Hemenway, *Zora Neale Hurston*.

80. Zora completed her degree in anthropology at Barnard in 1928 followed by two years at Columbia; throughout that time, she was conducting ethnographic research. See Kennedy-Epstein, *Unfinished Spirit*, 135–59, on Rukeyser's planned biography of Boas.

81. Muriel Rukeyser to Alice Walker, May 1975. Muriel Rukeyser Papers, General Correspondence, part 2, box 3, Library of Congress.

82. Probyn, *Blush*, xi–xii.

83. Telegrams, Nancy Naumburg to Muriel Rukeyser, May and June 1932, Muriel Rukeyser Papers, Berg Collection.

84. Muriel Rukeyser to Alice Walker, May 1975, Muriel Rukeyser Papers, General Correspondence, part 2, box 3, Library of Congress.

85. Muriel Rukeyser to Alice Walker, May 1975.

86. The letter closes with a reading of the situation as "a demonstration of Muriel's magnificent devotion to you," which in time made Alice "feel exceedingly wretched." As Alice explains, she felt that Muriel saw "what had happened between us [Alice and Monica] (essentially business partners) as something more personal, more spiritually indelible, than it was." And therefore Muriel "blamed me for insults against you I had not dreamed of thinking about." Alice Walker to Monica McCall, February 20, 1976, Muriel Rukeyser Papers, General Correspondence, part 2, box 3.

87. White, *Alice Walker*, 274.

88. Walker, "Turning into Love."

89. Kennedy-Epstein, *Unfinished Spirit*, 117.

90. In 1935 Abbott began sharing a loft with art critic Elizabeth McCausland, with whom she lived for thirty years. See Kennedy-Epstein, *Unfinished Spirit*, 113–34, on Rukeyser's relationship with Abbott; and Geyer's brief bio of Abbott, "Revolt, They Said."

91. Geyer, "Revolt, They Said"; Howard Greenberg Gallery, "Berenice Abbott."

92. Chandler, *X*, 127.

93. Chandler, *X*, 127.

94. Rukeyser, *Willard Gibbs*, 151.

Bibliography

Alaimo, Stacy. *Bodily Natures: Science, the Environment, and the Material Self.* Bloomington: Indiana University Press, 2010.

Alcoff, Linda Martín. *The Future of Whiteness.* Malden, Mass.: Polity Press, 2015.

Allen, Julia M. "'Dear Comrade': Marian Wharton of the People's College, Fort Scott, Kansas, 1914–1917." *Women's Studies Quarterly* 1, 2 (1994): 119–33.

———. "'We Must Have Writers': An Introduction to the Narrative Rhetorical Theory of Meridel Le Sueur." Paper presented at the Annual Meeting of the Conference on College Composition and Communication. Minneapolis, Minn., April 12–15, 2000. https://files.eric.ed.gov/fulltext/ED442100.pdf.

Allen, Philippa [Bernard Allen, pseud.]. "Two Thousand Dying on a Job." *New Masses,* January 1935, 18–19.

Allred, Jeff. *American Modernism and Depression Documentary.* Oxford: Oxford University Press, 2010.

Apel, Dora, and Shawn Michelle Smith. *Lynching Photographs.* Oakland: University of California Press, 2007.

Arico, Ashley Fiutko, and Kierra Foley. "Ancient Egyptian Amulets: Heart Scarab." Johns Hopkins Archaeological Museum. https://archaeologicalmuseum.jhu.edu/the-collection/object-stories/ancient-egyptian-amulets/heart-scarab.

Arruzza, Cinzia, and Kelly Gawel, eds. "The Politics of Social Reproduction." Special issue, *CLCWeb: Comparative Literature and Culture* 22, no. 2 (June 2020).

Azoulay, Ariella. *The Civil Contract of Photography.* New York: Zone Books, 2012.

Baker, Ella, and Marvel Cooke. "The Bronx Slave Market." *The Crisis,* November 1935, 330–32.

Balthasar, Benjamin. *Anti-Imperialist Modernism: Race and Transnational Radical Culture from the Depression to the Cold War.* Ann Arbor: University of Michigan Press, 2016.

———. "'Don't Work' and Other Lessons from the Marxist Feminism of Meridel Le Sueur." *In These Times,* March 8, 2022. https://inthesetimes.com/article/depression-era-marxist-feminist-writer-activist-working-class-labor-movement.

Barraclough, Ruth, Heather Bowen-Struyk, and Paula Rabinowitz. "Introduction: Sex, Texts, Comrades." In *Red Love across the Pacific: Political and Sexual Revolutions of the Twentieth Century,* edited by Ruth Barraclough, Heather Bowen-Struyk, and Paula Rabinowitz, xi–xviii. New York: Palgrave, 2015.

Bartram, William. *Travels of William Bartram.* Edited by Mark Van Doren. New York: Dover, 1928.

Bascom, Lionel C., ed. *Renaissance in Harlem: Lost Essays of the WPA, by Ralph Ellison, Dorothy West, and Other Voices of a Generation.* New York: HarperCollins, 1999.

Bellamy, Jay. "The Scottsboro Boys: Injustice in Alabama," *Prologue,* Spring 2014. https://www.archives.gov/files/publications/prologue/2014/spring /scottsboro.pdf.

Bennholdt-Thomsen, Veronika, and Maria Mies. *The Subsistence Perspective: Beyond the Globalized Economy.* London: Zed, 1999.

Bernard, Jay, and Walt Hunter. "Roses Full of Flame: The Poems of Claudia Jones." Young Poets Network, Poetry Society. https://ypn.poetrysociety .org.uk/features/roses-full-of-flame-the-poems-of-claudia-jones/.

Bewes, Timothy. *The Event of Postcolonial Shame.* Princeton: Princeton University Press, 2010.

Bhattacharya, Tithi, ed. *Social Reproduction Theory: Remapping Class, Recentering Oppression.* London: Pluto Press, 2017.

———. "What Is Social Reproduction Theory?" YouTube video, November 22, 2017. https://www.youtube.com/watch?v=Uur-pMk7XjY.

Bourne, Jenny. "The Midwest Farmers Movement That Challenged Gilded Age Capitalism." "What It Means to Be American": A National Conversation Hosted by the Smithsonian and Arizona State University, November 12, 2018. https://www.whatitmeanstobeamerican.org /engagements/the-midwest-farmers-movement-that-challenged -gilded-age-capitalism/.

Boyd, Valerie. *Wrapped in Rainbows: The Life of Zora Neale Hurston.* New York: Scribner, 2003.

Braund, Kathryn E. Holland. "The Real Worlds of William Bartram's Travels." In *William Bartram's Living Legacy,* edited by Dorinda G. Dallmeyer, 439–54. Atlanta: Mercer University Press, 2010.

Brodkin, Karen. *How Jews Became White Folks and What That Says about Race in America.* New Brunswick, N.J.: Rutgers University Press, 1998.

Brown, Kathleen A. "The Savagely Fathered and Unmothered World of the Communist Party: Feminism, Motherhood, and Mother Bloor." *Feminist Studies* 25, no. 3 (1999): 537–70.

Brown, Kathleen A., and Elizabeth Faue. "Revolutionary Desire: Redefining the Politics of Sexuality of American Radicals, 1919–1945." In *Sexual Borderlands: Constructing an American Sexual Past,* edited by Kathleen Kennedy and Sharon Rena Ullman, 273–302. Cleveland: Ohio University Press, 2003.

Burden-Stelly, Cherisse. "Radical Blackness and Mutual Comradeship at

409 Edgecombe." *Black Perspectives,* July 16, 2019. https://www.aaihs
.org/radical-Blackness-and-mutual-comradeship-at-409-edgecombe/.

Burkett, Paul. *Marx and Nature: A Red and Green Perspective.* Chicago:
Haymarket, 2014.

Byrd, Jodi A. *The Transit of Empire: Indigenous Critiques of Colonialism.*
Minneapolis: University of Minnesota Press, 2011.

Cabeza de Vaca, Alvár Nuñez. *Relación de Alvár Nuñez Cabeza de Vaca.*
1542. Edited and translated by Enrique Peña. Sydney: Wentworth Press,
2018.

"A Call for an American Writers' Congress." *New Masses,* January 22, 1935,
20.

Carter, Dan T. *Scottsboro: A Tragedy of the American South.* Baton Rouge:
Louisiana State University Press, 1979.

Chandler, Nahum Dimitri. *X: The Problem of the Negro as a Problem for
Thought.* New York: Fordham University Press, 2014.

Cherniak, Martin. *The Hawk's Nest Incident: America's Worst Industrial
Disaster.* New Haven: Yale University Press, 1986.

Childress, Alice. *Like One of the Family.* Boston: Beacon Press, 1986.

Childress, Alice, Paule Marshall, and Sarah E. Wright. "The Negro Woman
in American Literature." *Freedomways* 1 (1966): 8–25.

Coiner, Constance. *Better Red: The Writing and Resistance of Tillie Olsen
and Meridel Le Sueur.* London: Oxford University Press, 1995.

Cooke, Marvel. Recorded by Kathleen Currie. Washington Press Club
Foundation, Women in Journalism Oral History Project, 1989. http://
beta.wpcf.org/oralhistory/cook.html.

———. Interview by Mary Licht. August 16, 1984. Communist Party of the
United States of America Oral History Collection. Tamiment Library/
Robert F. Wagner Labor Archives, New York University. Audio, http://
digitaltamiment.hosting.nyu.edu/s/cpoh/item/3960.

———. "I Was Part of the Bronx Slave Market." *Daily Compass,* January 8,
1950.

———. "'Mrs. Legree' Hires on the Street, Always 'Nice' Girls." *Daily Compass,* January 11, 1950.

———. "Occupation: Streetwalker." *Daily Compass,* April 16, 1950.

———. "Some Ways to Kill the Slave Market." *Daily Compass,* January 12,
1950.

———. "Where Men Prowl and Women Prey on Needy Job Seekers." *Daily
Compass,* January 9, 1950.

Cooper, Esther. "The Negro Woman Domestic Worker in Relation to Trade
Unionism." MA thesis, Fisk University, 1940.

Crawford, Evelyn Louise, and Mary Louise Patterson, eds. *Letters from
Langston.* Oakland: University of California Press, 2016.

Crawford, John F. "A Note on the History of Ludlow." In *The Dread Road,*
by Meridel Le Sueur, 55–57. Albuquerque: West End Press, 1991.

Damon, Anna. "The Scottsboro Mothers Look to You." *Working Woman,* December 1934, 10.

Daniel, F. Raymond. "Challenges Story by Victoria Price." *New York Times,* July 14, 1937.

Däumer, Elisabeth. "Introduction: Muriel Rukeyser's Presumptions." Special issue on Muriel Rukeyser, *Journal of Narrative Theory* 43, no. 3 (2013): 247–57.

Däumer, Elisabeth, and Bill Ruykeyser. Muriel Rukeyser: A Living Archive. http://murielrukeyser.emuenglish.org/.

Davidson, Michael. *Ghostlier Demarcations: Modern Poetry and the Material World.* Berkeley: University of California Press, 1997.

Davies, Carole Boyce, ed. *Claudia Jones: Beyond Containment.* Banbury, UK: Ayebia Clarke Publishing Limited, 2011.

——. *Left of Karl Marx: The Political Life of Black Communist Claudia Jones.* Durham, N.C.: Duke University Press, 2007.

Dayton, Tim. *Muriel Rukeyser's "Book of the Dead."* Columbia: University of Missouri Press, 2015.

Debo, Angie. *And Still the Waters Run: The Betrayal of the Five Civilized Tribes.* 1940. Reprint, Princeton: Princeton University Press, 1991.

Debs, Eugene. "The School for the Masses: The People's College of Fort Scott, Kansas." *American Socialist* 2, no. 10 (1915): 2–3.

Delegard, Kirsten. "Hemmed In: Three Families Confront American Apartheid in Minneapolis." *Mapping Prejudice,* February 2018.

Deloria, Vine, Jr. *God Is Red: A Native View of Religion.* 1973. Reprint, New York: Putnam, 2003.

Denning, Michael. *The Cultural Front: The Laboring of American Culture in the Twentieth Century.* New York: Verso, 1996.

Dillon, Elizabeth Maddock. *New World Drama: The Performative Commons in the Atlantic World, 1649–1849.* Durham, N.C.: Duke University Press, 2014.

Duberman, Martin. *The Martin Duberman Reader: The Essential Historical, Biographical, and Autobiographical Writings.* New York: New Press, 2013.

Du Bois, W. E. B. *Dusk of Dawn: An Essay toward an Autobiography of a Race Concept.* 1940. Reprint, London: Oxford University Press, 2007.

Dunbar-Ortiz, Roxanne. *An Indigenous Peoples' History of the United States.* Boston: Beacon Press, 2014.

Ehlers, Sarah. *Left of Poetry: Depression America and the Formation of Modern Poetics.* Chapel Hill: University of North Carolina Press, 2019.

Ehrhardt, Julia C. *Writers of Conviction: The Personal Politics of Zona Gale, Dorothy Canfield Fisher, Rose Wilder Lane, and Josephine Herbst.* Columbia: University of Missouri Press, 2004.

Eiland, Howard, and Kevin McLaughlin. Translator's introduction to *The Arcades Project,* by Walter Benjamin. Cambridge, Mass.: Harvard University Press, 1999.

Engelhardt, Helen. "Muriel's Gift: Rukeyser's Poems on Jewish Themes."
    Muriel Rukeyser: A Living Archive. http://murielrukeyser.emuenglish.
    org/2016/02/05/helen-engelhardt.
Engels, Friedrich. *Dialectics of Nature.* New York: Lawrence and Wishart,
    1977.
Federici, Silvia. *Beyond the Periphery of the Skin: Rethinking, Remaking,
    and Reclaiming the Body in Contemporary Capitalism.* Oakland, Calif.:
    PM Press, 2020.
———. *Caliban and the Witch: Women, the Body, and Primitive Accumula-
    tion.* New York: Autonomedia, 2004.
———. *Re-enchanting the World: Feminism and the Politics of the Commons.*
    Oakland, Calif.: PM Press, 2018.
Feimster, Crystal Nicole. *Southern Horrors: Women and the Politics
    of Rape and Lynching.* Cambridge, Mass.: Harvard University Press,
    2011.
Ferguson, Susan. *Women and Work: Feminism, Labour, and Social Repro-
    duction.* London: Pluto Press, 2020.
Fields, Karen E., and Barbara J. Fields. *Racecraft: The Soul of Inequality in
    American Life.* London: Verso, 2012.
Flynn, Elizabeth Gurley. *The Alderson Story: My Life as a Political Pris-
    oner.* New York: International Publishers, 1963.
Foley, Barbara. *Radical Representations: Politics and Form in U.S. Prole-
    tarian Fiction, 1929–1941.* Durham, N.C.: Duke University Press, 1993.
———. *Spectres of 1919: Class and Nation in the Making of the New Negro.*
    Urbana: University of Illinois Press, 2008.
Foster, John Belamy. *Marx's Ecology: Materialism and Nature.* New York:
    Monthly Review Press, 2000.
Foster, John Belamy, and John Burkett. *Marx and the Earth: An Anti-
    Critique.* Chicago: Haymarket, 2016.
Friedman, Murray. *What Went Wrong? The Creation and Collapse of the
    Black–Jewish Alliance.* New York: Free Press, 1995.
Fulfilling a Prophecy: The Past and Present of the Lenape in Pennsylvania.
    Exhibition organized by the Penn Museum and the Lenape Nation of
    Pennsylvania. Penn Museum, September 13, 2008–July 2010, Philadel-
    phia. https://www.penn.museum/sites/fap/index.shtml.
Gander, Catherine. "Facing the Fact: Word and Image in Muriel
    Rukeyser's 'Worlds Alongside.'" *Journal of Narrative Theory* 43, no. 3
    (2013): 288–328.
———. *Muriel Rukeyser and Documentary: The Poetics of Connection.*
    Edinburgh: Edinburgh University Press, 2013.
Geyer, Andrea. "Revolt, They Said." 2012–. https://andreageyer.info
    /revolttheysaid/a.html.
Gilio-Whitaker, Dina. *As Long As the Grass Grows: The Indigenous Fight
    for Environmental Justice, from Colonization to Standing Rock.* Boston:
    Beacon Press, 2019.

Gilyard, Keith. *Louise Thompson Patterson: A Life of Struggle for Justice.* Durham, N.C.: Duke University Press, 2017.

Giménez, Martha. *Marx, Women, and Capitalist Social Reproduction.* Leiden, Neth.: Brill, 2019.

Goldsby, Jacqueline. *A Spectacular Secret: Lynching in American Life and Literature.* Chicago: University of Chicago Press, 2006.

Goldstein, Eric L. *The Price of Whiteness: Jews, Race, and Identity.* Princeton: Princeton University Press, 2006.

Goodman, James. *Stories of Scottsboro.* New York: Pantheon, 1994.

Gore, Dayo. *Radicalism at the Crossroads: African American Women Activists in the Cold War.* New York: New York University Press, 2011.

Gornick, Vivian. *The Romance of American Communism.* 2nd ed. New York: Verso, 2020.

Gosse, Van. "'To Organize in Every Neighborhood, in Every Home': The Gender Politics of American Communists between the Wars." *Radical History Review* 50 (1991): 109–41.

Greer, Jane. "No Smiling Madonna: Marian Wharton and the Struggle to Construct a Critical Pedagogy for the Working Class, 1914–1917." *College Composition and Communication* 2, no. 51 (1999): 248–71.

Grenier, John. *The First Way of War: American War Making on the Frontier, 1607–1814.* Cambridge: Cambridge University Press, 2005.

Griffin, Brent Garrett. "Geographies of (In)Justice: Radical Regionalism in the American Midwest, 1930–1950." PhD diss., Northeastern University, 2015.

Hapke, Laura. *Daughters of the Great Depression: Women, Work, and Fiction in the American 1930s.* Athens: University of Georgia Press, 1995.

———. "Who Are You Calling Un-American? Harlem Voices in New Deal Narratives." *Americana: The Journal of American Popular Culture* 18, no. 2 (Fall 2019). https://americanpopularculture.com/journal/articles/fall_2019/hapke.htm.

Harris, LaShawn. "Marvel Cooke: Investigative Journalist, Communist and Black Radical Subject." *Journal for the Study of Radicalism* 6, no. 2 (2012): 91–126.

———. "Running with the Reds: African American Women and the Communist Party during the Great Depression." *Journal of African American History* 94, no. 1 (2009): 21–43.

Harris, Trudier. *From Mammies to Militants: Domestics in Black American Literature.* Philadelphia: Temple University Press, 1982.

———. Introduction to *Like One of the Family,* by Alice Childress, xi–xxxiv. Boston: Beacon Press, 1986.

Harrow. "The Factory Farm." *Communist* 8, no. 3 (February–March 1929): 142–49.

Hart, Henry, ed. *American Writers' Congress.* New York: International Publishers, 1935.

Hartman, Saidiya. *Wayward Lives, Beautiful Experiments: Intimate His-*

tories of Riotous Black Girls, Troublesome Women, and Queer Radicals. New York: Norton, 2019.

Hedges, Elaine, ed. Introduction to *Ripening: Selected Work, 1927–1980,* by Meridel Le Sueur, 1–30. Old Westbury, N.Y.: Feminist Press, 1982.

Hemenway, Robert. *Zora Neale Hurston: A Literary Biography.* Urbana: University of Illinois Press, 1977.

Hennessy, Rosemary. "Toward an Ecology of Life-Making: The Remembering of Meridel Le Sueur." *CLCWeb: Comparative Literature and Culture* 22, no. 2 (2020). http://docs.lib.purdue.edu/clcweb/vol22/iss2/6.

Herbst, Josephine. "Cuba Sick for Freedom." *New Masses,* April 2, 1935, 17–20.

———. "The Farmer Looks Ahead." *American Mercury,* February 1935, 212–19.

———. "Farmers Form a United Front." *New Masses,* January 2, 1934, 20–22.

———. "Feet in the Grass Roots." *Scribner's Magazine,* January 1933, 46–51.

———. *New Green World.* New York: Hastings House, 1954.

———. "Passport from Realengo 18." *New Masses,* July 16, 1935, 10–11.

———. *Rope of Gold.* 1939. Reprint, New York: Feminist Press, 1984.

———. "Soviet in Cuba." *New Masses,* March 19, 1935, 9–12.

———. *The Starched Blue Sky of Spain and Other Memoirs.* New York: HarperCollins, 1991.

Higashida, Cheryl. *Black Internationalist Feminism: Women Writers of the Black Left, 1945–1995.* Urbana: University of Illinois Press, 2011.

Hine, Darlene Clark. "Rape and the Inner Lives of Black Women in the Middle West: Preliminary Thoughts on the Culture of Dissemblance." *Signs* 14, no. 4 (1989): 912–20.

Holland, Sharon. *The Erotic Life of Racism.* Durham, N.C.: Duke University Press, 2012.

Holt, Alex, ed. *Alexandra Kollontai: Selected Writings.* Translated by Alex Holt. New York: Norton, 1976.

Horne, Gerald. "The Red and the Black: The Communist Party and African Americans in Historical Perspective." In *New Studies in U.S. Communism,* edited by Michael E. Brown, Randy Martin, Frank Rosengarten, and George Snedeker, 199–237. New York: Monthly Review Press, 1993.

Howard Greenberg Gallery. "Berenice Abbott." Blog entry. https://www.howardgreenberg.com/artists/berenice-abbott/featured-works?view=thumbnails.

Inman, Mary. *In Woman's Defense.* Los Angeles: Committee to Organize the Advancement of Women, 1940.

Jacobson, Matthew Frye. *Whiteness of a Different Color: European Immigrants and the Alchemy of Race.* Cambridge, Mass.: Harvard University Press, 1998.

Jameson, Fredric. *Allegory and Ideology.* New York: Verso, 2019.

Johnson, Diane. Introduction to *The Starched Blue Sky of Spain and Other*

Memoirs, by Josephine Herbst. Boston: Northeastern University Press, 1999.

Jones, Claudia. "Autobiographical History." In *Claudia Jones: Beyond Containment,* edited by Carole Boyce Davies, 10–16. Oxfordshire: Ayebia Clarke Publishing Limited, 2011.

———. "An End to the Neglect of the Problems of the Negro Woman!" *Political Affairs* 28, no. 6 (1949): 51–67.

———. "Sojourners for Peace and Justice." *Daily Worker,* February 10, 1952.

Jones, Jacqueline. *Labor of Love, Labor of Sorrow: Black Women, Work and the Family from Slavery to the Present.* New York: Basic Books, 2010.

Kadlec, David. "X-ray Testimonials in Muriel Rukeyser." *Modernism/Modernity* 5, no. 1 (1998): 23–47.

Kalaidjian, Walter. *American Culture between the Wars: Revisionary Modernism and Postmodern Critique.* New York: Columbia University Press, 1993.

Kansas Geological Survey. "Lead and Zinc Mining." University of Kansas. https://geokansas.ku.edu/lead-and-zinc-mining.

Kaplan, Carla. *Miss Anne in Harlem: The White Women of the Harlem Renaissance.* New York: HarperCollins, 2013.

Katz, Cindi. "Vagabond Capitalism." *Antipode* 33, no. 4 (2001): 709–28.

Kaufman, Janet. "'But Not the Study': Writing as a Jew." In *"How Shall We Tell Each Other of the Poet?" The Life and Writing of Muriel Rukeyser,* edited by Anne F. Herzog and Janet E. Kaufman, 45–62. New York: St. Martin's Press, 1999.

Keenaghan, Eric. "Biocracy: Reading Poetic Politics through the Traces of Muriel Rukeyser's Life-Writing." *Journal of Narrative Theory* 43, no. 3 (2013): 258–87.

Kelley, Robin. *Hammer and Hoe: Alabama Communists in the Great Depression.* Chapel Hill: University of North Carolina Press, 1990.

Kennedy-Epstein, Rowena. *Unfinished Spirit: Muriel Rukeyser's Twentieth Century.* Ithaca: Cornell University Press, 2022.

Kertesz, Louise. *The Poetic Vision of Muriel Rukeyser.* Baton Rouge: Louisiana State University Press, 1980.

Kimmerer, Robin Wall. *Braiding Sweetgrass: Indigenous Wisdom, Scientific Knowledge, and the Teachings of Plants.* Minneapolis: Milkweed, 2013.

King, Tiffany Lethabo. *The Black Shoals: Offshore Formations of Black and Native Studies.* Durham, N.C.: Duke University Press, 2019.

Kollontai, Alexandra. "Make Way for Winged Eros: A Letter to Working Youth." In *Alexandra Kollontai: Selected Writings,* edited and translated by Alex Holt, 276–92. New York: Norton, 1977.

———. "Sexual Relations and the Class Struggle." In *Alexandra Kollontai: Selected Writings,* edited and translated by Alex Holt, 237–49. New York: Norton, 1977.

Kosiba, Sara. "Feet in the Grassroots." In *Regionalists on the Left: Radical*

Voices from the American West, edited by Michael Steiner, 47–64. Norman: University of Oklahoma Press, 2013.

Koszarski, Richard. "Nancy Naumburg." Women Film Pioneers Project, edited by Jane Gaines, Radha Vatsal, and Monica Dall'Asta, 2013. https://wfpp.columbia.edu/pioneer/ccp-nancy-naumburg/.

Kuokkanen, Rauna. *Reshaping the University: Responsibility, Indigenous Epistemes, and the Logic of the Gift.* Vancouver: UBC Press, 2007.

Landers, Jane. "Africans and Native Americans on the Spanish Florida Frontier." In *Beyond Black and Red: African–Native Relations in Colonial Latin America,* edited by Matthew Restall, 53–80. Albuquerque: University of New Mexico Press, 2005.

———. *Black Society in Spanish Florida.* Urbana: University of Illinois Press, 1999.

Langer, Elinor. *Josephine Herbst: The Story She Could Never Tell.* New York: Little, Brown, 1983.

Larsen, Neil. *Modernism and Hegemony.* Minneapolis: University of Minnesota Press, 1990.

Lecklider, Aaron S. *Love's Next Meeting: The Forgotten History of Homosexuality and the Left in American Culture.* Oakland: University of California Press, 2021.

Lenin, V. I. "Capitalism and Agriculture in America." *Communist* 8, no. 6 (June 1929): 313–18.

Le Sueur, Meridel. "American Bus." 1953. In *Harvest Song: Collected Essays and Stories,* 134–39. Albuquerque: West End Press, 1990.

———. "The Ancient People and the Newly Come." 1955. In *Ripening: Selected Work, 1927–1980,* 39–62. Old Westbury, N.Y.: Feminist Press, 1982.

———. "Annunciation." In *Ripening: Selected Work, 1927–1980,* 124–32. Old Westbury, N.Y.: Feminist Press, 1982.

———. Author's note to *The Dread Road,* 61–62. Albuquerque: West End Press, 1991.

———. *Crusaders.* New York: Blue Heron Press, 1955.

———. "The Dakotas Look Back on a Trail of Broken Treaties." *Worker,* March 19, 1950, 4–5.

———. "The Dark of the Time." 1956. In *Ripening: Selected Work, 1927–1980,* 231–39. Old Westbury, N.Y.: Feminist Press, 1982.

———. *The Dread Road.* Albuquerque: West End Press, 1991.

———. "Eroded Woman." 1948. In *Ripening: Selected Work, 1927–1980,* 225–31. Old Westbury, N.Y.: Feminist Press, 1982.

———. "The First Farmers' Revolt: A Tale of the American Indian's Fight for His Land." *Mainstream* 15, no. 3 (March 1962): 20–26.

———. *The Girl.* New York: West End Press, 1978.

———. *I Hear Men Talking, and Other Stories.* Albuquerque: West End Press, 1984.

———. "Iron Country." *Masses and Mainstream* 2, no. 3 (March 1949): 53–60.

———. "Meridel Le Sueur." In *Minnesota Writers: A Collection of Autobiographical Stories,* edited by Carmen Nelson Richards, 192–96. Minneapolis: T. S. Dennison, 1961.

———. *The Mound Builders.* New York: Franklin Watts, 1974.

———. *North Star Country.* New York: Book Find Club, 1945.

———. "The Origins of Corn." 1976. In *Ripening: Selected Work, 1927–1980,* 261. Old Westbury, N.Y.: Feminist Press, 1982.

———. *Ripening: Selected Work, 1927–1980.* Old Westbury, N.Y.: Feminist Press, 1982.

———. "Women Are Hungry." 1934. In *Ripening: Selected Work, 1927–1980,* 144–57. Old Westbury, N.Y.: Feminist Press, 1982.

———. *Women on the Breadlines.* 1932. Reprint, Albuquerque: West End Press, 1984.

———. "Women on the Breadlines." 1932. In *Ripening: Selected Work, 1927–1980,* 137–43. Old Westbury, N.Y.: Feminist Press, 1982.

———. "Salvation Home." In *New Masses: An Anthology of the Rebel Thirties,* edited by Joseph North, 125–28. New York: International Publishers, 1969.

———. *Sparrow Hawk.* 1950. Reprint, Stevens Point, Wisc.: Holy Cow Press, 1987.

———. "Zapata!" Unpublished manuscript made available to me by David and Barbara Tilsen.

Le Sueur, Meridel, and Twin Cities Women's Film Collective. *My People Are My Home.* Film. Oakland, Calif.: Serious Business, 1976. https://archive.org/details/mypeoplearemyhome.

Lindsey, Lydia. "Black Lives Matter: Grace P. Campbell and Claudia Jones; An Analysis of the Negro Question, Self-Determination, Black Belt Thesis." *Journal of Pan African Studies* 12, no. 9 (2019): 110–43.

Lira, Natalie, and Alexandra Minna Stern. "Mexican Americans and Eugenic Sterilization." *Aztlan* 39, no. 2 (2014): 9–34.

Lorde, Audre. "Uses of the Erotic: The Erotic as Power." In *Sister Outsider: Essays and Speeches,* 41–48. Berkeley, Calif.: Crossing Press, 1984.

Löwy, Michael. "Jewish Radical Intellectuals in Europe and the United States." In *Lineages of the Literary Left: Essays in Honor of Alan M. Wald,* edited by Howard Brick, Robbie Lieberman, and Paula Rabinowitz, 325–44. Ann Arbor: Michigan Publishing, 2015.

———. "Marx, Engels and Ecology." *Capitalism, Nature, Socialism* 28, no. 2 (2017): 10–21.

Lynd, Helen Merrell. *On Shame and the Search for Identity.* London: Routledge and Kegan Paul, 1958.

Marx, Leo. "The Idea of Nature." *Daedalus,* 2008: 8–21.

Maxwell, William J. *New Negro, Old Left.* New York: Columbia University Press, 1999.

May, Claudia. "Airing Dirty Laundry: Representations of Domestic Laborers in the Works of African American Women Writers." *Feminist Formations* 27, no. 1 (2015): 141–66.

McDuffie, Erik S. *Sojourning for Freedom: Black Women, American Communism and the Making of Black Left Feminism.* Durham, N.C.: Duke University Press, 2011.

McGlamery, J. Gabriel. "Race Based Underwriting and the Death of Burial Insurance." *Connecticut Insurance Law Journal* 15, no. 2 (Spring 2009): 531–70.

Merchant, Carolyn. *The Death of Nature: Women, Ecology, and the Scientific Revolution.* New York: Harper, 1980.

———. *Radical Ecology: The Search for a Livable World.* London: Routledge, 2000.

Michaels, David. "Silicosis Outbreak Highlights the 'Malignant Neglect' of OSHA That Is Killing American Workers." First Opinion. Stat, October 10, 2019. https://www.statnews.com/2019/10/10/silicosis-outbreak -malignant-neglect-of-osha/.

Mickenberg, Julia. *American Girls in Russia: Chasing the Soviet Dream.* Chicago: University of Chicago Press, 2017.

———. "Writing the Midwest: Le Sueur and the Making of a Radical Regional Tradition." In *Breaking Boundaries: New Perspectives on Women's Regional Writing,* edited by Sherrie A. Inness and Diana Royer, 143–60. Iowa City: University of Iowa Press, 1997.

Middleton, Thomas C. "Some Memoirs of Our Lady's Shrine at Chestnut Hill, PA: A.D. 1855–1900 (Continued)." *Records of the Catholic Historical Society of Philadelphia* 12, no. 4 (1901): 385–418.

Mies, Maria, and Vandana Shiva. *Ecofeminism.* London: Zed, 1993.

Miles, Tiya. *Ties That Bind: The Story of an Afro-Cherokee Family in Slavery and Freedom.* 2nd ed. Oakland: University of California Press, 2015.

Miller, James A., Susan D. Pennybacker, and Eve Rosenhaft. "Mother Ada Wright and the International Campaign to Free the Scottsboro Boys, 1931–1934." *American Historical Review* 106, no. 2 (April 2001): 387–430.

Miller, Susan A. "Seminoles and Africans under Seminole Law." In *Native Historians Write Back: Decolonizing American Indian History,* edited by Susan A. Miller and James Riding, 187–206. Lubbock: Texas Tech University Press, 2011.

Miller, Susan A., and James Riding In, eds. *Native Historians Write Back: Decolonizing American Indian History.* Lubbock: Texas Tech University Press, 2011.

Milton, David. *The Politics of U.S. Labor from the Great Depression to the New Deal.* New York: Monthly Review Press, 1982.

Minneapolis Tribune. "Negro Building House in Spite of Protests." October 29, 1909.

Minneapolis Tribune. "Race War Started in Prospect Park." October 22, 1909.

Moore, Catherine Venable. "The Book of the Dead." *Oxford American* 94 (Fall 2016). https://main.oxfordamerican.org/magazine/item/1049-the -book-of-the-dead.

——. Introduction to *The Book of the Dead by Muriel Rukeyser*. Morgantown: West Virginia University Press, 2018.

Moore, Jason W. *Capitalism in the Web of Life: Ecology and the Accumulation of Capital*. New York: Verso, 2015.

Moore, Richard. "Think of Them." *Working Woman,* August 1934, 13.

Morehead, Craig. "Negative Entropy and the Energy of Utopian Potential in Muriel Rukeyser's *The Book of the Dead*." *Journal of Narrative Theory* 43, no. 3 (2013): 329–52.

Moreton-Robinson, Aileen. "Whiteness, Epistemology, and Indigenous Representation." In *Whitening Race,* edited by Aileen Moreton-Robinson, 75–88. Canberra: Aboriginal Studies Press, 2004.

——. *The White Possessive: Property, Power, and Indigenous Sovereignty*. Minneapolis: University of Minnesota Press, 2015.

Morris, Vivian. "Domestic Workers Union." Library of Congress. https:// www.loc.gov/resource/wpalh2.22042106/?sp=2&st=text.

Murphy, Michelle. "Chemical Regimes of Living." *Environmental History* 3, no. 4 (2008): 695–703.

Naison, Mark. *Communists in Harlem during the Depression*. Urbana: University of Illinois Press, 1983.

——. "From Eviction Resistance to Rent Control: Tenant Activism in the Great Depression." TenantNet. http://www.tenant.net/Community /history/hist03f.html.

——. "Remaking America: Communists and Liberals in the Popular Front." In *New Studies in American Communism,* edited by Michael E. Brown, Randy Martin, Frank Rosengarten, and George Snedeker, 45–73. New York: Monthly Review Press, 1993.

Naumburg, Nancy, ed. *We Make the Movies*. London: Faber and Faber, 1938.

Nekola, Charlotte, and Paula Rabinowitz, eds. *Writing Red: An Anthology of American Women Writers, 1930–1940*. 1987. Reprint, Chicago: Haymarket, 2022.

New York Times. "Josephine Herbst, Novelist and Political Reporter, Dead." January 29, 1969, 38.

Orlick, Annelise. "'We Are That Mythical Thing Called the Public': Militant Housewives during the Great Depression." *Feminist Studies* 19, no. 1 (1993): 147–72.

Palmer, Bryan D. "Rethinking the Historiography of United States Communism." *American Communist History* 2, no. 2 (December 2003): 139–74.

——. *Revolutionary Teamsters: The Minneapolis Truckers' Strikes of 1934*. Chicago: Haymarket, 2014.

Palmer, Bryan D., and Joan Sangster. "Legacies of 1917: Revolution's Longue Durée." *American Communist History* 16, nos. 1–2 (2017): 1–45.

Pratt, Linda Ray. Afterword to *I Hear Men Talking, and Other Stories,* by Meridel Le Sueur, 225–36. Minneapolis: West End Press, 1984.

———. "Woman Writer in the CP: The Case of Meridel Le Sueur." *Women's Studies* 14 (1988): 247–64.

Probyn, Elsbeth. *Blush: Faces of Shame.* Minneapolis: University of Minnesota Press, 2005.

Rabinowitz, Paula. "'Between the Outhouse and the Garbage Dump.'" *American Literary History* 23, no. 1 (Spring 2011): 32–55.

———. *Black and White and Noir.* New York: Columbia University Press, 2002.

———. "Class Ventriloquism: Women's Letters, Lectures, Lyrics—and Love." In *Red Love across the Pacific: Political and Sexual Revolutions of the Twentieth Century,* edited by Ruth Barraclough, Heather Bowen-Struyk, and Paula Rabinowitz, 201–20. New York: Palgrave, 2015.

———. "Domestic Labor: Film Noir, Proletarian Literature, and Black Women's Fiction." *Modern Fiction Studies* 47, no. 1 (2001): 229–54.

———. *Labor and Desire: Women's Revolutionary Fiction in Depression America.* Chapel Hill: University of North Carolina Press, 1991.

Ransby, Barbara. *Ella Baker and the Black Freedom Movement: A Radical Democratic Vision.* Chapel Hill: University of North Carolina Press, 2003.

Reilly, P. R. "Involuntary Sterilization in the United States: A Surgical Solution." *Quarterly Review of Biology* 62, no. 2 (June 1987): 153–70. https://pubmed.ncbi.nlm.nih.gov/3299450/.

Rich, Adrienne. Introduction to *A Muriel Rukeyser Reader,* edited by Ann Heller Levi, xiii. New York: Norton, 1994.

———. "Muriel Rukeyser, 1913–1978: Poet, Woman, American, Jew." *Bridges* 1, no. 1 (1990): 23–26.

Richman, A. J. "The Mass Migration of American Farmers." *Communist* 8, no. 5 (May 1929): 255–62.

Roberts, Alison. *My Heart My Mother: Death and Rebirth in Ancient Egypt.* Rottingdean, UK: NorthGate, 2000.

Roberts, Nora Ruth. *Three Radical Women Writers: Class and Gender in Meridel Le Sueur, Tillie Olsen, and Josephine Herbst.* New York: Garland, 1996.

Roediger, David R. *Working toward Whiteness: How Immigrants Became White.* New York: Basic Books, 2005.

Rosenfelt, Deborah. "Getting into the Game." *Women's Studies International Forum* 9 (1986): 563–72.

Rukeyser, Muriel. *The Collected Poems.* Edited by Janet E. Kaufman and Anne F. Herzog. Pittsburgh: University of Pittsburgh Press, 2005.

———. "From Scottsboro to Decatur." *Student Review,* April 1933: 12–15.

——. "Gauley Bridge." *Films* 1, no. 3 (1940): 51–64.

——. "Josiah Willard Gibbs." *Physics Today* 2, no. 2 (1949): 6–13, 27.

——. *The Life of Poetry.* 1949. Reprint, Ashfield, Mass.: Paris Press, 1996.

——. "Under Forty." *Bridges* 1, no. 1 (1990): 26–29.

——. *Willard Gibbs.* 1942. Reprint, New York: Dutton, 1964.

——. "Women of Scottsboro." Muriel Rukeyser Papers, part 2, box 19. Library of Congress, Manuscript Division, Washington, D.C.

——. "Worlds Alongside: A Portfolio of Photographs with Narrative by Muriel Rukeyser." *Cornet,* October 1939, 83–98.

Russell, Thomas Holt. "Who Was Vivian Morris?" Medium, September 4, 2018. https://medium.com/@thruss09/who-was-vivian-morris-70a050eac90b.

Sagarin, Edward [Donald Webster Cory]. *The Homosexual in America.* New York: Greenberg, 1951.

Saito, Kohei. *Karl Marx's Ecosocialism: Capital, Nature, and the Unfinished Critique of Political Economy.* New York: Monthly Review Press, 2017.

Salleh, Ariel, ed. *Eco-sufficiency and Global Justice: Women Write Political Ecology.* New York: Pluto Press, 1984.

Sawyer, Bobbie Jean. "The Story behind America's Most Toxic Ghost Town." Wide Open Country, February 2, 2021. https://www.wideopencountry.com/picher-oklahoma/.

Schafer, Daniel L. *William Bartram and the Ghost Plantations of British East Florida.* Gainesville: University Press of Florida, 2010.

Schere, Laura. "Irene Paull as Jewish Woman Radical." *Upper Midwest Jewish History* 1 (Fall 1998): 19–35.

Schleuning, Neala. *America: Song We Sang without Knowing; The Life and Ideas of Meridel Le Sueur.* Mankato, Minn.: Little Red Hen Press, 1983.

——. "Meridel Le Sueur: Toward a New Regionalism." *Books at Iowa* 33 (November 1980): 22–41.

Schwieder, Dorothy. "History of Iowa." Iowa Official Register. http://publications.iowa.gov/135/1/history/7-1.html.

Sherwood, Marika. *Claudia Jones: A Life in Exile.* London: Lawrence and Wishart, 1999.

Shover, John L. *Cornbelt Rebellion: The Farmers' Holiday Association.* Urbana: University of Illinois Press, 1965.

Smethurst, James Edward. *The New Red Negro: The Literary Left and African American Poetry, 1930–1946.* New York: Oxford University Press, 1999.

Smith, Neil. *Uneven Development: Nature, Capital, and the Production of Space.* 3rd ed. Athens: University of Georgia Press, 2008.

Smith, Shawn Michelle. *At the Edge of Sight: Photographs and the Unseen.* Durham, N.C.: Duke University Press, 2013.

Solomon, Mark. *The Cry Was Unity: Communists and African Americans, 1917–36.* Jackson: University Press of Mississippi, 1998.

Sowinska, Suzanne. "American Women Writers and the Radical Tradition." PhD diss., University of Washington, 1992.

Spillers, Hortense J. "Mama's Baby, Papa's Maybe: An American Grammar Book." *Diacritics* 17, no. 2 (1987): 64–81.

Steiner, Michael C., ed. *Regionalists on the Left: Radical Voices from the American West.* Norman: University of Oklahoma Press, 2013.

Streitmatter, Rodger. "Marvel Cooke: An African American Woman Journalist Who Agitated for Racial Reform." *African Americans in New York Life and History* 16, no. 2 (1992): 47.

Sullivan, Shannon. *Revealing Whiteness: The Unconscious Habits of Racial Privilege.* Bloomington: Indiana University Press, 2006.

Swanger, Joanna. *Rebel Lands of Cuba: The Campesino Struggles of Oriente and Escambray, 1934–1974.* Lanham, Md.: Lexington Press, 2015.

Tajima-Peña, Renee, director. *No más bebés.* Moon Canyon Films, 2015.

Taylor, David Vassar. *African Americans in Minnesota.* St. Paul: Minnesota Historical Society Press, 2002.

Taylor, Yuval. *Zora and Langston: A Story of Friendship and Betrayal.* New York: Norton, 2019.

Thompson (Patterson), Louise. "And So We Marched." *Woman Today,* June 1933, 6.

———. "Southern Terror." *Crisis,* November 1934, 328.

———. "Toward a Brighter Dawn." *Woman Today,* April 1936, 14, 30.

Thurston, Michael. *Making Something Happen: American Poetry between the Wars.* Chapel Hill: University of North Carolina Press, 2001.

Tilsen, David, and Barbara Tilsen. Interview by the author. June 21, 2021.

Trethewey, Natasha. Introduction to *The Essential Muriel Rukeyser: Poems,* ix–xiii. New York: HarperCollins, 2021.

U.S. House of Representatives, Subcommittee on Labor Hearings. H.R. Res. 449. 74th Cong., second sess., 1936.

Van Deen, Sadie. "Save the Scottsboro Boys." *Working Woman,* March 1934, 5.

Vann, Mick. "A History of Pigs in America." *Austin Chronicle,* April 10, 2009.

Wald, Alan M. *American Night: The Literary Left in the Era of the Cold War.* Chapel Hill: University of North Carolina Press, 2012.

———. "Culture and Commitment." In *New Studies in U.S. Communism,* edited by Michael E. Brown, Randy Martin, Frank Rosengarten, and George Snedeker, 281–305. New York: Monthly Review Press, 1993.

———. *Exiles from a Future Time: The Forging of the Mid-Twentieth Century Literary Left.* Chapel Hill: University of North Carolina Press, 2002.

———. *The New York Intellectuals: The Rise and Decline of the Anti-Stalinist Left from the 1930s to the 1980s.* Chapel Hill: University of North Carolina Press, 1987.

Walker, Alice. "Turning into Love: Some Thoughts on Surviving and Meeting Langston Hughes." *Callaloo,* no. 41 (Autumn 1989): 663–66.

Ware, Susan. *Holding Their Own: American Women in the 1930s.* Woodbridge, Conn.: Twayne, 1982.

Washington, Mary Helen. "Alice Childress, Lorraine Hansberry, and Claudia Jones: Black Women Write the Popular Front." In *Left of the Color Line: Race, Radicalism and Twentieth Century Literature,* edited by Bill V. Mullen and James Smethurst, 183–204. Chapel Hill: University of North Carolina Press, 2003.

———. *The Other Blacklist: The African American Literary and Cultural Left of the 1950s.* New York: Columbia University Press, 2014.

Wells, Ida B. *Southern Horrors, and Other Writings.* Edited by Jacqueline Jones Royster. Boston: Bedford / St. Martin's Press, 2016.

White, Evelyn C. *Alice Walker: A Life.* New York: Norton, 2004.

Wiedmann, Barbara. *Josephine Herbst's Short Fiction: A Window to Her Life and Times.* Selinsgrove, Pa.: Susquehanna University Press, 1998.

Wiegand, Kate. *Red Feminism: American Communism and the Making of Women's Liberation.* Baltimore: The Johns Hopkins University Press, 2001.

Willis, Ellen. "The Myth of the Powerful Jew." In *Beginning to See the Light: Sex, Hope and Rock-and-Roll,* 228–244. Minneapolis: University of Minnesota Press, 2012.

Wixson, Douglas. *Worker-Writer in America: Jack Conroy and the Tradition of Midwestern Literary Radicalism, 1898–1990.* Urbana: University of Illinois Press, 1994.

Wolfe, Patrick. "Settler Colonialism and the Elimination of the Native." *Journal of Genocide Research,* December 21, 2006, 387–409.

———. *Settler Colonialism and the Transformation of Anthropology: Politics and Poetics of an Ethnographic Event.* London: Cassell, 1999.

Wolosky, Shira. "What Do Jews Stand For? Muriel Rukeyser's Ethics of Identity." *NASHIM: A Journal of Jewish Women's Studies and Gender Issues* 19 (2012): 199–226.

Wood, Peter H. *Black Majority: Negroes in Colonial South Carolina, from 1670 to the Stono Rebellion.* New York: Knopf, 1975.

Wynter, Sylvia. "Rethinking 'Aesthetics': Notes towards a Deciphering Practice." In *Ex-Isles: Essays on Caribbean Cinema,* edited by Mbye Cham, 237–79. Trenton, N.J.: Africa World Press, 1992.

Zadik, Benjamin Joseph. "The Iberian Pig in Spain and the Americas at the Time of Columbus." MA thesis, University of California, Berkeley, 2000. https://www.bzhumdrum.com/pig/iberianpigintheamericas.pdf.

Zavialova, Maria. "Red Venus: Alexandra Kollontai's Red Love and Women in Soviet Art." In *Red Love,* edited by Ruth Barraclough, Heather Bowen Struyk, and Paula Rabinowitz, 221–31. New York: Palgrave, 2015.

Archives

Alice Childress Papers. Schomburg Center for Research in Black Culture. Manuscripts, Archives and Rare Books Division, New York Public Library.

Josephine Herbst Papers. Yale Collection of American Literature. Beinecke Rare Book and Manuscript Library, Yale University. https://archives .yale.edu/repositories/11/resources/1616.

Claudia Jones Memorial Collection. Schomburg Center for Research in Black Culture. Manuscripts, Archives, and Rare Books Division, New York Public Library.

Meridel Le Sueur Papers. Manuscripts Collection, Minnesota Historical Society, St. Paul.

Muriel Rukeyser Papers. Berg Collection of English and American Literature, New York Public Library, Astor, Lenox, and Tilden Foundations.

Muriel Rukeyser Papers. Library of Congress, Manuscript Division, Washington, D.C.

Neala Schleuning–Meridel Le Sueur Collection. Special Collections, University of Delaware Library, Newark.

Louise Thompson Patterson Collection. Stuart A. Rose Manuscript, Archives, and Rare Book Library, Emory University.

Index

Abbott, Bernice, 243–44, 245, 269n29, 273nn90–91
abortion, 16, 18, 65, 112
Adams, Henry, 195
Adams, John Quincy, 195
African Americans, 58, 199, 254n10; Jews and, 11; oppression of, 113, 227; relief efforts and, 15. *See also* Black people
African Blood Brotherhood, 33
Afro-Cubans, 120, 121
Agricultural Adjustment Administration, 261n30
agricultural establishments, U.S.-owned/in Cuba, 261n40
agriculture, 114; political supremacy of, 165
Akiba, Rabbi, 216
Alabama Constitutional Convention, 210
Alaimo, Stacy, 150–51
Alcoff, Linda, 99
Alderson prison, 68, 69
Alderson Story, The (Flynn), 257n74
Alien Registration Act (1940), 256n64
allegory, 88, 128, 130, 131, 135, 138, 139, 140, 143; form of, 24; historical, 145
Allen, Philippa, 237
Allred, Jeff, 230
Alvarez, Leon, 121
America (Schleuning), 263n2
"American Bus" (Le Sueur), 171
American Communism, 4, 8, 9, 12, 13, 18, 23, 27, 37, 38, 205, 251n17, 264n8; capitalism and, 10, 14; East Coast focus of, 25; marginalization of, 9; political

discourse and, 15; racism and, 5; self-determination and, 65; social justice and, 11; vision/practice of, 248. *See also* Communism
American Federation of Labor (AFL), 64
American Fur Company, 164
American Indian Movement (AIM), 173
American Interracial Seminar (Congregational Church), 57
American Legion, 11, 97, 218
American Mercury, 9
American Negro Theater, 79
American Poetry Review, 243
American Writers' Congress, 157
Amsterdam News, 32, 44, 51
"Ancient People and the Newly Come, The" (Le Sueur), 174, 178
Anderson, Margaret, 261n29
Anderson, Maxwell, 112, 261n29
"And So We Marched" (Thompson), 56, 57
Angelou, Maya, 256n65
Anishinaabe, uprising of, 174
Anna Lucasta (Yordan), 79
"Annunciation" (Le Sueur), 160
anti-Communism, 87, 103
anti-imperialism, 121, 122
antiracism, 5, 7, 12, 33, 208
anti-Semitism, 5, 6–7, 8, 9, 211, 217
Anvil, 9, 157
appropriate/appropriation, 169
Aptheker, Bettina, 256n65
Aptheker, Herbert, 256n65, 258n101
Arawak, 124
assimilation, 7, 8, 144, 217
Associación de Productores Agricolas del Realengo 18 y Colandantes, 121

293

Rosemary Hennessy is L. H. Favrot Professor of Humanities and professor of English at Rice University. She is author of *Materialist Feminism and the Politics of Discourse*; *Profit and Pleasure: Sexual Identities in Late Capitalism*; and *Fires on the Border: The Passionate Politics of Labor Organizing on the Mexican Frontera* (Minnesota, 2013).